PEASANT LIFE IN CHINA

INTERNATIONAL LIBRARY OF SOCIOLOGY AND SOCIAL RECONSTRUCTION

Founded by Karl Mannheim

Editor : W. J. H. Sprott

A catalogue of the books available in the INTERNATIONAL LIBRARY OF SOCIOLOGY AND SOCIAL RECONSTRUCTION, and new books in preparation for the Library, will be found at the end of this volume.

PEASANT LIFE IN CHINA

CHINA

A Field Study of Country Life in the Yangtze Valley

By

HSIAO-TUNG FEI

B.A. (Yenching), M.A. (Tsing Hua), Ph.D. (London)

With a Preface by
PROFESSOR BRONISLAW MALINOWSKI

LONDON
ROUTLEDGE & KEGAN PAUL LTD
BROADWAY HOUSE: 68-74 CARTER LANE E.C.4

First published . . . 1939
Second impression . . 1943
Third impression . . 1945
Fourth impression . . 1947
Fifth impression . . 1962

江村經濟

費孝通著

To My Wife
TUNG-WEI WANG

Printed in Great Britain by
Lowe and Brydone (Printers) Limited, London, N.W.10

CONTENTS

v

CONTENTS

A*

LIST OF ILLUSTRATIONS

ACKNOWLEDGEMENTS

I HAVE to thank all those who have encouraged and helped me in my field investigation and in my preparation of this book. Above all, I must acknowledge my indebtedness to the following teachers and friends :

To Professors Wu Wen-tsao and S. M. Shirokogoroff I owe my early training in sociology and ethnology, and encouragement in introducing the intensive field investigation in studying Chinese culture. My sister, whose devotion to the rehabilitation of the livelihood of the villagers has actually inspired me to take up this investigation, had introduced me to the village and financed my work. Later, I was awarded a scholarship by Tsing Hua University, which enabled me to pursue my study in England and, so to speak, " to enter under the door " of Professor B. Malinowski. His intellectual inspiration and paternal affection during the past two years has imposed on me a life-long filial duty—a duty, as I understand, to share his heavy burden in building up a science of man, and in realizing a genuine co-operation among all civilizations.

I must thank Mr. G. F. A. Wint, Dr. and Mrs. Raymond Firth, Dr. M. H. Read, Mr. C. Wrong and Miss M. Wrong for their kindness in reading my manuscript and in correcting my English. I was also assisted in various ways by members of the Seminar in the London School of Economics, especially Mr. P. L. Haksar and L. K. Hsü.

Finally, let me remember my wife, who died for Anthropology in our expedition to the Yao Mountains in 1935. Her solemn sacrifice leaves me no alternative but to follow her always. To her this book is dedicated.

PREFACE

By B. Malinowski

I venture to foretell that *Peasant Life in China* by Dr. Hsiao-Tung Fei will be counted as a landmark in the development of anthropological field-work and theory. The book has a number of outstanding merits, each of them marking a new departure. Our attention is here directed not to a small, insignificant tribe, but to the greatest nation in the world. The book is not written by an outsider looking out for exotic impressions in a strange land ; it contains observations carried on by a citizen upon his own people. It is the result of work done by a native among natives. If it be true that self-knowledge is the most difficult to gain, then undoubtedly an anthropology of one's own people is the most arduous, but also the most valuable achievement of a field-worker.

The book, moreover, though it takes in the traditional background of Chinese life, does not remain satisfied with the mere reconstruction of the static past. It grapples fully and deliberately with that most elusive and difficult phase of modern life : the transformation of traditional culture under Western impact. The writer is courageous enough to cast away all academic pretence at scientific detachment. Dr. Fei fully realizes that knowledge is indispensable to the right solution of practical difficulties. He sees that science, in rendering real service to mankind, is not degraded. It indeed receives the acid test of its validity. Truth will work, because truth is nothing else but man's adaptation to real facts and forces. Science becomes only prostituted when the scholar is forced, as in some countries of

Europe, to adapt his facts and his convictions to the
demands of a dictated doctrine.

Dr. Fei as a young Chinese patriot is fully alive,
not only to the present tragedy of China, but to the
much bigger issues involved in the dilemma of his
great Mother-country to westernize or to perish.
And since as an anthropologist he knows how difficult
a process is that of readaptation ; how this process
must be built on the old foundations, and built slowly,
gradually, and wisely, he is deeply concerned that all
change should be planned, and that the planning be
based on the solid foundation of fact and knowledge.

Some passages of this book can indeed be taken as a
charter of practical sociology and anthropology.
" The need of such knowledge has become more and
more urgent in China because the country cannot
afford to waste any more of her wealth and energy in
making mistakes." Dr. Fei sees clearly that with the
best intentions and the most desirable end clearly in
view, planning must remain faulty if the initial situation
of change be misconceived. " An inaccurate definition
of a situation, either due to deliberate aberration or to
ignorance, is dangerous for a group," because it pre-
supposes forces which do not exist, and ignores
obstacles which obstruct the way of progress.

I feel I have to quote one more paragraph from the
Introduction. " An adequate definition of the situation, if it is to organize successful actions and attain
the desired end, must be reached through a careful
analysis of the functions of the social institutions, in
relation to the need that they purport to satisfy and
in relation to other institutions on which their working
depends. This is the work of a social scientist. Social
science therefore should play an important rôle in
directing cultural change." This expresses well the
greatest need, not only of the Chinese but of our own
civilization, the need, that is, to recognize that even as
in mechanical engineering only a fool or a madman

would plan, design, and calculate without reference to scientific physics and mathematics, so also in political action, reason and experience must be given the fullest play.

Our modern civilization is perhaps now facing its final destruction. We are careful to use only the most qualified specialists in all mechanical engineering. Yet as regards the control of political, social, and moral forces, we Europeans are yielding more and more to madmen, fanatics, and gangsters. A tremendous arraignment of force, controlled by individuals without a sense of responsibility or any moral obligation to keep faith is accumulating on the one side of the dividing line. On the other side, where wealth, power, and effectives could still be made overwhelmingly strong, we have had during the last few years a consistent and progressive display of weakness, lack of unity, and a gradual whittling down of the sense of honour and of the sanctity of obligations undertaken.

I have read Dr. Fei's clear and convincing arguments as well as his vivid and well-documented accounts with genuine admiration, at times not untinged with envy. His book embodies many of the precepts and principles which I have been preaching for some time past, without, alas, having the opportunity of practising them myself. Most of us forward-looking anthropologists have felt impatient with our own work for its remoteness, exoticism, and irrelevancy—though perhaps these may be more apparent than real. But there is no doubt that my own confession that " Anthropology, to me at least, was a romantic escape from our over-standardized culture," was essentially true.

The remedy, however, is at hand. If I may be allowed to quote some of my other reflections, " the progress of anthropology towards a really effective analytic science of human society, of human conduct, and of human nature, cannot be staved off." To achieve this, however, the science of man has first

and foremost to move from so-called savagery into
the study of more advanced cultures of the numerically,
economically, and politically important peoples of the
world.   The present book and the wider work in China
and elsewhere, of which it is a part, justifies my forecast : " The anthropology of the future will be . . .
as interested in the Hindu as in the Tasmanian, in the
Chinese peasants as in the Australian aborigines, in the
West Indian negro as in the Melanesian Trobriander,
in the detribalized African of Haarlem as in the
Pygmy of Perak."   In this quotation is implied another
important postulate of modern field-work and theory :
the study of culture change ; of the phenomena of
contact, and of present-day diffusion.

It was therefore a great pleasure when some two
years ago I received the visit of a distinguished Chinese
sociologist, Professor Wu Wen-Tsao of Yenching
University, and learnt from him that independently and
spontaneously there had been organized in China a
sociological attack on the real problems of culture
change and applied anthropology, an attack which
embodies all my dreams and desiderata.

Professor Wu and the young scholars whom he
was able to train and inspire had realised first of all
that to understand the civilization of their great
country and to make it comprehensible to others, it
was necessary to read in the open book of Chinese life,
and learn how the live Chinese mind works in reality.
Just because that country has had the longest unbroken
tradition, the understanding of Chinese history must
proceed from the appreciation of what China is to-day.
Such an anthropological approach is indispensable as a
supplement to important historical work carried out
by modern Chinese scholars, and by a body of sino-
logists in Europe, on the basis of written records.
History can be read back, taking the present as its
living version, quite as much as it can be read forward,
starting with the archæological remains of the dimmest

past and the earliest written records. The two
approaches are complementary and they must be used
concurrently.

The principles and the substance of Dr. Fei's book
reveal to us how sound are the methodological foundations of the modern Chinese School of Sociology.
Take the main subject-matter of the book. It is a
field-study of country life on one of those riverine
plains which for thousands of years have nourished the
Chinese people both materially and spiritually. It is
axiomatic that the foundation of an essentially agrarian
culture will be found in village life, in rural economy,
and in the needs and interests of a peasant population.
By becoming acquainted with the life of a small village,
we study, under a microscope as it were, the epitome of
China at large.

Two main motives dominate the story of this book :
the exploitation of the soil, and the reproductive
processes within the household and the family. In
this book, Dr. Fei limits himself to the fundamental
aspects of peasant life in China. He proposes, I
know, in his subsequent studies, to give a fuller account
of ancestor-worship ; of the more complicated systems
of belief and knowledge which flourish in village
and township alike. He also hopes sooner or later to
make a wider synthesis of his own works and that of his
colleagues, giving us a comprehensive picture of the
cultural, religious, and political systems of China.
For such a synthesis, monographic accounts such as the
present one are the first step. Dr. Fei's book and the
contributions of his fellow-workers will become
valuable pieces for the mosaic which it will be possible
to construct from them.[1]

---

[1] The work already completed, mostly in Chinese, includes such subjects as : *The
Marketing System in Shangtung*, by C. K. Yang ; *Litigation in a Village Community of Hopei*,
by Y. S. Hsu ; *Peasant Custom in Hopei*, by S. Huang ; *A Clan-Village in Fukien*, by Y. H.
Lin ; *Chinese Rural Education (in Shangtung) in Change*, by T. C. Liao ; *The Social Organization of Hua Lan Yao (in Kwangsi)*, by Dr. and Mrs. Fei. Further studies are now being
made of Land Tenure in Shansi, by Y. I. Li ; and problems of emigrant relations between
Fukien and overseas outpost, by A. L. Cheng.

It is not the task of a preface writer to retell a story so admirably told as the one of this book. The reader will find himself introduced into the setting : the charming riverine village of Kaihsienkung. He will be able to visualize its lay-out with its streams and bridges, its temples, rice-fields, and mulberry trees. In this the excellent photographs will prove an additional help. He will appreciate the good balance of concrete, at times numerical data, and the clear descriptions. The account of agricultural life, of the means of livelihood, and the typical occupations of the villagers ; the excellent seasonal calendar, and the precise definition of land tenure, give a type of intimate and at the same time tangible information not to be found anywhere else in the literature on China.

I am allowed to quote from a statement by Sir E. Denison Ross, who read the book in manuscript, and thus defines its position in scientific literature : " I regard this treatise as quite exceptional. I know of no other work which describes at first hand and with intimate understanding the full story of life in a Chinese village community. We have had works dealing with statistics, economic studies, and novels full of local colour—but in no book have I found the answer to every kind of inquiry which the curious stranger might make." The "curious stranger," when he appears in the person of Sir Denison Ross, is a man of science, a historian, and one of the world's experts in Oriental Studies.

To me personally, the chapter on the silk industry is perhaps the most significant achievement of the book. It is an account of a planned change from domestic industry into a readaptation to co-operative work compatible with modern conditions. It vindicates some of the claims of sociology to be a practical and relevant study for social engineering. It raises a number of collateral questions, and will become, I think, the starting point of other inquiries both in China and elsewhere.

In the argument of this chapter and in many other passages we can discover a moral quality of the book which I may be allowed to underline. There is no trace of special pleading or self-justification, although the book is written by a Chinese to be placed before Western readers. It is rather a criticism or self-criticism. Thus in the chapter on " Agrarian Problems in China " we read " The national government with all its promises and policies on paper was not able to carry out any practical measures owing to the fact that most of the revenue was spent in its anti-communist campaign, while, as I have pointed out, the real nature of the communist movement was a peasant revolt due to their dissatisfaction with the land system. Despite all kinds of justification on either side, one thing is clear : that the conditions of the peasants are getting worse and worse. So far no permanent land reform has been accomplished in any part of China since the recovery of the Red Area by the government." That a type of sociological work which openly criticizes the inadequacy of government action is yet carried on with the encouragement of the government speaks for itself. It proves on the one hand the integrity of the young sociologists in China and on the other the good-will and wisdom of their official patrons.

A dispassioned, detached, and dignified attitude characterises all the Author's observations. That a Chinese must to-day have bitter feelings against Western civilization and the political rule of Western nations, is understandable. Yet no trace of this will be found in the present book. In fact, throughout my personal acquaintance with Dr. Fei and some of his colleagues, I had to admire the absence of national prejudice and national hatred—a moral attitude from which we Europeans could learn a great deal. The Chinese seem to be able to distinguish between nationhood and the political system. There is no hatred even of the Japanese as a people. On the first page of this book the Author refers to the invading country only in terms of dispassionate appreciation of its rôle in consolidating the Chinese nation and forcing it to build up a united front, and to readjust some of its fundamental problems, economic and social. The very village which we have learnt to know, to appreciate, to which we have almost become attached, has probably now been destroyed. We can only echo the writer's prophetic desire that in the ruin of that village and many others, "the internal conflicts and follies should find their last resting-place " and that " from the ruin a new China shall emerge."

B. MALINOWSKI

DEPARTMENT OF ANTHROPOLOGY,
  UNIVERSITY OF LONDON.
    15th October, 1938

CHAPTER I

INTRODUCTION

This is a descriptive account of the system of consumption, production, distribution and exchange of wealth among Chinese peasants as observed in a village, Kaihsienkung, south of Lake Tai, in Eastern China. It aims at showing the relation of this economic system to a specific geographical setting and to the social structure of the community. The village under investigation, like most Chinese villages, is undergoing a tremendous process of change. This account, therefore, will show the forces and problems in a changing village economy.

An intensive investigation of a small field of this kind is a necessary supplement of the broad surveys made of present-day economic problems in China. It will exemplify the importance of regional factors in analysing these problems and will provide empirical illustrations.

This type of study will enable us to realize the importance of the background of the traditional economy, and the effect of the new forces on the everyday life of the people.

To stress the equal importance of the traditional and the new forces is necessary because the real process of change of Chinese economic life is neither a direct transference of social institutions from the West nor a mere disturbance of a traditional equilibrium. The problems arising from the present situation are results of the interaction of these two forces. In the village under our examination, for instance, the financial issues can only be understood by taking into consideration the decline of the price of silk due to the world industrial development on the one hand, and on the other, the importance of domestic industry in the family budget based on the traditional system of land tenure. Underestimation of either aspect will distort the real situation. Moreover, the product of the interaction of these two forces, as we shall see in the later description, cannot be a reproduction of the West or a restoration of the past. The result will depend on how the people solve their own problems. A correct understanding of the existing situation based on empirical facts will assist in directing the change towards a desired end. Herein lies the function of social science.

Culture is a set of material equipment and a body of knowledge. It is man who uses the equipment and the knowledge in order to live. Culture is changed by men for definite purposes. When a man throws away a tool to acquire a new one, he does so because he believes that the new tool suits his purpose better. Therefore in any process of change, there is an integration of his past experience, his understanding of the present situation and his expectation of the future consequences. Past experiences are not always a real picture of past events because they have been transformed through the selective process of memory. The present situation is not always accurately comprehended because it attracts attention only in so far as interest directs. The future consequences do not always come up to expectations because they are the products of many other forces besides wishes and efforts. So the new tool may at last prove not to be suitable to man's purpose.

It is more difficult to achieve successful changes in social institutions. Even when an institution has failed to meet the need of the people, there may be no substitute. The difficulty lies in the fact that since a social institution consists of human relations, it can be changed only through concerted actions which cannot readily be organized. Moreover, the social situation is usually complicated and expectation varies among the individuals involved. Therefore in the process of social change, it is always necessary in order to organize collective actions to have a more or less accepted definition of the situation and a formulated programme. Such preparatory activities generally take a linguistic form. It can be seen in its simplest form in the command of a captain to his crew when directing the course of a ship. It can also be observed in the well staged debates in parliament or congress. Different definitions of the situation and varying expectations about the results form the centre of the debates. Nevertheless, such preparatory activities are always present in an innovation in socially organized activities.

An inaccurate definition of situation, either due to deliberate aberrations or to ignorance, is dangerous for the group because it may lead to an undesired future. There are many instances in the present account to illustrate the importance of an empirical definition of the situation. In anticipation of the following pages, I shall mention a few of them. In kinship organization, the present practice of inheritance is defined by the legislature as an instance of inequality between sexes. Since the situation is so defined, once the idea of sex equality has been accepted, the resultant actions would involve a revision of the unilateral kinship principle. As I shall show, the transmission of property is a part of the reciprocal relation between generations ; the obligation of supporting the old, in a society where that responsibility falls upon the children, cannot be equally shared by sons and daughters under the present system of patrilocal marriage. Therefore the bilateral inheritance combined with unilateral affiliation creates inequality between the sexes. Seen in this light, the consequences of the legislation are obviously contrary to expectation (IV–6).

A definition of situation sometimes may be accurate but not complete. In the silk industry, for instance, the reformers have defined the situation mainly in technical terms. The omission of the factor of international trade in the decline of the price of silk had resulted in their failure for many years to fulfil their promise to the villagers of big incomes from the industry (XII–8).

An adequate definition of situation, if it is to organize successful actions and attain the desired end, must be reached through a careful analysis of the functions of the social institutions, in relation to the need that they purport to satisfy and in relation to other institutions on which their working depends. This is the work of a social scientist. Social science therefore should play an important rôle in directing cultural change.

The need of such knowledge has become more and more urgent in China because the country cannot afford to waste any more of her wealth and energy in making mistakes. The fundamental end is evident ; it is the satisfaction of the basic requirements common

to every Chinese. This should be recognized by all.
A village which stands on the verge of starvation profits
nobody, not even the usurers. In this sense there
should be no political differences among the Chinese
upon these fundamental measures. Where differences
exist, they are due to misrepresentation of facts. A
systematic presentation of the actual conditions of the
people will convince the nation of the urgent policies
necessary for rehabilitating the lives of the masses.
It is not a matter for philosophical speculation, much
less should it be a matter for dispute between schools
of thought. What is really needed is a common-sense
judgment based on reliable information.

The present study is only one of the initial attempts
of a group of young Chinese students who have
realized the importance of this task. Similar studies
have been carried out in Fukien, Shantung, Shansi,
Hopei, and Kwangsi and will be pursued in the future
by more extensive and better organized efforts. I am
reluctant to present this premature account, premature
because I have been deprived of chances of further
field investigation in the immediate future on account
of the Japanese occupation and destruction of the village
here described. But I am presenting this study in the
hopes that it may give a realistic picture to western
readers of the huge task that has been imposed on my
people and the agony of the present struggle. Without
being pessimistic, let me assure my readers that the
struggle is evidently to be a long and grave one. We
are ready for the worst and it may be a thousand times
worse than the Japanese bombs and poisonous gas.
I am, however, confident that, despite the past errors
and present misfortunes, China will emerge once more
a great nation, through the unswerving effort of her

people. The present account is not a record of a vanished history but a prelude to a new chapter of the world history that will be written not in ink but in the blood of millions.

CHAPTER II

THE FIELD

Delimitation of Field — Geographical Foundation — Economic Background — Village Site — The People — Reasons for Choosing the Field

I. DELIMITATION OF FIELD

To carry out intensive study of the life of the people, it is necessary to confine oneself to the investigation of a small social unit. This is due to practical considerations. The people under investigation must be within easy reach of the investigator in order that the latter can observe personally and intimately. The unit of study, on the other hand, should not be too small. It should provide a fair cross-section of the social life of the people.

This general problem has been discussed by Professor A. Radcliffe-Brown, Dr. Wu Wen-tsao, and Dr. Raymond Firth.[1] It is agreed that in the first stage of such a study, a village would be the most appropriate unit. " To start with a single village as a centre," says Dr. Firth, " investigate the relationships of the persons composing it, in terms of kinship, the distribution of authority, economic organization, religious

[1] Professor A. Radcliffe-Brown gave a lecture in Yenching University, Peiping, in 1935 on the problem of intensive study of Chinese villages. Following this lecture, Dr. Wu Wen-tsao has published a series of articles on the problem in *Social Research Weekly*, Yih Shih Pao, Tientsin. Recently Dr. Raymond Firth has discussed the problem in his article, " Stability in North China Village Life," *The Sociological World*, Vol. X, in Chinese.

affiliations, and other social ties, and try to see how
these relationships affect one another and determine
the co-operative life of the small community.   From
this centre the investigation will radiate out following
the personal relationships into other units in adjacent
villages, economic linkage and social co-operation." [1]

A village is a community characterized by its being
an aggregate of households on a compact residential
area, separated from other similar units by a considerable distance (this may not hold good in some parts of
China where households are scattered), organized in
various social activities as a group, and possessing a
special name of its own.   It is a *de facto* social unit
recognized by the people themselves.

A village as such does not enter formally into the
new administrative system in China—Pao, Chea [2]—
which is artificially created for certain specific purposes
(VI–5).   Since this system was introduced to Kaihsienkung only in 1935, it is very difficult to say when these
de jure units, through increasing administrative function, will cause a shift in the existing *de facto* groupings.
But at present, in actual practice, the Pao Chea system
is still largely a formality.   Thus the unit of our study,
the aim of which is to understand the life of the people,
must follow the real existing functioning unit—the
village.

To take the village as the unit of study at the present
stage of investigation, does not mean that it is a self-
contained unit.   The inter-dependence of territorial
groups, especially in economic life, is very close in
China.   It can even be said that the Chinese people

---

[1] *Op. cit.*, English Abstract, p. 435.
[2] Chinese terms are transcribed in this book following the conventional
Wade system.   But for special local terms, broad phonetic transcriptions
are used, and printed in italics.   In phonetic transcription, I adopt *j* as
sign for jetisation.

have during the last half century entered into the world community. Western goods as well as ideas have reached very remote villages. The conomic and political pressure of the Western powers is the prime factor in the present change of Chinese culture. In this connection, one can ask what understanding of these changes and of the external forces causing them can be gained by a field investigation in a small area, such as a village.

It is obvious that the investigator in the village cannot analyse the outside forces in their wide perspective. For instance, the decline of the price of native silk in the world market as a result of the world economic depression and of the technical improvement of the silk industry in general, has produced such effects in the village as deficiency in the family budget, shortage of food, postponement of marriage and the partial breakdown of the domestic industry. The field investigator in this case must record as fully as possible the forces that affect village life but he will of course leave the further analysis of these forces themselves to other sicences. He will take these facts for granted and limit himself to tracing the effects which can be directly observed in the life of the village.

Generalizations made from such an intensive study of a small social unit may not be applicable to other units. But they can be used as hypotheses and as comparative material for further investigation in other fields. This is the soundest way to obtain really scientific generalizations.

2. GEOGRAPHICAL FOUNDATION

The village chosen for my investigation is called Kaihsienkung, locally pronounced *kejiug'on*. It is situated on the south-east bank of Lake Tai, in the lower course of the Yangtze River and about eighty miles west of Shanghai. It is in the geographical region of the Yangtze Plain. The geographical foundation of this region has been described by G. B. Cressey : " The Yangtze Plain is a land of rivers and canals. Probably nowhere else in the world is there an area with so many navigable waterways. The Yangtze Kiang, the Hwai Ho, and their tributaries provide a splendid highway through the length of the region. In addition to the many rivers there are a series of great lakes, chief among which are Tungting, Poyang, Tai, and Hungtse Hu. It is the canals, however, which give the most characteristic note to the landscape. These canals are the very arteries of life. In the region of Yangtze Delta they form an intricate network and serve as an artificial drainage system which takes the place of rivers. Their length in the south delta alone is estimated by F. H. King, at twenty-five thousand miles.

" This region is compound alluvial plain, the accumulation of sediment laid down by the rivers during long ages. There are a few isolated hills, but for the most part the land is level. The country is flat, but innumerable grave mounds and the trees about the villages break the view. Both rural and urban settlement is more congested than in the region of the North, but factors of climate and location combine to make this the most prosperous part of China.[1]

" The Yangtze Plain is . . . distinctly influenced by summer-monsoon conditions. . . . Here, too, are felt the greatest effects of continental cyclonic storms.

" Owing to the southernly latitude, the summers are

[1] *China's Geographical Foundation,* 1934, p. 283.

subtropical with temperatures which frequently rise to 38° C. (100° F.). . . . The average (rainfall) for the entire region is about 1,200 mm. (45 in.). . . . Most of the rain falls during the spring and summer, with June the rainiest month. The period from October to February is comparatively dry with clear skies and stimulating temperatures, making this the most pleasant season of the year.

" Winter temperatures seldom remain below freezing for more than a few days at a time. Ice forms only in thin sheets on the colder nights and there is little snow. . . . The average of summer maximum temperature for Shanghai is 37° C. (91° F.), and the average of winter minimum is −7° C. (19° F.).

" The Yangtze Plain has climate conditions which are favourable for agriculture during most of the year so that the growing season lasts for about 300 days." [1]

The commanding position of this region in Chinese economy is due partly to its superior natural environment and partly to its favourable position in the system of communications. It is located at the crossing point of the two main water routes : namely, the Yangtze River and the Grand Canal. They connect this region with the immense territory of western and northern China. Being a coastal region, it has become more and more important since the development of international trade by ocean transport. Shanghai, the seaport of this region, has developed into the biggest metropolis in the Far East. The railway system in this region is also well developed. From Shanghai, two important lines have been built, one to Nanking, passing Soochow, and one to Hongchow, passing Chianhsing. Recently in 1936 a new line between

[1] *Op. cit.*, p. 295.

Soochow and Chianhsing was added to form a circuit between the above-mentioned two main lines. Motor roads have been built for the intra-regional communication ; and besides there is an extensive use of the canals and canalized streams.

This region has supported a very dense population, most of which is resident in villages. A bird's-eye view shows a cluster of villages. Each village is separated from its neighbour by only a walking distance of, on an average, twenty minutes. Kaihsienkung is but one of these thousands of villages crowding on this land.

In the centre of several tens of villages there is a town. The town is the collecting centre of the basic produce from the surrounding villages and the distributing point for manufactured goods brought from the outside cities. The town on which Kaihsienkung depends is called Chên Tsê, about four miles south of the village. It takes about two and a half hours for a single trip by boat. Chên Tsê lies about six miles south-east of Lake Tai and eight miles west of the Grand Canal and the Soochow-Chianhsing line. At present it is connected with the nearest station, Ping Wang, both by motor boat and bus services. By the existing railway lines, one can reach Shanghai from the town within eight hours. The geographical position of Kaihsienkung in relation to the above-mentioned towns and cities is shown in the accompanying maps (Map I and II).

3. ECONOMIC BACKGROUND

Here the human geographer will be right in inferring the occupation of the people from the natural conditions of the land they occupy. A traveller in a train,

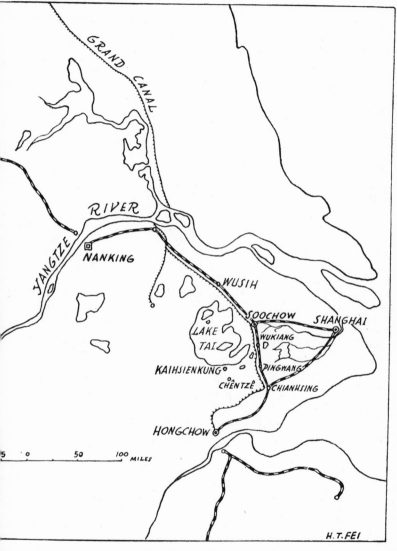

MAP I.—The Lower Yangtze Valley

B

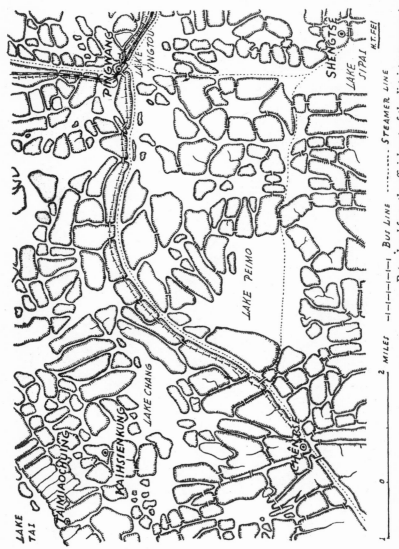

Reproduced from the official map of the district government

passing through that region, would not lose sight of the rice fields for more than intervals of a few minutes. In Kaihsienkung, according to estimates, more than ninety per cent. of the land is used for rice cultivation. This single village produces, on the average, eighteen thousand bushels of rice every year (X–2). Only a little more than half of the produce is consumed by the people themselves (VII–5). Very few households in the village are entirely free from agricultural work. About seventy-six per cent. of the total number of households are engaged in agriculture as their main occupation (VIII–1). The time spent in cultivating rice amounts to six months in the year (IX–3). From this crop the people earn more than half of their income (XII–2). Thus from any angle, rice is of primary importance.

But rice is not the only produce of the land. Wheat, rapeseeds and various vegetables are grown too, although they are insignificant as compared with the chief crop. Moreover, the water provides fish, shrimps, crabs, and different kinds of water plants which are all used locally as food.

The mulberry tree plays an important part in the economic life of the villagers. It enables them to develop their silk industry. Wright wrote early in 1908, " Raw white silk, the *tsatlee* silk of European markets, is produced by the hand reeling of the Chinese silkworm farms. . . . The best white silk comes from the district surrounding Shanghai, which contributes by far the greatest proportion of the value exported." [1]

Silk industry is common to the whole region but it

[1] Arnold Wright, ed. *Twentieth Century Impressions of Hongkong, Shanghai and Other Treaty Ports of China*, p. 291.

is specially well developed in the villages around Lake Tai. This specialization is due, according to the local people, to the good quality of the water. It is said that the so-called *tsatlee* silk is produced only in the area about four miles in diameter around Kaihsienkung. How far this statement is true is another question, but the importance of the village in rural industry is beyond doubt. During its prosperous period, this area not only contributed a large part of China's silk export but also supplied the demand for raw material for the domestic weaving industry of the neighbouring town Shang Tsê (Map II). The weaving industry of that town before its decline had been known to be able to produce " ten thousand pieces a day."

The rural silk industry began to decline when the modern factory for silk manufacturing with its improved technique of production was introduced both into Japan and China. This industrial revolution changed the fortunes of the domestic rural industry.

" Previous to 1909 . . . the quantity of Chinese silk exported had been larger than that of Japanese silk. In 1907, for instance, the two were almost the same. It was only in 1909, however, that Japanese silk export began to exceed that of China, and this advantage the former has been able to keep up ever since. In fact, in recent years, the Japanese export was nearly three times that of this country. From the point of view of our foreign trade, silk also decreased in significance since 1909. Before that date it used to constitute from 20 to 30 per cent. of our total exports, but the average for the years 1909–1916 fell to 17 per cent." [1]

The amount of produce, however, had been increasing although irregularly up to 1923. But owing

[1] D. K. Lieu, *The Silk Reeling Industry in Shanghai*, 1933, p. 9.

to the fall in price, the increasing amount of export did not mean necessarily an increase of return. The amount of export has declined steadily ever since that time. During 1928 to 1930, the percentage of decrease was about twenty.[1] The rate of decrease was more rapid in the period between 1930 to 1934. " As Japanese silk was dumped on the American market in the latter part of the year (1934), China's silk export dropped to the lowest point accordingly. The volume of silk exported amounted to only one-fifth of that in 1930, a fact which is indicative of the depression of the Chinese silk trade.

" The price of raw silk dropped to a new low level in 1934. . . . The 1934 price level for the same quality of silk was only one-third of the 1930 price level." [2]

The internal market for silk has shrunk at the same time due to the same forces of industrial revolution affecting the weaving industry. The consequence of the shrinkage of the market is the break-down of the traditional domestic silk industry in the rural district. The traditional specialization in the silk industry and its recent decline form the background of the economic life of the village in the present analysis.

4. THE VILLAGE SITE

Let us examine the village itself. The land occupied by the people in this village consists of eleven *yu*. *Yu* is the local term for the unit of land surrounded by water. Each *yu* has its own name. Its size is determined by the distribution of streams and thus varies. The total area of land of this village is 3,065

---

[1] *Op. cit.*, p. 9.
[2] *The Chinese Year Book*, 1935–36, " Foreign Trade," p. 1094.

mow or 461 acres. The names and size of these eleven *yu* are given in the following table, according to the official survey of 1932. Two of the *yu* belong in part to other villages, and, since there are no clear boundaries, I can only make a rough estimate of the portion belonging to Kaihsienkung.

Hsi Chang *yu*	986·402 *mow*
Ch'eng Kioh Hsi Tou *yu* . . .	546·141
Kuei Tsŭ *yu*	458·010
Ch'eng Kioh *yu*	275·110
Liang Kioh *yu*	261·320
Hsi Tou *yu*	174·146
P'an Hsiang Pa	173·263
Tou Tsŭ *yu*	70·540
Wu Tsŭ *yu*	56·469
Peh Cheng Kioh	55·858
Hsin Tien *yu*	8·545
TOTAL	3,065·804
or . . .	461·12 acres

The land can be roughly divided into two parts; namely, that used for cultivation and that used for dwellings. The residential area occupies rather a small portion. It is found at the junction of three streams and the houses are distributed on the margin of four *yu*. Names of these *yu* and number of houses on each are given in the following table:

I. Ch'eng Kioh *yu*	133
II. Liang Kioh *yu*	95
III. Hsi Chang *yu*	75
IV. T'an Chia Têng (Wu Tsŭ *yu*). . .	57
TOTAL	360

The plan of the residential area must be studied in relation to the communication system of the village. In this region, boats are extensively used for heavy and long-distance traffic. The land routes connecting different villages and towns are mainly used for pulling the boats against unfavourable currents and winds. People usually come to the village by boats, except a few pedlars. Nearly every household possesses at least one boat. The importance of the boat in communication means that the houses must be near the water and consequently determines the plan of the village. Villages grow up along the streams ; at the junction of several streams, bigger villages are found. As we can see from the accompanying map, the backbone of Kaihsienkung village is formed by three streams, designated here as A, B, and C. Stream A, the main one, runs like an arc, and from this the village gets its name. Kaihsienkung literally means open-string-bow.

Boats are not convenient for short distances or very light traffic inside the residential area. Roads are built for communication between the houses. In this case, the streams represent obstacles to communication and the separated *yu* must be connected by bridges.

The road system of this village does not form a complete circle. In the northern part of *yu* III, a large part of the land is used for farming. In that part, there are only small paths among the farms, and they are not convenient for walking, especially during wet weather. Owing to this fact the bridge at the west end of stream A is the central point in the system. Small shops are concentrated largely around the bridges, especially the bridge at the west end (XIV-8).

Nevertheless, in the village plan, there is no special place where the public life of the people is concentrated. Except for the informal gatherings in the summer evenings around the bridges, there has been no organized public gathering for more than ten years, since the annual opera performance was suspended.

The headquarters of the village headmen is at the east end in the co-operative silk factory. The position of the factory was selected for technical reasons. The

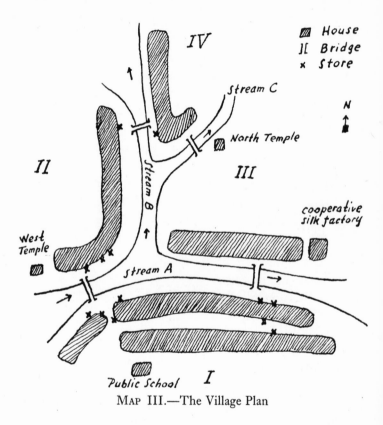

MAP III.—The Village Plan

current of Stream A runs from west to east. To avoid adding the dirt of the factory to the stream which provides the daily water supply of the people along the stream, the factory was built at the lower course.

Two temples are found on the outskirts of the

residential area ; one at the west end and the other at
the north end.   But the position of the temples does
not mean that the religious life of the people is concentrated on the outskirts.   In fact, their religious life
is largely carried on in their own houses.   It would
be more correct to regard the temples as the residences
of priests and gods, who are not only segregated some
distance apart from the ordinary people but are also
separated from everyday community life except on
special ceremonial occasions.

The public school is at the south end.   The building
was originally used as the office of the silk reform
bureau.   It was given to the school when the factory
was established.

The residential area is surrounded by farming land,
which is low owing to the irrigation system (X–1).
The area suitable for buildings has been covered by
houses and for a long time has not expanded.   The
newly introduced public institutions such as the school
and the silk factory could only find their location at
the outskirt of the old residential area.   Their location
is an expression of the process of change in the community life.

5. THE PEOPLE

A census of the village was taken in 1935.   Because
no continuous registration of births and deaths has
been properly carried out, I can take this census only
as the basis for my analysis.   In the census, all the
residents in this village, including those temporarily
absent, are recorded.   The figures are summarized in
the following table :

B *

Age	Male	Female	Total
71+	4	15	19
66–70	10	19	29
61–65	14	32	46
56–60	30	39	69
51–55	40	38	78
46–50	26	29	55
41–45	45	38	83
36–40	69	55	124
31–35	64	45	109
26–30	75	61	136
21–25	63	52	115
16–20	68	54	122
11–15	72	61	133
6–10	73	59	132
– 5	118	87	205
?	—	—	3
Total	771	684	1,458

Those temporarily residing in the village but living in definite households are recorded in the census in a special class called " Persons living together " ; these are not included in the above table. The total number in this class is 25.

The density of population (excluding surface of water in computation) is about 1,980 per square mile. This cannot be compared with the average density of the province. The latter is calculated from the general area of the province which includes the surface of water and uncultivated land ; it is a gross density. My figure represents the actual ratio between men and land used. The gross density of the province (Kiangau), as quoted by Professor Tawney, is 896 per square mile.[1]

Not all those who reside in the village are indiscriminately considered as villagers. If the inhabitants are asked which are the people who belong to the village, we shall discover that distinction is made locally

[1] *Land and Labour in China*, p. 24.

between natives and outsiders. This is not a legal distinction ; from the legal point of view those who reside in a district for more than three years become members of the local community.[1] But this does not constitute, in the people's eyes, real membership of the village.

To analyse this distinction, it may be better to take concrete cases of those who are considered as outsiders in the village. There are ten such households, and their professions and birth-places are as follows :

Barber	2	Chenkiang (Kiangsu)
Miller and shoemaker	1	Tanyang (Kiangsu)
Grocer	1	Hengshan (A village in the same district)
Spinner	1	Wuchiashen (A village in the same district)
Priest	1	Chên Tsê
Operator of the pumping machine	1	Ningpo (Chekiang)
Silversmith	1	Shaohsing (Chekiang)
Bamboo artisan	1	Chinhua (Chekiang)
Medicine dealer	1	Wuchen (Chekiang)

Their common characters are (1) that they are immigrants and (2) that they are engaged in special professions. But I have no information about the necessary period of residence in order to attain the status of being a native villager. I have, however, known cases of children of the " outsiders " born in the village being treated like their parents. It appears that the distinction is not made solely on the consideration of period of residence.

On the other hand, the fact that none of the outsiders are farmers is significant. Although not all special professions are filled by them, they constitute one-third of the whole group (VIII–2). It prevents them from quick assimilation.

[1] Law Governing the Population Registration, December 12, 1931.

The villagers as a group possess certain cultural peculiarities. One of my informants mentioned three outstanding items to me : (1) that the villagers tend to palatalize the words such as *gon*, *jeu*, etc., in speech, (2) their women do not work on the farm, and (3) their women always wear skirts even in the hot summer. In these respects, they differ even from the people from the nearest town, Chên Tsê.

Those who are regarded as outsiders have not been culturally assimilated. I noticed their non-native accent in speech and non-native way of dressing ; for instance, the women in the medicine shop did not wear skirts.

As long as the outsiders preserve their own linguistic and cultural difference, and those are noticed by the natives, they will live on more or less symbiotically in the community. The distinction of natives and outsiders is significant because it has been translated into social relations. The fact that outsiders are all engaged in special professions and possess no land is alone sufficient to indicate that the distinction has far-reaching economic consequences.

6. REASONS FOR SELECTING THE FIELD

The village as described is of interest in the following respects.

(1) It has been one of the important centres of domestic silk industry in China. The village can therefore be taken as a representative case of the process of change in Chinese industry ; the change has been chiefly concerned with the substitution of the factory for the domestic system and the social problems rising therefrom. This is a general process, still going on in China, and also has parallels in different parts of

the world. The problem of industrial development in China has its practical significance, but has never been studied intensively with a full knowledge of the social organization of the village. Moreover, in this village an experiment at industrial reform has been made during the past ten years. The social reform activities are of great relevance to the social changes in China ; they should be carefully analysed in an objective way. It is possible that through such an analysis certain important but hitherto unnoticed problems may be revealed.

(2) Kaihsienkung is located in an area where, owing to superb natural resources, agriculture has been developed to a very high degree. The institution of land tenure also has here peculiar elaborations. The village would provide a good field for the study of land problems in China.

(3) The extensive use of water communication in that region, with its net-like distribution of water ways, has led to a special relation between town and village, which is different from that found in North China. We are thus able to study a typical case of a marketing system based on water transport.

Besides these considerations, I had special facilities in investigating this village. My investigation had to be limited to a period of two months. It would have been impossible in this short time to carry out any intensive study, if I had worked in an entirely unfamiliar field. Kaihsienkung is a village belonging to the district of Wukiang of which I am a native. I thus started with certain linguistic advantages. Differences in Chinese dialect is one of the practical difficulties in carrying out field investigation. The people in villages usually cannot understand any other dialect beside their own. Being a native of the district, it was not necessary for me to spend time in learning the local dialect. The community feeling of being a native of the same district also enabled me to penetrate into more intimate life without arousing suspicion.

Above all, in this village I could fully utilize the personal connections of my sister, who, being responsible for the silk reform, had gained the confidence of practically every person in the village. I could without any difficulty secure the best possible co-operation of the villagers in general and the village heads in particular. Having understood my intention, they not only supplied me with all possible material, but made very intelligent and valuable suggestions and explanations to facilitate my investigation. Furthermore, I had visited the village several times before and had been kept continuously informed by my sister about the conditions there. Thus I could go directly into the problem without wasting my time in preliminary work.

My investigation covered the two months of July to August, 1936. Within this time limit, I was naturally not able to follow the complete annual cycle of social activities. However, these two months are significant in their economic life. They cover the last part of the silk industry and the first part of the agricultural work. Supplemented by oral information and my past experiences, the material so far gathered concerning their economic life and the related social institutions is enough for a preliminary analysis.

CHAPTER III

THE CHIA

Chia as an Expanded Family — Continuity of " Incense and Fire " — Population Control — Parents and Children — Education — Marriage — The Daughter-in-Law in the Chia — Cross-Cousin Marriage and Siaosiv.

The basic social group in the village is the Chia, an expanded family. The members of this group possess a common property, keep a common budget and co-operate together to pursue a common living through division of labour. It is also in this group that children are born and brought up and material objects, knowledge, and social positions are inherited.

Larger social groups in the village are formed by combining a number of Chia for various purposes and along kinship or territorial principles. Associations based on individual membership are few and secondary. The following four chapters will provide a social background of the village for our study of its economic life.

I. CHIA AS AN EXPANDED FAMILY

The term family, as commonly used by anthropologists, refers to the procreative unit consisting of parents and immature children. A Chia is essentially a family but it sometimes includes children even when they have grown and married. Sometimes it also includes some relatively remote patrilineal kinsmen.

27

We can call it an expanded family, because it is an expansion of a family due to the reluctance of the sons to separate from their parents after marriage.

Chia emphasizes the inter-dependence of parents and children. It gives security to the old who are no longer able to work. It tends to ensure social continuity and co-operation among the members.

In a given economy, the indefinite expansion of the group may not be advantageous. In the process of expansion social friction among the members increases. As we shall see presently, the Chia will divide whenever the division proves to be advisable. The size of the group is, therefore, maintained by the balance of the opposing forces working for integration on the one hand and for distintegration on the other. We shall analyse these two forces in the following sections.

Some quantitative data about the size of the Chia in the village may be helpful for our further discussion. In spite of the fact that most studies of China have stressed the importance of the large-family system in China, curiously enough, in this village a large-family is rare. In less than ten per cent. of the total number of Chia do we find more than one married couple.

The most common type is that which consists of a nucleus of a married couple and several dependent patrilineal relatives. In fact, more than half, or 58 per cent. of the total, are of this type. But there is not a married couple in every Chia. Sometimes, for instance, after the death of her husband, a woman lives with her children without joining another unit. It may also be the case that a father lives with his son without a woman in the house. These are cases resulting from social disorganization, mainly due to the death of working members of the group ; they are consequently unstable. Either the widower will re-marry or the child will marry in the earliest possible future so that a normal functioning of the group can be restored. This type of unstable Chia amounts to 27 per cent. of the total.[1]

An average Chia in the village consists of four persons. This is by no means an exception, and indicates the smallness of the group. Evidences from other rural districts in China give a similar conclusion. The variation lies between six to four persons per family.[2] The so-called large-family is chiefly found in towns and evidently has a different economic basis. For the present material, it can be said that in the village here described, the Chia is a small kinship group consisting of a family as its nucleus and several dependent relatives.

2. CONTINUITY OF " INCENSE AND FIRE "

The parent-child and the husband-wife relations are two fundamental axes in the family organization. But in the Chia the former seems more important. The essential character of the Chia is that married sons do not always leave their parents, especially when either father or mother is dead. Furthermore, to find a bride

[1] The following table gives the number of each type of Chia :

I. Those which do not include a married couple . .		99
(a) Without extended relatives	62	
(b) With extended relatives	37	
II. Those containing a single married couple . . .		223
(a) Corresponding exactly to " family " . . .	85	
(b) With extended relatives	138	
III. Those with more than one married couple . . .		37
(a) Parents with one married son and his wife .	25	
(b) One of the parents with two married sons and their wives	9	
(c) Parents with two married sons and their wives .	3	
TOTAL (excluding the priest)	359	

[2] R. H. Tawney, *Land and Labour in China*, p. 43, note 1.

for a young man is regarded as part of the parental obligation. Mates are selected and ceremonies arranged by the parents. On the other hand, the legal act of marriage, although preceding the birth of the child, always anticipates the realization of parenthood. The main purpose of marriage, in the village, is to secure the continuity of descent. To ensure posterity is the chief consideration in the selection of a daughter-in-law and this is explicitly expressed in the consultations which are held with the fortune-tellers. The incapacity of a daughter-in-law to fulfil her obligations may be taken as a strong ground for her repudiation without compensation. Again, the full status of a woman is acquired after the birth of her child. Similarly, the affinal relation remains impotent unless a child is born. It is, therefore, justifiable to start our description of the organization of Chia from the parent-child relation.

The importance of the posterity is conceived in religious and ethical terms. The local term for the continuity of descent is " continuity of incense and fire " ; this means a continuity of ancestor worship. Beliefs connected with the relation of living descendants to the spirits of their ancestors are not clearly and systematically formulated among the people. The general view is that the spirits live in a world very similar to ours, but that economically they are partially dependent on the contributions of their descendents which are made by periodically burning paper money, paper clothes, and paper articles. Therefore it is essential to have someone to look after one's well-being in the after-world.

Some explain the importance of having children on purely ethical grounds. They conceive it to be their

duty because it is through their children that they can
pay back their debt to their own parents. Thus the
desire to have children is backed up by a two-fold
motive : it ensures, in the first place, the continuity
of the line of descent ; and, in the second place, it is a
concrete expression of filial piety by the future father
towards his ancestors.

These beliefs, while undoubtedly connected with
religious and ethical ideas, have also practical value.
In later sections I shall show how the child helps the
development of intimate relations between husband
and wife, who are little acquainted with one another
before marriage. The child stabilizes the relations in
the domestic circle. The economic value of the child
is also important. A child starts contributing very
early to the family welfare, often before he is ten years
of age, in such tasks as collecting grass to feed sheep.
A girl is specially useful in the daily house work and
in the silk industry. Moreover, when a boy grows up
and gets married, his parents are relieved by the young
couple of the full burden of work on the land and in the
house. When the parents are old and unable to work,
they are supported by their sons. This is illustrated
by the following fact : there are 145 widows in this
village who are unable to live on their own resources,
but this does not constitute a serious social problem
because most of them are supported by their adult
children. Children in this sense are insurance for old
age.

Social continuity in kinship is complicated by the
unilateral emphasis of affiliation. Membership and
property of a person is not transmitted equally to the
son and daughter. Emphasis is on the male side.
During childhood both male and female children are

cared for by their parents. Both assume their father's surname, but when they grow up, and get married, the son will continuously live in the parents' house before division while the daughter will leave her parents and live with her husband. She will add her husband's surname to her own. She has no claim on the property of her parents except what she gets as dowry. She also has no obligation to support them except by offering periodical gifts and occasional financial help as their affinal relations (XV-2). Property is inherited by the son whose obligation it is to support the old (IV-3). In the third generation, only the children of the son carry on the continuous line of affiliation. The children of the daughter are regarded as affinal relatives, and assume their father's surname. Therefore, in the village, the principle of descent is patrilineal.

This principle, however, can be modified in case of need. By agreement, a daughter's husband may add his wife's surname to his own and their children will carry their mother's line. Sometimes the husband and wife may carry both lines of their parents. These however are minor obliterations of the general principle and appear only in specific circumstances (IV-4). The present legal system has attempted to alter the traditional unilateral emphasis of kinship affiliation owing to the new conception of sex equality (IV-6). We will discuss these obliterations later.

3. POPULATION CONTROL

In spite of the fact that the villagers recognize the importance of posterity, there is a limiting factor for population. It is true that children can contribute labour to the domestic economy, but there must be enough work on which it can be utilized. With land holdings of limited size, and with limits to the extent of silkworm raising, surplus members of a Chia will be merely a burden to the unit. This brings us to an examination of the average size of a land holding in the village.

The total area of cultivated land is 3,065 *mow* or 461 acres. If this area were equally allotted to 360 households, it would mean that each household could only occupy a piece of land about 9·5 *mow* or 1·2 acres in size. Each *mow* of land can produce in a normal year six bushels of rice. About twenty-seven bushels of rice is needed for the consumption of one man, one woman, and one child (VII–5). In other words, to obtain sufficient food, a family group needs a piece of land of about five *mow*. The present size of land holdings is hardly sufficient to provide an average household with a normal livelihood which requires sufficient food and other necessities. The pressure of population on the land is thus a strong limiting factor on the number of children. For example, a family, with a small holding of nine *mow*, will face a serious problem if a second boy is born. According to local custom, the children when grown up will divide the estate. This will mean poverty for both sons. The usual solution is infanticide or abortion. The people do not attempt to justify these practices and admit that they are bad. But there is no alternative except poverty and " crime." The result can be seen in the figures of the total number of children in the village : there are only 470 children under sixteen years of age, 1·3 per Chia.

The practice of infanticide is more often for the female children. The patrilineal descent and the patrilocal marriage have effected the social status of women. A girl is of less value in the eyes of the parents because she cannot continue the " incense and fire " and because as soon as she is mature, she will leave her parents. In consequences, the ratio of females in the age group 0–5 is unusually low. There are only 100 girls to 135 boys (II–5). Only in 131 Chia, or 37 per cent. of the total, are there girls (under sixteen) among their children (excluding *siaosiv*), and in only fourteen Chia is there more than one girl.

Since population control is considered as a precaution against poverty, families with comparatively large estates are free to have more children. They are proud of their numerous children, and these are taken as a sign of their wealth in the eyes of the people. The desire for posterity, the dislike of infanticide and abortion, and economic pressure—these factors work together to equalize land holdings (XI–6).

4. PARENTS AND CHILDREN

Before the birth of a child, the mother has already definite obligations toward it. During pregnancy, the mother must abstain from violent emotion, from looking at abhorrent things, and from eating certain types of food. There is an idea that the fœtus needs education. Good behaviour by the mother is expected to affect the future personality of the child. No special obligations are, however, incurred by the father, except perhaps abstaining from sex relations with his wife, since this is considered unfavourable to the physiological development of the child and may lead to its early death.

Expectation and fear cause a general tension in the house. The pregnant woman is recognized to be in a special position and is exempted from her various household duties. The exemption is associated with the sense of uncleanliness of sex matters. Her own parents share the tension. Shortly before the child is delivered, they will offer a kind of medical soup to their daughter. Her mother will stay in her room for several days to look after her. It is also the duty of her own mother to clean all the soiled clothes and wait on her daughter after delivery.

It is not customary for the mother to take a long period of rest after the child is born. She resumes her work in the household within a week. This practice was regarded by my informant as the cause of the high death rate of women after childbirth. The actual death rate is not known. But in the population statistics, there is an apparent fall in numbers in the age group of females of 26–30 and 41–45 (II–5) ; this indicates the fact.

Infantile mortality is also high. If we compare the number of individuals in the age group 0–5 with that in the age group 6–10, a big decrease is observed. The difference between the groups is 73 individuals, or 33 per cent. of the group. This phenomenon is also reflected in the belief in " spirit sadism." In the ceremony of *menyu*, literally " child-reaching-full-month," the child will be shaved and given a personal name by his maternal uncle. This is usually a name of abuse, such as dog, cat, or monk. The people believe that the lives of the children, particularly those who are specially regarded by their parents, are sought by devil spirits. A way of protecting the child is to show the spirits that there is no one interested in it ; the theory is that spirits, being sadists, will then discontinue their intervention. This is sometimes carried so far that children are nominally given for protection to somebody who is considered to have greater influence, or even to gods. This pseudo-adoption will be described later (V–3). The parents' outward expression of love of their children is thus carefully concealed.

The attitude of the parents and elder relatives towards children must be understood in relation to these factors—the need for population control due to economic pressure, the small number of children, the high infant mortality, the belief in spirit sadism, the desire for posterity and the connected religious and ethical ideas. As a result of these factors, we can see that the children who survive are highly valued, even though there is an outward show of indifference.

The children in the village cling to their mothers all the day long. The cradle is little used if there are arms available for nursing the babies. The period of suckling lasts three or more years. The time of feeding is not fixed. Whenever the child cries, the mother will at once put her nipple into the child's mouth to keep the child quiet. Moreover, women in the village do not go to the farm, but work almost all the day in the house. Contact between mother and child is thus in ordinary circumstances almost uninterrupted.

The relation between the father and the child is slightly different. The husband has no special duties during his wife's pregnancy and child delivery. For more than half the year, men are at work outside the house. They go out in the early morning and come back in the evening, the chance of contact between them and the children is relatively less. During the child's infancy, so far as the child is concerned, its father is only an assistant of its mother and sometimes an occasional playmate. The husband will take over a part of his wife's work, even in the kitchen, to relieve his wife when she is nursing the child. I have seen young husbands holding their babies awkwardly in their arms in the evening when enjoying their leisure after hard work in the daytime.

As the child grows, the father's influence over the child increases. In the case of boys, the father is the source of discipline ; less so in the case of girls. The mother is more or less indulgent ; when a child is mischievous the mother often will not punish him directly but threaten to tell his father. The method adopted by the father is usually beating. Very often in the evening a big storm will burst out in a house and show that a child is being beaten by a bad-tempered father. As a rule this is ended by the mediation of the mother. Sometimes, the result is a dispute between husband and wife.

Children more than six years old are usually engaged in collecting grass to feed the sheep. This job is congenial to them because it permits a free run in the wild with their companions without any interference from the elders. Girls above twelve generally stay at home with their mothers and are engaged in household work and silk reeling, keeping apart from the children's group.

It is only through a gradual process that a dependent child becomes a full member of the community and it is also by a gradual process that the old retire to a dependent position. These two processes are actually two phases of a general process, that is, the transmission of social functions from one generation to the other—whereby social continuity is secured in spite of biological discontinuity. The social functions of the newcomers, owing to the limited material environment of the community, cannot be acquired without displacing the old. It is specially true in the village where material expansion is very slow. For instance, the total amount of labour required for the land, under the unchanged technique of production, is more or less constant. The introduction of a young man to the land means the displacement of an old man in the working team.

This process is gradual but nevertheless the older generation is retreating step by step. In the process, knowledge and material objects are transmitted from the old to the young, and the latter gradually takes over at the same time his obligation towards the community and the older generation. Here we find the problems of education, inheritance and filial obligation.

5. EDUCATION

Children receive their education from their families. Boys of fourteen begin to learn the technique of agriculture from their fathers by practical instruction and participation in the farm work. They become full workers before they are twenty. Girls learn the technique of the silk industry, sewing and other household work from their mothers.

A few words may be added on the school education in the village. The public school is conducted according to general prescriptions of the Minister of Education. The total term for attendance is six years. Instruction is exclusively literary. If a child starts his school days at six, he will still have enough time to learn his main occupations, in agriculture and the silk industry, after twelve. But in the past ten years, sheep raising has become an important domestic industry.

As I shall describe later, these sheep are kept in huts
and their food must be collected for them (XIII).
This has become the children's job. Thus the
village economy comes into conflict with the school
curriculum.

Furthermore, literary training has not been proved
to be very useful in community life. Illiterate parents
do not take school education very seriously. Without
the help of the parents, primary school education is not
very successful. The enrollment is more than a
hundred but the actual attendance as some students
told me, rarely exceeds twenty, except when the inspector visits the school. Vacations are long. My
stay in the village covered a period longer than the
official vacation, but I had had no opportunity to see
the school at work. The literary knowledge of the
students, so far as I could test, is suprisingly poor.

Chen, a village head, who had himself been a schoolmaster, complained to me that the new school system
cannot work in the village. His reasons are worth
quoting here : Firstly, the school terms are not adjusted
to the calendar of work in the village (IX–3). Students
in the school are generally about twelve years old, and
have reached the age when practical education must be
started. The leisure periods in the calendar of work
are two ; from January to April and from July to
September. But during these periods, the school is
closed for the vacation. While the people are busy at
the silk industry and agriculture, the school is open.
Secondly, the system of education in the school is the
so-called " collective " method, that is, the giving of
lessons one after another without considering individual
absence. Since absence is frequent, the student who
has been absent cannot follow the class when he comes

back. In consequence students cannot keep up their interest and this causes further absence. Thirdly, the present girl teacher does not command prestige in the village.

I cannot go into the problem in detail here but it is clear that there is a maladjustment of the present educational system to the general social condition in the village. A field study of the educational system in a district is Shantung by Mr. Liao Tai-chu [1] shows that the maladjustment is not limited to this village but is a general phenomenon in Chinese villages. This deserves further systematic investigation from which practical suggestions may be drawn.

6. MARRIAGE

The problems of inheritance and filial obligation do not arise in normal conditions until the children grow up and get married. Therefore, we can come to the problem of marriage first.

In the village, sons and daughters give their parents a free hand in arranging their marriage affairs and will obey accordingly. It is considered as improper and shameful to talk about one's own marriage. Therefore there is no such thing as courtship. The parties to this transaction are not acquainted with one another and after the engagement is fixed, must avoid each other.

Arrangements for marriage are made early in the child's life, usually when it is six or seven years of age. This is necessary if there is to be a large range for selection, because children of good families are usually promised very early. My informants repeatedly ob

[1] *Chinese Rural Education in Change*, Yenching University, 1936 (in Chinese).

served that if a girl is engaged too late, she will not be able to make a good match. But it is improper for a girl's mother to initiate a proposal. Moreover, as mentioned, the relation between mother and daughter is very strong. Marriage means the separation of a girl from her parents, and the mother is therefore usually reluctant to contemplate it. Indeed the girl cannot be retained too long in her parents' house. Under the patrilineal system, a woman has no rights of inheritance to the property of her parents. Her future, even a proper livelihood, can only be received through marriage. A third party is thus needed for making arrangements for the marriage. The villagers state that match-making is a good job, because the service is well paid.

The first step by the match-maker is to ascertain the time of birth of the girl. This is written on a red paper with eight characters defining the year, month, date, and hour of the birth. The parents will not object to anyone to whom these papers are sent by the match-maker—at least so they pretend. The match-maker carries the paper to the family of an eligible boy and lays it before the kitchen god. She then explains her mission. A boy of an ordinary family usually receives more than one such red paper at a time. Thus his parents are able to make a choice.

The next step is for the boy's mother to bring the red papers to a professional fortune-teller, who will answer questions (according to a special system of calculation based on the eight characters) as to the compatibility of the girls in question and the members of the boy's Chia. He will suggest the relative merits of each girl, tactfully leaving his client to express her real attitude, and give a decision accordingly. Even if the fortune-teller gives a judgment against his client's wishes, which are usually uncertain, the latter is not bound to take this as final. She can seek a further consultation with the same fortune-teller or with another.

A rational selection of a daughter-in-law is a very difficult matter. No girl is perfect, but everyone seeks the best. It is easy to be mistaken. If no other reason for error can be found, the selector will be blamed. The fortune-teller thus serves not only as a means of reaching a decision, but also for shifting responsibility for human error to the supernatural will. If the marriage turns out to be an unhappy one, it is fate. This attitude is a very practical aid in the adjustment of husband and wife. But it must be clearly understood that the real factor in the selection is the personal preference of the boy's parents, as specially seen in cross-cousin marriage (III–8), although this is disguised under the cover of a supernatural judgment.

The chief considerations in the selection are two : physical health that insures posterity, and skill in the silk industry. These represent the two main functions that are expected from a daughter-in-law: the continuity of the family, and the economic contribution to the household.

When in the manner described a candidate has been selected, the match-maker will go to persuade the girl's parents to accept the match. The custom is first to refuse the proposal. But a diplomatic match-maker will not find very much difficulty in obtaining consent if there is no competition. Lengthy negotiation is needed to determine the marriage settlement. The negotiation between the parties involved is carried out through the third party—the match-maker—and the villagers remarked that at this period the principals behave to each other like enemies. The girl's parents will make exorbitant demands for gifts ; the boy's parents will bargain ; and the match-maker goes between them. The marriage gift, including money, dress, and ornaments, will be sent on three ceremonial occasions. The total amount of a proper marriage gift varies from two to four hundred dollars.[1]

It is far from correct to regard the bargaining as a kind of economic transaction. It is not a compensation to the girl's parents. All the gifts, except that offered to the girl's relatives, will be returned to the boy's Chia as the dowry, to which the girl's parents will add nearly as much as the marriage gift. How much the girl's parents will add it is difficult to estimate, but according to the rule generally accepted, they will be disgraced if they cannot match at least the marriage gift, and the girl's position in her new Chia will be an embarrassing one.

The keen bargaining, hotly carried on, has a twofold meaning. It is a psychological expression of the conflict between mother-love and patrilineal descent. As the people put it, " We cannot let them have our girls without making a fuss." On the sociological side, it is important because the marriage gifts and dowry are, in fact, the contribution of the parents on both sides to provide the material basis for the new family, and a periodic renewing of the material basis of the household for each generation.

The point must be made clear that from the economic point of view the marriage is disadvantageous to the girl's parents. The girl, as soon as she is mature and

---

[1] A Chinese dollar equals in English currency about 1s.—1s. 3d. in normal exchange rate.

can assume her full share of work, is taken from her own parents, who have had all the expense of her upbringing. The marriage gifts do not belong to them, but are returned to the daughter in the form of a dowry with an addition which nominally is at least equal in amount. Since the bride will live and work at her husband's house, this means a net loss to her parents. Furthermore, when the girl is married, her parents and brothers assume a new series of obligations towards their relatives, specially to the children of their girls. In actual life, interest is taken in a child by relatives both on the father's and mother's side. But descent is unilateral, and the child has fewer obligations to its relatives on the mother's side (IV–5 and V–2). The immediate reaction on the side of the girl's parents towards their disadvantages in their girl's marriage is reflected in the whole process of arrangement and wedding ceremony and also in the high rate of female infanticide and its resulting unbalanced sexual ratio.

The wedding ceremony takes as a rule the following forms. The bridegroom goes in person to meet his bride, travelling by a special " meeting-boat " used for this purpose. He puts on a humble and self-deprecating air, and he must face a crowd of the bride's relatives whose attitude to him is usually by no means friendly. He must behave strictly according to custom, and there are experts in this who direct him. A mistake will lead to the suspension of the proceedings. Sometimes the ceremony lasts for a whole night. The culminating scene is when the bride makes a final effort at resistance and buries herself in tears before leaving her father's house. This is ended by the ritual of " throwing the bride " by her father, or, if she has

THE AUTHOR AND VILLAGE GIRLS

The background is the open space before the houses, along the Stream A, piled with threshed rice-stalks and a pump not in use.

[face p. 44

Plate II.

A BRIDGE

At the west entrance of the village.

no father, by her nearest male relative on her father's side, into the sedan chair. As soon as the bride enters the chair, the bridegroom's party leaves very quickly and quietly, and no music is played until they are clear of the village. The symbolic expression of antagonism on the part of the girl's relatives often causes unpleasant feelings between the newly established affinal relatives, especially if they have not a sense of humour.

The next stages of the procedure are the transporting of the bride by " the meeting-boat," the act of union, the ritual recommendation of the bride to her husband's relatives, and the worshipping of her husband's ancestors ; these I cannot describe here. A big feast is prepared by the bridegroom's parents for their relatives and friends. This is one of the occasions for the kinship group to assemble, and the ties of relationship between them are thus reinforced. Each relative or friend offers a gift in cash, the amount of which is determined by the proximity of kinship and friendship. The expenses of the ceremony amount to two to four hundred dollars.

7. THE DAUGHTER-IN-LAW IN THE CHIA

The girl has now entered her husband's house. She finds herself among strangers, but in the most intimate relations with them. Her position is dictated by custom. At night, she sleeps with her husband and she must respond submissively to him. With him alone she can have sexual relations. By day, she shares in the housework under the supervision of her mother-in-law, who has authority over her. She must treat her father-in-law with respect but not with intimacy. She must deal tactfully with her husband's sisters and

C

brothers or they will intrigue against her. She will undertake the cooking and at meals will take the lowest place at table—or even not appear at the table at all.

It must be remembered that in her own family, she enjoyed a rather free life, and one can then imagine what a new world she has now entered. This is her time for discipline. Occasionally, she is allowed to go back to her mother and sob for comfort, as every newly married girl will do. But as the traditional verse runs, " Spilled water cannot be gathered up " : so no one can help her. She accepts her position. This is facilitated by religious beliefs. Human marriage is believed to be held together by the old man in the moon, *yulou*, with invisible red and green threads. This knitting together is symbolically performed in the wedding ceremony. The paper inscription of the god is in evidence in every marriage ceremony. Human helplessness breeds such religious beliefs and they help to relieve the situation. At least in this case they mitigate the tendency of the bride to rebel.

The process of adjusting herself in her husband's house does not in ordinary conditions last very long. She is useful in the house especially in the silk industry, which, as will be shown later, is of great importance in domestic economy (XII–2). In the first spring after marriage, a new daughter-in-law must pass a kind of test. Her mother sends her a sheet of specially selected good silkworm eggs. She will raise these worms entirely by herself. If as a result she proves her skill, she will, so to speak, win the favour of her mother-in-law. This is considered an important event in the life of a girl and on it depends her position in her husband's house.

Similarly her position will be strengthened if she

bears a child, especially a boy. Before the birth of the child, her husband, at least overtly, is indifferent to her. He will not mention her in conversation. Even in the house, in anyone's presence, if he shows any intimate feeling for his wife it will be considered improper and consequently will become a topic for gossiping. Husband and wife do not sit near each other and very seldom talk to each other in that situation. Rather they talk through a third party and they have no special terms for addressing one another. But when a child is born, the husband can refer to his wife as the mother of his child. Thereafter, they can converse freely and behave naturally towards each other. It is the same with other relatives. It is the child that actually admits a woman to her husband's household. The care of the child is an integrative force in the domestic circle.

There are, however, difficulties in the adjustment of relations between a bride and her new relatives. She may not take a quick liking to her husband with whom she has had no previous acquaintance. The people are prejudiced against any intimate relations of a woman with men outside wedlock. To prevent such a possibility prenuptial chastity is strictly maintained by social disapproval of any intimate association between grown-up girls and boys. Any lapse of this code on the girls' side may lead to invalidating their marriage arrangement and difficulties in making other arrangements. Adultery of married women is still more grave. Husbands, in theory, can murder the adulterers with impunity. But in practice it is seldom done. The expense of marriage prevents people even from repudiating a misbehaved daughter-in-law. Sexual intrigues are talked about without seriousness in the evening gatherings. In one case, as my informant told me, the husband indulges his wife in holding a man for economic purposes. But unfaithfulness of a wife is undoubtedly a factor for domestic conflict.

Domestic conflicts are more frequently found between the daughter-in-law and her mother-in-law. It comes to be taken more or less for granted that the mother-in-law is a potential enemy of the daughter-in-law. Friction between them is taken as usual and harmony as worth special praise. Anyone who has listened to gossips among the elder women, will confirm this statement. They are never tired of cursing their daughters-in-law. The potential conflict between them can be understood considering the daily life of the household. The husband and father-in-law do not spend their whole time in the house, but work outside. But the mother-in-law is always there. The daughter-in-law starts with no affection for her. When she comes into the house, she finds herself being watched by her, criticized and constantly scolded. She must obey her, otherwise she may be beaten by her husband on behalf of her mother-in-law. The mother-in-law represents authority.

Similarly from the point of view of the old woman, the daughter-in-law is not always pleasant. I have pointed out in the above section that the tie between parent and child is strong. The relation between husband and wife is in a certain sense a disturbing factor in the parent-child relation. If there is any conflict between the daughter-in-law and the mother-in-law, the husband cannot keep entirely aloof. If he takes sides with his mother, as is usually the case at the beginning of married life, the quarrel becomes one between husband and wife. If he takes side with his wife, the conflict becomes one between mother and son. I witnessed a case where the son became so furious with his mother, owing to a conflict between her and his wife, that he beat his mother. With this triangular relation in the house it is often very difficult to maintain harmony.

If the conflict becomes intolerable, the daughter-in-law may be repudiated. Repudiation is usually on the initiation of the mother-in-law even against the will of her son. If she could find any recognized ground of such action, such as adultery or sterility of the daughter-in-law, no compensation would be asked ; otherwise, sixty to seventy dollars must be given to the repudiated party. The daughter-in-law has no right of redress against such action, but she may be able to persuade her husband to stand firm for her. In the latter case, a division of Chia will result.

The daughter-in-law has no right to request a divorce. The positive action open to her is desertion of the home. She may run away to the town, where she can find a job to maintain herself until a compromise becomes possible. If her husband supports his mother too firmly and there is no hope of reconciliation, she may take a more desperate course : committing suicide. According to popular belief she then becomes a spirit and is able to revenge herself ; furthermore her own parents and brothers will seek redress, sometimes even destroying part of her husband's house. Therefore the mere threat of suicide is enough for practical purposes to effect a reunion. Moreover, since the mother-in-law has to face this possibility, she will usually not drive the daughter-in-law so far as to provoke the result she so much fears.

Disharmony in the Chia should not be exaggerated.

In the group, co-operation is essential.   It is true that the mother-in-law has a privileged position, so long as she is supported by her husband and her son, but the educational value of her discipline should also be taken into consideration.   The discipline which a boy receives from his father, a girl gets from her mother-in-law.   And, as the people themselves say, in the long run justice is done ; for when the girl's own son takes a wife, the mother will enjoy the same privilege as her own   mother-in-law.   The   economic   value   of   a daughter-in-law, and the common interest in the child, make for a harmonious give and take.

8. CROSS-COUSIN MARRIAGE AND *siaosiv*

I have now briefly reviewed the parent-child relation and the husband-wife relation.   I have brought out the fact that there is an apparent lack of economic reciprocity between the boy's and girl's families : and that owing to the marriages being arranged without regard for the inclinations of husband and wife, there is the possibility of domestic disharmony which may lead to the instability of the Chia.   Admittedly in the long run, there is a reciprocity of economic advantage, and this is the fundamental stabilizing force in the kinship institutions ; but the temporary grievances of the daughter-in-law are not favourable to the smooth working of the group.   Cross-cousin marriage is one of the solutions.

In the village, two kinds of " cross-cousin " marriage can be distinguished.   A girl married to the son of her father's sister is called *saonseodiu*, meaning a girl going up the hill.   " Up the hill " signifies the prosperity of the family.   A girl married to the son of mother's brother is called *wesienodiu*, meaning a girl going back

to the native place. This is interpreted as a sign of
ruin of the family. As these terms show, the people
prefer the up-hill type and dislike the " reverting "
type.

Let us see what is the real difference between these
two types. If family A in the first generation gives a
girl to family B to be the latter's daughter-in-law, and
in the next generation the process is repeated, the process is an " up-hill " one. If the process is reversed
in the next generation, the girl is the " reverting " type.
In the first case the girl will be the daughter-in-law of
her father's sister, who is from the father's Chia and
still stands in an intimate relation to her father ; while
in the second case, the girl will be the daughter-in-law
of her mother's brother's wife, who has suffered from
her own mother-in-law who is the girl's mother's
mother. An intimate relation of a mother towards
her married daughter is usually jealously resented by
her son's wife. When the girl comes under her control, she will take her as a target for revenge.

In this family situation, we can see that the psychological factor is stronger than the economic factor,
because from the economic point of view the second
type is much preferable for a balancing of obligations.

I could not ascertain the actual number of cases of
each type of cross-cousin marriage. But my informant admitted that if there is an opportunity of a
suitable match of the up-hill type, it will usually be
made. In a neighbouring village, there is only one
case of the " reverting " type, and that was cited as
fresh evidence of its unhappy results. Furthermore,
comparative materials from South China confirms the
conclusion here suggested. The same type of patrilineal family system and the potential conflict between

the mother-in-law and daughter-in-law is found, together with the same preference for the up-hill type of cross-cousin marriage.[1]

The economic burden of girl children has led to a high rate of female infanticide. This I have already shown in the previous section. The sex ratio which results actually makes it difficult for poorer boys to get a mate. If we take 16 as the lower age limit for marriage, we find that there are 128 marriageable men, or 25 per cent. of the total, who are still single. On the other hand there are only 29 women above 16, or 8 per cent. of the total, who are unmarried. Not a single woman above 25 is a spinster. But there are still 43 bachelors above 25.

The unbalanced sex ratio also affects the age difference between husband and wife. The average difference is as seen in 294 cases 4·9 years while the husbands are older than wives by an average of 3·65 years. We must remember that very young wives are not looked upon with favour, because they are unable to perform their share of the labour of the household. There are many cases where the wife is older than the husband. Indeed in one case the wife was eleven years older than her husband.

I must add that the figures given above were confined to this village ; but marriage is, in most cases, inter-village. Thus, I am assuming a similarity of conditions in other villages. Such an assumption is justified by the fact that the marriage area is identical with the industrial area, and that the silk industry in this area makes identical demands upon girls. In the town conditions are different. The sex ratio in the town is

[1] Lin Yueh-hwa, *Clan Village in Foochow*, unpublished monography, Yenching University (in Chinese), also Kulp II, *Country Life in South China*, p. 167–168.

unknown. But the villagers, instead of practising infanticide often send their girls to the town as foster maids in big families as well as to special philanthropic institutions. Moreover, in the town, I found that infanticide was less practised. In consequence it is to be expected that the sex ratio will be higher than in the village. The difference in the sex ratio between town and village has led to the practice of women being supplied from the town to the village. For instance, when a maid servant in the town comes of age, her master will arrange a marriage for her with villagers. In the village, I know eleven such cases (representing 2·5 per cent. of the married women).

Late marriage is also due to the high expense of the ceremony. Though I could not discover a definite figure for such expenses, a rough estimate is about five hundred dollars (VII–7). This amount is equivalent to the total yearly family expenditure. During the past few years of depression, marriage has been entirely suspended. The depression of rural industry has fundamentally challenged the existing marriage proceedings. But since marriage cannot be postponed indefinitely, another type of marriage is found. This is the so-called *siaosiv* system : *siaosiv* meaning small daughter-in-law or more precisely the foster daughter-in-law.

The parents of the boy will take a girl as foster-child at a very early age, the future mother-in-law even feeding her at her breast, and will take care of her up to marriage. All the elaborate proceedings such as match-making, marriage gifts, the sending of the meeting-boat and sedan chair, will not be needed, if the daughter-in-law has been brought up in her husband's house. Some of the *siaosiv* even do not

C*

know their own parents. Those who have still maintained contact with their own parents, owing to early separation, will not be of special interest to them. The wedding ceremony can be curtailed to cost less than one hundred dollars.

The relations among the members of the Chia and between the affinal relatives are greatly modified by the new institution. The girl brought up from an early age by her future mother-in-law, becomes, as I have observed in many cases, very closely attached to the latter and feels towards her just like a daughter, especially in the frequent cases where there is no real daughter. Even those who are badly treated by the future mother-in-law become used to their position and do not thus experience a crisis after marriage. Thus the conflict between the mother-in-law and the daughter-in-law is often not so acute, even if not entirely avoided. Affinal relation is very loose, and in many cases is entirely eliminated.

The number of *siaosiv* has increased during the last decade. Among the married women, 74 out of 439, or 17 per cent. had been *siaosiv* before marriage. But among the unmarried girls, there are 95 *siaosiv* against 149 non-*siaosiv*. This amounts to 39 per cent. On the average there is one *siaosiv* for each 2.7 households. This figure is very instructive. But it is too early to predict the further development of the institution. Traditional marriage is still the predominant institution, both in frequency of occurrence and in the regard of the people. The *siaosiv* system is despised, since it develops at times of economic depression and is usually practised by poorer families. Moreover, its effect in loosening ties of affinal relationship, affects the normal working of kinship organization. It is also unfavourable to the status of women and to the possibility of the young couple forming an independent family, since they lack the contribution of their parents in marriage gifts and dowry. It is significant that, according to my informants, this type of marriage had in rather similar circumstances become very popular after the Taiping Rebellion (1848–1865), which was followed by a general economic depression. But it had given way to the traditional type as soon as normal conditions had been recovered.

CHAPTER IV

PROPERTY AND INHERITANCE

Ownership — Property of the Chia — Transmission of Property — Effects of Inheritance on Marriage and Descent — Obligation of the Young — New Legislation on Inheritance

1. OWNERSHIP

Before we proceed to discuss the problems of property and inheritance, it is necessary to add a section on ownership in this chapter. I will reserve the problem of land ownership to a later chapter.

Ownership is a certain relation between an object and an individual or a group of individuals. The owner can use, enjoy the benefits of, and dispose of the object under the prescription of custom and law. There are three subjects to be studied, namely : the owner, the object, and the relation between them. From the villagers, we can get a classification of property based on the nature of the owner.

(1) " No man's property." Everyone without discrimination has free access to such property—air, road, water ways, etc. But free access is qualified by the essential fact that one individual should not deprive another of its use. Take the example of water routes : everyone can use the village streams, but they are not allowed to use the route to the detriment of the villagers. The streams are closed during the night. No one can then pass unless he gets permission from

the night guards. Again, even in daytime, boats are not allowed to block the passage. When a boat stops, it must be close to the bank and must leave room for others to pass.

(2) Village property. The inhabitants of the village have equal rights to use and to be benefited by such property—the water products in the surrounding lakes and streams, the grass on the public roads and on the " tomb-land." But the right of disposing of such property is in some cases in the hands of the village heads. This kind of property will be described more fully in the chapter on land tenure (XI–1).

Objects belonging to other territory groups are few. Perhaps we may mention the idol of *luiwan* which is " owned " by the group *de* (VI–3).

(3) Property of extended kinship groups. The clan in the village does not own any common property. But among brothers, after the process of division of Chia, they may still use the same front room of the house (VII–2). The ancestral tombs do not come under property in the real sense because they cannot be used for any benefit of the descendants, but the descendants are on the contrary obliged to keep them in repair. The obligation is shared among the sibling Chia.

(4) Chia property. This category will be the main subject of the next section.

These four categories have exhausted those about which a villager will inform you, and with them all the objects in the village can be classified accordingly. It may be surprising to note the essential omission of individual ownership. The fact is that individual ownership is always included under the name of Chia ownership. For instance, when you ask a person whether his pipe belongs to him or to his Chia, he will answer that it belongs to both. When he says the pipe belongs to his Chia he is trying to exclude members of other Chia from using it ; and when he says it is his personal belonging, he is trying to indicate that his fellow members in the Chia do not use it. These two types of ownership do not seem to him mutually exclusive. Everything owned by an individual is recognized as a part of the property of his Chia. Members of a Chia are under an obligation to protect any article belonging to any particular member in the group. This does not mean that there is no discrimination in the rights over the object of the different members of the group. What it really indicates is only a title under which there is a wide range of intermediary gradations between property jointly owned by the group and individually owned by each member.

Objects may be classified again by types of use.

(1) Those used as a means of production, such as the land, the house so far as it is used for the silk industry, the hut used for raising sheep, the implement, the kitchen, etc.

(2) Those used for consumption.

> (a) Those not destroyed or exhausted after being used, such as rooms, clothes, furniture, ornaments, etc.
>
> (b) Those destroyed and exhausted after being used, such as food, etc.

(3) Those immaterial objects, such as purchasing power (as represented by money), credit, services, and, on the negative side, liabilities, and debts.

2. PROPERTY OF THE CHIA

Among the property-owning groups, the Chia is the fundamental one. It is the basic social unit of production and consumption and thus becomes the basis of the collective aspect of ownership. But, as mentioned, the collective aspect of ownership of the Chia does not entirely rule out the group. It is therefore necessary to analyse how different kinds of objects are owned by different members and how different types of ownerhip are diffused among them.

Land is cultivated by all or some of the male adult members of the household. Boys assist occasionally and women only in irrigation. The produce is partly stored for the consumption of the household and partly sold to pay taxes, rent, and wages and to buy other goods for consumption. The right of using the land as well as the right to a share of the produce is sometimes extended to the employees by definite contract. The right of the tax and rent collectors is limited to that of deriving benefits from the land. In the village, with exceptions, the right of using and right of disposing are generally reserved by the cultivator. He may be regarded as a full owner if he does not pay rent to any one, but pays taxes to the government. If he has lost his legal title of his holding, he must pay rent to the title holder who will pay the taxes out of the rent. In any case the cultivators are protected by law and custom from alienation of the land and from interference by the title holders. In other words, the cultivator owns the land with an attached liability to share a part of the produce with the person who holds the title (XI–4).

The right of disposing of the land is in the hands of

the head of the Chia. But in daily management—such as the determining of the crop to be sown, date of sowing, etc.—the head, especially if it is a woman, does not exercise the right but leaves the decision to persons competent in the technique. But in selling or leasing the land, no one except the head can make a decision. Indeed, in practice, his action may be compelled by other members or he may act on their advice, but the responsibility is his own. In the ownership of land, we can see how the right of use, the right of enjoying the benefit and the right of disposal have been diffused among the members of the group.

The house is used for the silk industry, for threshing rice, for cooking, and for other productive work. It is also used for shelter, for sleeping and for comfort. These different functions derive from quite different types of ownership. In case of silk raising, much space is needed specially during the last two weeks of the raising period. In that period, all the rooms except the kitchen may be used for sheltering silkworms. All the members of the household will crowd in one bedroom. The individual allotment of bedrooms disappears temporarily. In threshing rice, the central hall is used in common and even sometimes shared with the newly divided siblings. The kitchen is chiefly used by women. But the food prepared is shared by all members of the household, except occasionally for special members.

Individual ownership, as meaning the exclusive use of certain objects by certain individuals, is found mostly in goods for consumption. It is clear that those goods which will be exhausted after use are necessarily owned by individuals. But those articles that can be repeatedly used may be shared by several persons successively. The clothes are shared among brothers or among sisters, and between parents and children in different periods, but during certain periods they are used more or less exclusively by one person. Valuable ornaments are exclusive to individual members. They belong mostly to women and are a part of the dowry. Dowry is considered as the " private " property of the woman and shared with her husband and children. It is the family property within the Chia. But at a financial crisis, the family property may be mortgaged for common relief of the Chia. In this case, the willingness of the woman must be secured. Selling a wife's ornaments without her consent will cause domestic disputes.

The room allotted for individual use is more or less exclusive to the family group. The furniture is partly supplied by the wife's parents. The door can be locked by the daughter-in-law although this is not considered as very polite to the mother-in-law. The keys to the boxes and drawers in the room are kept by the daughter-in-law which marks the exclusiveness of family property in the Chia.

The private use of the bedroom by the family does not undermine the final right of disposal of the house to the head of the Chia. The junior members cannot sell or exchange their rooms with anyone. As in the case of land, the head of the Chia has the final decision in any transaction concerning immovable property. It is also true for the produce of the land and the industry. Raw silk may be sold by the woman. If she is not the head, she must hand the money to the head. In this sense, the head of the Chia possesses a superior right to the property over that of anyone in the group.

The rights over immaterial goods, which includes money as purchasing power, are more complicated. The main source of income derived from rice, silk, and sheep, is controlled by the head. Thus money is largely in his hand. It is he who determines the buying of implements and fertilizer, or the acquisition of new land or a new house. Theoretically, according to the ideal system, other members, whenever they get money from other sources, must hand it to the head ; and when they need things must ask the head to buy them. It is a very centralized economy. But in practice the earner usually reserves the whole or a part of his or her earnings. For instance, a girl who works in the factory usually gives her wage not to her grandfather but to her mother to save for her own future use. A daughter-in-law will consider her wage as her own. If a daughter-in-law does not earn money directly, she will ask for more than the real cost of the daily commodities and save the surplus. In this way, she gets a little saving of her own which is called *sivon*, her " private room." It is kept in secret but always watched closely by her mother-in-law and consequently becomes a source of conflict.

The daily expenditure of the household is paid from the common source. But individual members may have a sum each month as their pocket money for free disposal. The main items such as taxes, wages, food, clothes, and other services are controlled by the head. Permission is necessary before any individual member can execute any transactions of these kinds. They are not allowed to secure loans. If a son, a bad one indeed in the eyes of the villagers, is in debt to somebody secretly, his father may refuse to repay as long as he is living. The son can only pay back the loan when he gets a share in inheritance. Therefore the interest is usually very high.

From his economic position, the head of the Chia derives the actual authority in the group. The right over objects enjoyed by a person who is not the head of a Chia is limited and incomplete.

3. TRANSMISSION OF PROPERTY

Inheritance in its wide sense is the entire process of transmission of property according to kinship affiliation. But it is limited in legal usage to referring the claim of an heir to the property of his deceased progenitor.[1] As studied by anthropologists, the problem is usually that of the disposal of the property of a deceased person.[2]

But to limit the study in this way is to leave out various facts, such as the transmission of property during the parents' lifetime and the economic obligation of the descendants towards their deceased ancestors. Ownership is a composite concept of various rights over an object. The process of transmission usually takes place bit by bit. It is not completed even when the progenitor is dead. The fear of displeasing the spirits of the ancestors or the ethical consideration of filial piety indicate the lingering influence of the dead on the free disposal of the inheritance by the heir. Therefore for the present analysis, I shall use the term inheritance in its wider sense.

A child is born into the world without possessing anything. Owing to his physical incapacity to acquire objects the infant is solely dependent upon other's

---

[1] Chinese Civil Code, article 1147. The term succession to property is used in English translation of the code (C. L. Hsia, etc., Kelling and Walsh, Ltd., 1930). I follow the definition given by W. H. R. Rivers : inheritance for the transmission of property and succession for transmission of office (*Social Organization*, p. 87).

[2] R. H. Lowie, *Primitive Society*, pp. 243–255.

provision. It is the function of the family to bring up a dependent infant to become a full member of the community. The parental obligation towards the child is the basis for the universal principle of transmission of property according to the kinship affiliation.

The relation between a child and the objects that satisfy his need is through his parents. At the beginning, he cannot use anything without the consent of his parents. For instance, the basic need of nutrition is dependent on the consent of his mother. Indeed, this consent is to a certain extent guaranteed by human sentiment and social rules, but even this is not always secured. In case the child is not welcomed to the house, he may be killed by the refusal of milk. As he grows up, the objects allotted for his use increase. But he has no free access to those things. The clothes he wears are put on him or taken off according to the will of his mother. Food is put before him. He cannot take things without the permission of his mother. The gifts given by his relatives are kept by his mother. The control of the elders over the child in his relation with objects is mainly for the welfare of the child and for preventing damage to the object by the child's unskilful use. Therefore when the child knows how to take care of itself and learns the proper use of objects the control diminishes. As technical knowledge increases and he participates in productive work, the child gradually acquires the right of use over objects that belong to the Chia. But there are very few objects exclusively and freely used by him. The type and amount of goods he consumes are also always under the control of his elders.

An important step in the process of transmission of property takes place at marriage. In the marriage, the parents of both bride and bridegroom contribute to the new couple, in terms of marriage gifts and dowry, a set of objects, consisting of personal belongings, as a nucleus of family property. The new couple now have a room, more or less, for themselves. But from the point of view of the bride, she has at the same time lost at least a considerable amount of her right over the objects in her own parents' house. When she goes back after marriage, she is a guest, the more so if her parents are dead and the house is owned by her brother. She is admitted into her husband's house. But she cannot behave there freely as in her own parents' house. Her right to use objects is in practice very limited. She has no share in the personal objects of other members in the Chia except those of her husband. It is she who starts the disintegrative tendency in the collective economy of the Chia.

The centralized system in the domestic economy, as described in the above section, reduces the independence of the young couple. The parental control is necessary for the development of a child, but the persistence of such control over him after his marriage is a different matter. A full member of the community needs a certain amount of property under his own disposal and a normal functioning of a family requires a larger material basis ; but these are precluded by the centralized system of the Chia economy. The demand for economic independence of the young then becomes one of the disorganizing forces, and finally leads to the division of the group.

The process of division is one of the most important steps in the transmission of property from the parents to the child. Through the process the young acquire a legal title over a part of the property formerly belonging to the father and enjoy a more exclusive right to it.

The division between the parents and the married son usually takes place after some accident of domestic friction. The maternal uncle acts as mediator and proposes the division on behalf of the young man. He will negotiate with the old to decide the share to be allotted to the son. But the division between married brothers is automatic when their parents are dead.

Let us take an example of a Chia, consisting of a father, a mother, two sons, and a daughter. When the first son gets married and demands a division, the land will be divided into four parts. The first part is that reserved for the parents. The second share is the extra share for the first son. The rest is equally divided between the two brothers.

The share reserved for the parents will be sufficient to provide for their daily life as well as the marriage expenses of the second son and the daughter ; its size will therefore depend on the number of unmarried children and the living expenses of the parents.

The eldest son receives two shares, the extra share being a small one. The size of the extra share depends on the economic contribution that he has made to the collective unit. The first son, being older, will undoubtedly have made more contributions than his younger brother. Moreover, in the view of the villagers, he has also a greater ceremonial obligation towards the dead parents.

The share for the unmarried son is nominal. He will live with his parents and has no independent status. But he can demand the share when he is married. If one of the parents dies before his marriage, further division will be ruled out. The younger son who has not yet separated from his parents will support the remaining parent, who will hand over most of his or her economic authority to the married son even without division. When both parents are dead, the reserved share will go to the younger son, in consideration of the support he has given them. Thus he will also in the end inherit two shares. But if the elder brother shares in the support of their parents, he will have a claim on the reserved share. The final division will not necessarily be equal.

The house is divided in several ways. If the parents are living, the eldest son will have a house outside. In the case of Chou, the junior village head, he, being the younger son, lives with his parents in the old house. His elder brother moved, after the division of Chia, to a new house not far from the old one. If the division of Chia occurs after the death of the father, the elder son will occupy the old house and the younger son moves out with the mother. To build or to find a new house is difficult. Thus in most cases the old house is simply divided into two parts ; the elder takes the east part and the younger the west. (The orientation of the house is always to the south.) The front room is occupied in common.

If there is one son only, he will demand separation from his parents only in case of serious conflict. In this case it means no more than a demand for economic independence. The amount of the son's share is not important because it is only a temporary allotment. In the end all the property will be handed over to him ; when the parents are old and unable to work, they will be re-incorporated into their son's Chia. The process of re-incorporation does not undermine the rights acquired by the son, but, on the contrary, conveys to him the rights to the rest of the property.

Both the land and house are unilaterally inherited. The daughter has no share in them. When she is married her parents will give her a dowry, consisting of furniture, ornaments, clothes, and sometimes a sum of money ; but never land or house. Even the poorest parents furnish the coverlet of the bed for their daughter.

The son, after the process of division, has a separate house or a part of the house. He has a separate kitchen in which his wife will cook food for the family. He has a separate piece of land. The produce of the land is at his own disposal. But, in fact, his right over these allotments is still not complete. His father, as long as he is living, can strongly influence his use of the land and house. The son cannot sell them against the will of his father. He will send food to his parents in case of need. When the parents are old or one of them is dead, he is obliged to support them. Therefore the process of division does not completely end the economic relation between the parents and the child.

Moreover, the property divided in this way is limited to that used for production and a part of that used for consumption. Personal belongings of the parents will be reserved for them. The son usually gets a sum of money to start his new economic unit, but debts and liabilities, except his own secret loans, will be kept back until the death of the father.

The reserved part of the immovable property will be transmitted to the son when the parents are too old to work. The final transmission occurs at the death of the parents, specially of the father. A part of the personal belongings will be buried with the dead and a part will be burnt—to be used, as it is believed, by the spirits. The remainder will be divided not only between the sons but also between other relations who have served the deceased. The daughter will have a considerable share of her mother's leavings, including clothes and ornaments. This suggests, in some degree, the matrilineal inheritance ; but since the daughter-in-law also has her share, the rule is not absolute. The division of these types of property is subject more or less to the personal will of the deceased or her husband (or his wife) who has the right to decide the disposal of what is left.

4. EFFECTS OF INHERITANCE ON MARRIAGE AND DESCENT

As far as the land and house are concerned, the line of inheritance goes along the line of descent. But if a man has no son, to whom will the property be transmitted ? This problem appears in two circumstances : a man may be childless ; or may have a daughter but no son. Let us study the first case of the man who is childless.

Childlessness due to physiological sterility is rare. If a woman is sterile, she may be repudiated and her husband will remarry. In most cases childlessness is due to the death of the child. When a man is old and without a living child, he can adopt a boy. He is free to choose his adopted son. In adopting his son, he must invite his clansmen and before them he will sign a contract with the parents or other responsible person of the child. The contract consists of two parts. On the one hand the adopting father will give a formal promise to guarantee the full status of the adopted son, especially the right of inheritance ; and on the other side the person responsible for the adopted child will promise to sever his relation with the child and also guarantee in the child's name to support the adopting parents when they are old.

The endorsement of the fellow-clansmen of the contract is essential, for this action is counter to their interest. If the person dies without issue, his nearest kin in the next kinship grade will automatically become his descendant and inherit his property according to custom. But in this case, the heir will not sever social relations with his own parents. The child will live with his own parents and has done no work for his benefactors. The heir has, in fact, mainly ceremonial obligations.

From the economic point of view, it is considered preferable to adopt a child who can work for the adopted parents during their lifetime than to appoint an heir among kindred. But adopting an outsider means the loss on the side of the nearest kin of a potential claim on the property. Therefore the parents of the potential heir will do their best to prevent the action. The usual result is a compromise. Either the nearest kin will support the adopting parents or the old will adopt an outsider but promise a share to the potential heir in the inheritance. The share will not be land or house but a sum of money.

If the son dies after his marriage and leaves no grandson, his parents will find a substitute for his son as the second husband of their daughter-in-law. The substitute is called *wanipon*.[1] He will change his sur-

---

[1] Villagers explained the meaning of this term as yellow (*wan*) muddy (*ni*) leg (*pon*). But they did not know why he should be so called. Afterwards I found that a similar expression " muddy leg " is used in the Northern Chinese dialect, for example, in the classical novel *Red Chamber Dream*, chapter 45, referring to those wandering vagabonds. But another literary explanation of this term was given to me by the literate people in the town

name to that of his wife's former husband and live in the latter's house. His child will be regarded as a descendant of the deceased. The social status of such a substitute is low because no well-to-do person will accept this position. There are two *wanipon* in this village.

Levirate is practised in the similar condition if the deceased has a brother who has not yet been engaged. There are two cases of this type in the village. Levirate is common in case of *siaosiv* when her would-be husband dies before marriage.

We must now turn to the second case : that of the man who has only a daughter but no son. If the daughter has been married before the death of her brother, she cannot contribute anything to the continuity of her father's line. But if she has not been married, her parents, knowing that there is not hope of another son, can ask the parents of their daughter's fiancé to allow their daughter to carry on their descent. In other words, they will have the right to take one of their daughter's male children as their own grandson. This type of marriage is called *lendiugoxofen* ; meaning to attach two flowery flags on the ancestral shrines of both Chia. The flowery flag is a symbol of descent used in the wedding ceremony. In this village there is one case of this type.

If the daughter has not yet been engaged, her parents can adopt a son-in-law. The girl's parents will send marriage gifts to the boy's parents. The wedding

as " to prevent the wildness or lack of the child." The word for prevent, Fang, is pronounced by the local people as *ban* which has been changed as *wan* in this term. The word for child, Er, is pronounced as *ni* in the local dialect. The word for wild or lack, Huang, is pronounced as *whan*, and is changed here to *pon*. The phonetic changes such as *b* to *w* and *wh* to *p* are observed in other instances. The literary explanation gives the function of the substitute while the local explanation gives the nature of the substitute. They are both useful in understanding the practice.

ceremony will take place in the girl's house and the husband will live in his wife's house with the wife's parents. In addition to the general wedding ceremony, the girl's parents will sign a contract with the boy's parents, similar to that of adoption of a son and witnessed by their clansmen. The child of their daughter will take their surname and continue their descent. There are twelve such cases in this village. This number is significant if we take into consideration that there are relatively few cases of sonless parents and that the practice of late engagement is rare. When there is still hope for the parents to get a boy themselves, they will not arrange such a marriage. But if after the marriage, they got a boy, as seen in one case, the accomplished fact will continue to be valid. It is a generally accepted institution and has been legalized in the civil code.[1]

In the above-mentioned cases, the patrilineal principle of descent is obliterated and the marriage institution is modified. It shows that the problem of inheritance and descent should be viewed as a part of the reciprocal relation between the two generations: the transmission of property on the one hand and the obligation of supporting the old on the other. The obligation of the young to support the old is maintained not by legal force alone but by human affection. Owing to the tie of affection and economic security of the old, they prefer an adopted son from outside to an appointed heir among the kindred, and modify the patrilineal principle to adopt a son-in-law. The obligation of the young does not end when the old are dead. The care of the tomb and offering sacrifice to ancestor spirits are a part of this reciprocal relation.

[1] Code Nos. 1,000, 1,002, 1,059, and 1,060.

Furthermore, the right of free disposal of inherited property is again strongly conditioned by the religous and ethical belief of ancestor worship. Thus we must study the obligation of the young towards their parents in connection with the problem of inheritance.

5. OBLIGATION OF THE YOUNG

To begin with, in a childless family, the adults themselves will collect grass for the sheep. But when a child is born and able to work, they are relieved of this work. In rice growing, a boy will assist first in transplanting young shoots and in irrigation. As the boy grows older, he works side by side with his father and eventually undertakes more work than his father, even before he gets married. A girl will assist her mother in the daily household work and in the silk industry. When their contribution to the family exceeds their own consumption, they begin to support their parents, although their share is not apparent owing to the collective economy.

The problem of equality between parents and children in economic contribution does not arise, but it does arise between siblings. I was acquainted with one case of a man who did not work at all on the land but was supported by his brother. He prevented his younger brother from marrying in order to continue his parasitic way of living. He was severely criticized by the community. Public opinion has forced him to arrange a marriage for his younger brother which would be followed by a division of Chia, but it had not taken place before I left the village. The accepted idea is this, that since one owes a debt to one's parents in childhood and receives property from them, it is one's duty to work for them, but not for one's brother.

However, a sense of equality between parents and children is not altogether ruled out. When a young couple undertakes the greater part of the work in the household but still is without an independent status owing to the economic power being centralized in the hands of the older generation, there will be much dissatisfaction. It will eventually force the parents to relinquish their power along with their withdrawal from work.

The obligation to support becomes apparent when the son has secured his independence. If the parents have in their old age still a share of the land, and are not able to work it themselves, the son will cultivate it for them. This means in fact that the son must set apart a share of his labour for his parents. Another form common when one of the parents is dead, is that the remaining one will re-incorporate into the son's Chia and live there. The amount of support is then not fixed. If there are two sons, they may support their parent alternately. In any case, the authority of the parents is reduced in proportion to the degree of their dependence. From the point of view of types of ownership the general line of retreat of the parents is from the right to use to the right of disposal of the produce and finally to the right of disposal of the objects itself. From the point of view of types of objects, the retreat takes place from the means of production to goods for consumption and finally to immaterial privileges and liabilities. These steps of retreat correlated with the increase of obligation of the young from entire dependence to taking a co-operative rôle and finally to bearing responsibility for the whole livelihood of the parents. Even the death of the parents, as mentioned, does not completely eliminate the obligation of the young towards the old. The disposal of the corpse, the mourning and the periodical offering of sacrifices are a prolongation of filial obligations. Since the privileged party cannot exert direct control over these obligations, religious belief and public opinion enter more strongly into the sanctions.

A person approaching death will be attended by the members of the Chia. All the juniors will kneel beside him with the son in the closest position. Daughters are not necessarily among the group but will come promptly after their parent's death. A package of clothes will be burnt with a paper chair before the front door. Neighbours will then gather to assist the funeral business because the members of the Chia are under heavy mourning and not able to manage the business. The son, the daughter-in-law and the daughter will put on coarse hempen cloth and their heads will be tied with a long white belt down to the ground. Shorter belts and white clothes are worn by grandchildren.

On the second or third day, the corpse will be put into the coffin. The eldest son will hold the head of the deceased and the younger son the feet. On the next day, the coffin is closed and moved to the grave-yard. According to the practice of the village, which is different from the town, the coffin is not buried underground, but above the ground among the mulberry trees and covered with a shelter built in bricks and tiles. If the family cannot afford a brick-and-tile shelter, a simple straw one will do. In this way, no land is made waste for the burial.[1]

[1] The average percentage for grave land in the farm is 2·6 in Eastern Central China (Buck, *Chinese Farm Economy*, p. 33). The absence of special grave land, except the tombs for the rich in the town who bury their dead in the village, indicates the particularly high population pressure on land.

It is the duty of the descendants to repair the shelter of their ancestors' coffins up to five generations. Those decaying coffins, about which no one cares any more, will be removed by a special philanthropic institution and buried somewhere else.

The spirit of the dead, it is believed, has left the corpse and has been admitted to the world of spirits. It will come back to the house at the seventeenth or eighteenth day after death. On that day, the house will be prepared to welcome the spirit. The tablet with the name of the dead will then be put into a wooden pavilion presented by the husband of the daughter and set in the front room. Heavy mourning is observed for forty-nine days. Each meal will be prepared before the pavilion and a woman will wail beside it with dirges. This is the obligation of a wife towards her husband and a daughter-in-law towards her parents-in-law. Men never take part in such wailing.

During the funeral ceremony, the priest who keeps the genealogy of the Chia will be invited to recite buddhist classics before the dead. His recitation is believed to have pecuniary value in the spirit world. The name of the dead is thus put into the genealogical record by the priest and will be included on the list for worshipping.

Daily sacrifices will be ended on the forty-ninth day. The tablet pavilion will be burnt at the end of two years and two months. It concludes the mourning period. The tablet is then put in the ancestral shrine.

At ordinary time, special sacrifices are offered on the birth and death days of each particular ancestor, and collective offering for all lineal ancestors five times a year as shown in the time-table of social activities (IX–3). The mode of sacrifice is that a feast is pre-

Plate III.

HOUSES ALONG THE STREAM

Houses are built near the streams ; in front of each house there is
a stone platform for mooring boats.

[*face p.* 76

Plate IV.

THE STOVE AND THE PALACE OF THE KITCHEN GOD

The stove signifies the unit of Chia ; when the Chia divides, separated units must have their own stoves. On the top of the stove resides the kitchen god, who is the supernatural inspector of the house. Periodical sacrifices are offered on the platform where stand a pair of candlesticks.

pared for the spirits, at the conclusion of which paper money made in tin foils is burnt. This indicates directly the prolonged economic obligation of the young towards the old even after death.

The observance of these obligations by the descendants is in one sense the legal charter of descent and the claim on inheritance. The act of holding the head of the dead when the corpse is being placed into the coffin, for instance, is regarded as justifying the extra share of inheritance of the eldest son and is a determining fact in appointing an heir from the kindred. It is true that there are no two persons who stand in exactly the same kinship order with the deceased, but if the nearest kin failed to perform this act, the second one takes up his rôle and the claim of the nearest kin is forfeited. The one who observes the obligation will be the legal heir and will inherit the property.

Furthermore, at the death of an unmarried person who possesses no property of his own, the question of inheritance does not arise and therefore no descendant is appointed.

But the obligation of mourning is not unilateral. Mourning groupings are shown in the following table.

From the table, we can see that both the period and the act of mourning are not correlated with descent but to a certain extent with the actual social relations and their standardized ties of affection. Mourning is not thought to increase the welfare of the spirit but is regarded as an expression of affection. It is different from ancestor worship, which is thought to be a definite contribution to the welfare of the spirit.

The immediate control over objects and persons ceases at the time of death. But the belief in the existence of spirits even after death prolongs the in-

D

Relationship to the Dead	Period	Act of Mourning
Wife	Indefinitely, until the marriage of her son.	Coarse hempen skirt and shoes, white cord on the hair at the beginning then changing to white skirt and shoes ; wearing no silk.
Husband Son-in-law	Indefinite, a few months.	Blue button on the hat.
Son	2 years and 60 days.	Coarse hempen shoes, changing to white, if one parent is still living again changing to blue ; white button ; wearing no silk for one year.
Daughter (married or unmarried)	2 years and 60 days.	Coarse hempen skirt for 49 days ; white shoes changing to blue ; yellow cord.
Daughter-in-law	2 years and 60 days.	Coarse hempen skirt for 35 days, rest like the daughter.
Grandchild Brother's child Sister's child Daughter's child	1 year.	Blue button for male ; blue cord for female.

Elders of the deceased observe no obligatory mourning.

fluence of the deceased over property. Misfortunes and sickness are sometimes, not always, explained as the warning of ancestor spirits for some action that they do not approve, such as non-observance of the periodic sacrifice, damage to the coffin shelter, selling of land or house, etc. Pure ethical consideration is strong enough to prevent the person from selling his inheritance freely. The continuity of land holding is an expression of one's filial piety. Any act against it will be criticized by the community as bad. This is of considerable importance to the problem of land tenure.

5. NEW LEGISLATION ON INHERITANCE

Having described the actual process of transmission of property in the village, now we can turn to the legal provisions. In preparation of the new civil code in China which came into force in 1929, the legislators followed the fundamental policy of the Kuomintang, the National Party in China, to promote sex equality by granting an equal right of inheritance to men and women. This has made an important departure both from the old civil code and from the traditional practice as described above.

The principle of the old and the new codes on the problem of inheritance can be summarized as follows :

" Formerly, a woman had, save a simple exception, no right to inheritance according to Chinese law. For instance, suppose a Chinese died fifteen years ago, leaving his widow, a son and a daughter, the whole of the property left by the deceased was by law to be inherited by the son only. Neither the widow nor the daughter was entitled to any share. In case the deceased had no issue except the only daughter, the daughter and the widow were still entitled to nothing if the brother of the deceased had a son. The son of the deceased's brother was the legal heir to the deceased and the whole of the property was to go to him. Again, even if the deceased had no brother, or his brother had no son, yet, so long as the deceased had a male relative descending from their common male ancestor and belonging to a younger generation than that of the deceased, surviving him, that male relative had a legal claim to inherit the whole estate left by the deceased. So the daughter could have the right of inheritance only when her deceased father had neither a son, nor a nephew, nor a male relative existing at the time of his death. The widow was in no case entitled to succession.

" But now the law has been changed very greatly. Women's right of inheritance is expressly recognized in the civil code.[1] Suppose the above-mentioned man dies now, instead of fifteen years ago, his property will be equally divided between the widow, the son and the daughter. If he has no issue other than the daughter, the daughter and the widow will inherit jointly to the estate. The patrilineal nephew and the other male relatives have been deprived of the right of succession altogether."[2]

The old legal principle prescribed strict unilateral inheritance along the line of patrilineal descent. It followed the custom so long as a person had a son of his own. His daughter after marriage would live with her husband and join the economic unit of the latter. She had no obligation to support her own parents. In the mind of the people it was fair that a woman should be deprived of the right to inherit her own parents' property. But there were cases where a person had no son. According to the old law, he had

---

[1] The Chinese Civil Code, Article 1,138 : " Heirs to property other than the spouse come in the following order : (1) Lineal descendants by blood (2) Parents ; (3) Brothers and sisters ; and (4) Grand-parents." Lineal relatives are defined in Article 967 as " His relatives by blood from whom he is descended or those that are descended from him." They includ both son and daughter and their lineal descendants.

[2] This summary is supplied by Mr. H. P. Li, Barrister-at-law at Shanghai

no choice but to leave his property to his nearest kin. He might adopt a son or a son-in-law but the latter had no legal right of inheritance. Under these circumstances, the custom had provided compromises. It seemed to the people unreasonable to deprive one who had supported the deceased from inheriting what the latter left. But since they also recognized the potential claim of the nearest kin, as mentioned, compensation might be demanded.

The new code has altered the unilateral principle of inheritance because it is conceived as against the principle of sex equality. But how far it has altered the principle of descent is not very clear. It recognizes the daughter, even after marriage, as being as much a descendant of her parents as were her brothers (Article 967). But as a wife, she will " prefix to her surname that of the husband " (Article 1,000), and take " the domicile of her husband as her domicile " (Article 1,002), except her parent adopt a son-in-law for her. Her children will " assume the surname of the father " (Article 1,059), except there is an agreement for another arrangement, and the domicile of her child is that of the father (Article 1,060). As a descendant, she has obligations to maintain her own parents (Article 1,115). Therefore each family has the obligation to maintain relatives of both husband and wife while husband and wife have to live together.

These legal provisions when translated into actual social practice will lead to an organization based on a bilateral principle of kinship. Professor B. Malinowski has pointed out that " unilateral descent is also intimately bound up with the nature of filiation, that is, with the handing over of status, power, office and possessions, from one generation to the other. Order and simplicity in the rule of filiation are of the greatest importance for social cohesion." [1]

It would be interesting, therefore, to investigate the social consequences of this legal system. It provides an experiment for the anthropologists to study the process of change from unilateral kinship affiliation to a bilateral one. But so far as this village is concerned, I have yet found no indication of any actual change pointing in this direction, although the new law has existed for seven years.

[1] " Kingship," *Encyclopædia Britannica*, 14th ed.

CHAPTER V

KINSHIP EXTENSIONS

Paternal Extension — Maternal Extension — Pseudo-Adoption
— Kinship Basis of the Village

Kinship is the fundamental bond uniting the members of the Chia, but it does not confine itself within this group. It extends to a much wider circle and forms the principle of association of larger social groups which will be the subject-matter of this chapter.

I. PATERNAL EXTENSION

The Chia is an undivided expanded patrilineal family, because it excludes the relatives on the mother's side and also married daughters. The larger kinship group on the father's side is the group in which members have still preserved, to a certain degree, the social relations originated in the Chia after it is divided. As we have seen, when the family nucleus in the Chia increases in size, the group becomes unstable. This leads to division. But the divided units do not entirely separate from each other. Economically they become independent, in the sense that they have each a separate property and each has its own fire place. But they are still bound together by various social obligations. At the beginning, they usually live in adjacent houses and sometimes share the big front room in common. They stand very close to each other in matters of mutual help and in daily intercourse. In the second generation, children of both units share the intimacy of the relation between their parents. The intensity of daily intercourse and mutual help varies according to the kinship proximity and also to the territorial proximity of residence. If brothers after division reside in distant houses, the opportunity for mutual help is decreased, and this is still more so among siblings of the next generation.

According to accepted principle, all the patrilineal descendants and their wives that can be traced to a common ancestor within five kinship grades consider themselves as belonging to a kinship group called Tsu, and refer to each other as *tsezomenzon*, meaning " one who comes from the same door of my Tsu." But in practice this strict genealogical accounting is not important. Firstly, there is no written document of genealogy and memory of descent is not very exact. Family trees are kept by the priests, not for the purpose of recognizing living kindred but for keeping alive the memory of lineal ancestors to whom sacrifices should be offered. Siblings do not enter into the list of spirits. Spirits of ancestors farther back than five kinship grades are removed from the list to be worshipped. Secondly, if the principle were strictly observed, theoretically there would be a division of Tsu for each generation. But Tsu are seldom divided for this purpose.

The actual situation is as follows : The population in the village has been stationary for a long time. The Tsu will not be sub-divided if there is no increase of members. Furthermore, if there is an increase, there must also, owing to the pressure on the land, be a migration to some other place. When people move away, they will no longer take an active part in the kinship group. After one or more generations, kinship ties cease to function. That is why I have not yet found any Tsu with members permanently in other villages.

The following note given to me by a villager may be quoted here. " The average size of a Tsu is about eight Chia. This is because when my son marries, all the Tsu will come and sit at the same table. (Each table has eight seats, for one representative from each Chia ; men and women gather separately at different times.) When a table is not large enough, we do not invite our distant kindred to the celebration." Of course, this statement is not an actual rule, but indicates that the acknowledgement of membership of the unit allows individual discrimination. One can exclude those distant kin in ceremonial gatherings and they will not insist on their claim to be invited. A rich Chia is able to provide two or more tables for its clansmen, and will do so with pleasure and be praised for it. In this sense, the Tsu can be taken as no more than a ceremonial group which assembles periodically at wedding and funeral occasions, taking a common feast, offering sacrifices to the common ancestors together, and contributing a small sum barely enough to cover the food. Real social obligations of mutual aid exist between smaller groups, such as brothers with newly divided households. The people do not use the term *tzezomenzon* to describe their relation but the term *disho*, or brotherhood.

Another character of this unit is that its membership is the Chia. Therefore it is not a unilateral kinship as its individual members are concerned. A married woman entering her husband's Chia automatically

D *

becomes a member of her husband's Tsu. She takes the surname of her husband although she retains her father's surname in the second place. She kneels beside her husband in the joined offering of sacrifice to the ancestors during the ceremonial occasions of her husband's kin. When she is dead, she will receive sacrifices with her husband.

She loses her membership of her father's Tsu when she is married in the sense that she will not join the offerings of sacrifice to ancestors on the father's side and will not be offered sacrifices by them after her death.

The most important function of the Tsu is in the regulation of marriage. The Tsu is an exogamous unit except in case of levirate. Persons with the same surname are not barred from marriage, provided they are not of the same Tsu. It is true that the classical rule, as well as the old legal code, prohibited marriage between two persons with the same surname, but this does not apply in the village ; and so far as my informants remember, has never applied. The lack of clear distinction of Tsu does not hamper their exogamous function, because most of the marriages are inter-village and the organization of Tsu rarely goes beyond the village.

2. MATERNAL EXTENSION

In the above sections, we have already seen that the child keeps close contact with his relatives on his mother's side. His maternal grandmother comes to assist his mother in childbirth. The child will visit his maternal relatives many times a year. His maternal uncle has special obligations towards him. He is the guest of honour at the ceremony held when the child reaches one month, and is the one who selects a name for the child ; he escorts him when presenting him for the first time to his schoolmaster. He will present a valuable gift, ornament, or cash, when his sister's son gets married. On the child's side his maternal uncle is a protector against harsh treatment by his father. He can run to his maternal uncle in case of need. His maternal uncle will act as mediator in conflict between father and son. When property is divided between father and son or among brothers, the maternal uncle is the formal judge. When the maternal uncle dies, his sister's children will mourn for him.

The mother's sisters, especially those married to fellow villagers of the father, also, owing to local proximity, stand in very intimate relationship.

But the kinship relation does not extend beyond the group of Chia of maternal uncle or maternal aunt. Their extended kindred is excluded from the functional grouping.

Relatives on the wife's side do not come into intimate contact before a child is born. They do not participate in the wedding ceremonial of their daughter, but pay visits in the first month after it. The bridegroom goes with the bride to visit his new parents-in-law on the third day after the wedding. After those ceremonial visitings are over, they do not visit each other except the wife herself who may go back occasionally. When a child is born the wife's mother will spend a few nights with her daughter. From that time on relatives on the wife's side become maternal relatives of the child.

3. PSEUDO-ADOPTION

Pseudo-adoption is a system by which a person is partially included in another's kinship group without the connection of procreation or marriage. The local term for this system is *govan*, meaning " passing to another house " or *gochi*, meaning attaching. It is said to be originated from the belief in the malevolent spirits who will make trouble for those children who are specially regarded by their parents (III–4). By similar reasoning, anyone who has numerous children must possess stronger resisting power against the evil spirits. Thus by " attaching " a child to such a strong person, it will be protected. On the other hand, giving the child to others, though nominally, will be enough to show the spirits that the child is disregarded by its parents.

This belief, as shown, is related to the high infantile mortality, but the institution of pseudo-adoption means more than a spiritual protection of the child's welfare. It also provides a wider social connection for the child, if we remember that those who have numerous children, whether they really possess spiritual power or not, certainly possess wealth and social influence (III–3). By creating a pseudo-kinship relation with them, the child will acquire a better economic and social position in the community. On the other hand, the person who accepts pseudo-adopted children is pleased by the belief that this is an indication of his prestige and future prosperity.

The relation will be created by a ritual act, which consists of a sacrifice to a god called " new-official-horse " (the meaning of this term is not clear to me). The adopted child will offer a present of needles, peaches and wine, symbols of long life, to his " adopting " parents, who will in turn offer him a feast and give him a new personal name, and his " adopting " father's surname (which is in fact never used) and some ornaments and cash.

The child also acquires at the same time a new set of duties and privileges. He will address his " adopting " parents by relationship terms. In the new year, he must greet his " adopting " parents, offer regular gifts to them. He will participate in their ceremonial occasions, and mourn for them ; and he will not marry their children. He in return receives " rice of new year's eve," shoes, hats, and gowns for three years (symbolizing incorporation into the " adopting " parents' household), regular gifts and other regards.

This type of " adoption " is metaphorical ; the child does not sever its relation with its real parents. It acquires neither the right of inheritance nor the obligation of support. It nominally changes its surname but this is, as the villagers put it, only to fool the spirits. The real meaning therefore is to create a new social relation similar to kinship by metaphorical use of relationship terms and by ritual acts.

The extension of social relations facilitates social activities but is also expensive. During the economic depression, even real kinship relations are a burden, and there is a clear sign of the shrinking of kinship organization. Pseudo-adoption becomes less popular. As my informant told me, to seek protection against the evil spirits, they " attach " their children to the god or to their father's sister's husband. Thus no new relations will be created. Since girls are much less often pseudo-adopted, the special preference for a father's sister's husband to play the part may be linked up with the idea of unlucky marriage of the " reverting " type (III–8). It does not narrow down the marriage choice when girls of father's sisters are included in the exogamous unit.

4. KINSHIP BASIS OF THE VILLAGE

In pseudo-adoption, kinship terms are used in a metaphorical sense in order to establish new social relations which are similar and derived from kinship. This type of extension of the kinship relations to persons bound neither by procreation nor by marriage is very common in the village.

All the terms for relatives on the father's side, with the exceptions of those for father, mother, grandfather, and grandmother, are used for addressing fellow villagers according to their sex and age and the consanguinity and affinity to the village. The terms for mother-side relatives, with the exception of mother's parents are used for addressing the people in the village of mother's parents in similar manner. This type of usage of kinship terms serves the function of classifying local and age groups, and defines the different types of social relation towards each of them by that derived from the existing kinship relation.

There is a definite purpose in this extended use of relationship terms. To each term there has become attached certain psychological attitudes corresponding to the intimate relationships for which they were initially devised. These emotional attitudes may, by the extended use of the term, be taken up to persons not actually standing in such an intimate relationship. For instance, a person addressing his fellow senior villagers as father's brother will tend to show the same obedience and respect to them as to his father's brother. The attitude associated with the term used for the mother's brother, is different from that with the term for the father's brother. The nephew associates the idea of his maternal uncle with indulgence and friendliness. By addressing his mother's fellow villagers as mother's brother he behaves freely among that group of persons, and enjoys their treating him as a guest.

It should be noted that the extension of such emotional attitudes to persons not actually related as the terms would imply does not necessarily involve an extension of specific privileges and obligations. It does not imply a real extension of kinship relation, but it is useful in defining a person's status in the community where the old are respected and usually possess authority.

Recently the principle of distribution of authority according to age groups has been undergoing change. The old men in the village who are not able to keep up with the rapidly changing situation cannot fulfil the rôle of leaders in the community. Thus the present village head, Chou, is from the second age grade in the community. He addresses the senior grade who either work under him or are less influential in the community, by their personal names. Formerly this manner of address was possible only between a senior and his juniors. On the other hand a new term has been introduced, *sisan* (used in towns generally as the title of a teacher, or simply as a common title such as that of mister in English), by which he is addressed by the age grade senior to him. This case illustrates very clearly how sentiment is associated with the term. When the situation has changed in such a way that a person from the senior grade has become the subordinate, the original sentiment of respect is incompatible in the context. The changed social situation thus caused a psychological difficulty, and finally a change in language.

It must be pointed out that the extended use of relationship terms should not be taken as evidence of an existence of " clan village," at present or in the past, in this part of China. A study of the distribution of the surnames in the village can demonstrate that, although kinship groups tend to concentrate in compact areas, genealogical relation does not form a basis of local groups.

In the patrilineal society, the surname is handed down from father to son. But it does not imply that those who have the same surname can always trace their origin to a common ancestor. For instance, Chou told me that those who have the surname Chou in this village have two entirely separate origins. Furthermore, those with a common ancestor may not be recognized socially as kindred owing to the clan organization. But one thing is clear, those who have different surnames cannot be of the same patrilineal kinship group. Thus multiplicity of surnames in the village can be taken as an indication of their multiplicity of patrilineal kinship groups.

There are twenty-nine surnames in the village. The following table shows the number of Chia of each surname in each *yu* (II–3).

From this table, it is possible to see the distribution of the Chia of the same surname. There appears a tendency of concentration of kinship related groups. For instance, Chou and Yao are concentrated in *Yu* I ; Chen in *Yu* II ; and T'an in *Yu* III and IV. Some of the surnames, such as Lü and Chiu can be found only in one *yu*. These facts indicate a close relation between residence and kinship relations. In other words, there is a tendency for the Chia bearing the same surname, probably bound by kinship ties, to live in an

Surname	Yu I	Yu II	Yu III	Yu IV	Total
Chou . .	49	23	24	2	98
T'an . . .	7	4	17	28	56
Yao . . .	30	4	10	—	44
Hsü . . .	13	4	9	4	30
Shen . . .	2	4	13	7	26
Wang. . .	1	6	—	8	15
Lü . . .	—	14	—	—	14
Chiu . . .	—	10	—	—	10
Chao . . .	7	—	—	—	7
Ni . . .	4	3	—	—	7
Jao . . .	—	7	—	—	7
Wu . . .	—	4	2	—	6
Chiang . .	8	—	—	1	5
Lu . . .	—	—	—	5	5
Chen . . .	4	—	—	—	4
Fang . . .	4	—	—	—	4
Chin . . .	—	1	3	—	4
Ch'ien . .	—	—	—	4	4
Yang . . .	3	—	—	—	3
Ch'in . .	1	—	—	—	1
Chia . . .	1	—	—	—	1
Liu . . .	1	—	—	—	1
Fêng . . .	1	—	—	—	1
Ling . . .	1	—	—	—	1
Huang . .	—	1	—	—	1
Yu . . .	—	—	1	—	1
Li . . .	—	—	1	—	1
Ying . . .	—	—	1	—	1
Kuo . . .	—	—	—	1	1
TOTAL .	133	94	75	57	359 [1]

[1] Excluding the priest.

adjacent residential area. But it is also clear that the fact of numerous surnames and their dispersion indicate the multiple kinship groups and the low correlation of consanguinial and local ties.

Similar are the affinal relations. Strictly the village is neither an exogamous nor an endogamous unit. But, as mentioned, marriage is more frequently arranged among people of different villages. There is a tendency towards local exogamy although it is not formulated. Among the villages, no special preference is made of one as against another. Therefore, affinal relation does not preserve a strong tie among the people of the same village or among the villages.

CHAPTER VI

THE HOUSEHOLD AND VILLAGE

Household — Neighbourhood — Religious and Recreative Groups — Village Government — The Imposed Administrative System, Pao Chea

Beside kinship bonds, another fundamental social tie is that of territorial bonds. Those who live near each other find it easy to co-operate in matters of common interest demanding concerted action. In this chapter, we shall review various territorial groups.

1. HOUSEHOLD

The Chia, held together by kinship ties, is not necessarily an efficient working unit in economic life. Members of a Chia may be temporarily absent or removed by death. The introduction of new working members, through kinship ties such as birth, marriage and adoption, is not always easy to effect and sometimes is not advisable owing to questions of inheritance. On the other hand, members of a Chia, which has broken up may wish to be temporarily incorporated into another working unit without assuming new kinship relations. Therefore, those who live in the same house and participate in most of the economic pursuits may not be necessarily considered as members of Chia.[1]

---

[1] From the legal point of view, however, an individual not related in kinship but living permanently in the group is recognized as a member of the Chia (Code, No. 1122–1123). But this has not been accepted by the villagers. Even those who have lived a long time in the Chia are regarded as distinct from members of the Chia.

Here we may use the term household to refer to this basic territorial group.

In the village I found that in twenty-eight cases individuals have been introduced into the economic unit, living, eating, and working as members of the household but clearly distinguished from the members of the Chia. They were not connected with the Chia by the necessary kinship ties and did not permanently pool their property without discrimination into the Chia but usually joined the unit upon definite terms. The relation of such members to the group varies from that of a long-term guest to having practically no distinction from the members of the Chia except over the legal rights of property.

There are three ways in which non-Chia members may be introduced into a household. The member may be a guest of a certain family and have made a definite annual or monthly payment over a rather long period of residence. For instance, a medical doctor practising in the village had lived in the house of the owner of the medicine store for many years. He had a separate room and shared the daily life with his hosts. Another case was that of a child whose own family lived in another village, but who was brought up and nursed in a house in the village. The parents of the child made contributions each month to the family nursing it. There were five cases of persons related to their hosts by affinity. After the breaking up of their own Chia, they join their relatives on the mother's side. They could not be incorporated into the Chia but would remain as guests, although practically they lived in the house just as members of the Chia.

The institution of apprenticeship also provides a way of introducing a working member from outside.

There were four cases of this kind. An apprentice is provided with food and shelter by the master without tuition and in return is bound to work for his master for a certain period of years without wages, except in the last year when he can demand a small amount for " renewing his shoes and stockings."

The commonest way, however, is through employment. A person may be introduced into a household as an employee under a definite contract to work on the farm or at the silk industry. The employee receives accommodation in his employer's house. He participates in the household work, is entitled to use all the implements, and is provided with food and shelter. He has also a fixed amount of wage each year.

These are all the cases in the village in which members who do not belong to the Chia were introduced into the household.

The members of a Chia may not live in the house but pursue their work in distant places. Their temporary absence from the house does not affect their kinship affiliation. But during their absence, they cannot be considered as a member of the household, although they have definite economic relations with it.

In the village the total number of individuals not living in the house of their own family was fifty-four. Of these thirty-two are females and eighteen males ; they were at work in the town except four boys who lived in their master's houses in the village bound as apprentices. These numbers indicate the relatively strong movement of the population towards the town, especially among females.

2. NEIGHBOURHOOD

A number of Chia combined together to form larger territorial groups. The formation of larger groups depends on the common interests of those who live in a wider territory. For instance, there are natural menaces such as flood and drought and also the threat of invasion by an alien people, which do not affect single individuals but all those living in a locality. They must take concerted actions to defend themselves—as by building dikes, relief measures, magical and religious activities. Moreover, the satisfactory exploitation of his land by an individual requires co-operation with others : similarly with the distribution of the produce and with trade and industry. The need of relaxation and amusement is another factor which will bring together individuals in games and other forms of group recreation. Thus the fact of living together and near to each other produces the need of political, economic, religious, and recreative organizations. The following sections will give a general description of territorial groupings found in the village, but those groups formed specially for economic activities will be discussed in later chapters in detail.

A neighbourhood is the group of households combined for daily intimate contact and mutual help. Conventionally people take the five households on each side of their residence as being their neighbours. For these they have a special term *shanlin*. They have towards one another special social obligations.

When a new-born baby is one month of age, his mother will carry him to visit the neighbours. They will be courteously received with tea and entertainments. When they leave, a gift, which consists of cakes, will be bestowed on the baby. This is the first visit of the baby to a house other than his own, even before he goes to his mother's father's house.

In the case of marriage, the bridegroom's family will distribute a kind of cake as an anouncement and invitation to the wedding ceremony. Neighbours are included in the list. In return they will offer a present in cash on the wedding day and participate in the feast of celebration. In case of funerals, each house in the neighbourhood will send one person to assist without payment.　　　　　　　　*// 3314*

In daily life when one needs extra labour in household work, such as removing heavy articles, neighbours will come to help. In case of economic stress, money can be borrowed from them in small sums without interest. Such relations of mutual help are not rigidly confined to ten households, they depend more on personal intimacy than formal prescriptions.

3. RELIGIOUS AND RECREATIVE GROUPS

In the village, the god, besides the ancestor spirits, who receives sacrifices most frequently is the kitchen god—his wife being sometimes included.

The kitchen god, *zončen*, is the supernatural inspector of the household, sent by the emperor of heaven. His duty is to watch the daily life of the house and to report to his superior at the end of each year. The god is represented by a paper inscription, bought from the shop in the town and placed in the little palace on the stove. He receives sacrifices twice a month, regularly at the first day and the fifteenth day, and on other occasions as shown in the time-table of social activities (IX–3). The first dish of each seasonal food will also be shared with the god. The sacrifice is made by laying dishes on the platform before his little palace, lighting a pair of candles and burning a bundle of incense as an invocation.

At the end of the year, the twenty-fourth day of the twelfth month, a farewell sacrifice will be made. This sacrifice consists of a big feast and takes place in the front room. After the feast the paper inscription will be burnt with the pine sticks and a paper chair. Through the fire, as indicated by the flame, the god returns back to heaven. In this annual audience with the emperor, he will make a report about his findings on the particular house in his charge. Based on the report, the fortune of the household will be decided.

The criterion for pleasing and displeasing the god, a very important daily control of human behaviour, is the observance and non-observance of certain taboos. A full list of taboos does not exist in a precise form, but a vague feeling of fear of supernatural interference in daily life due to displeasing actions is definitely found in everyday occurrence. As far as I was able to note, those taboos fall into three categories. The first is based on reverence for rice. Rice should not be trampled underfoot or wasted. Even sour rice should not be thrown away carelessly. The proper manner is to eat all the rice cooked. If this cannot be done, it must be thrown into the river in order to feed the fish. The second category of taboo is connected with the sense of dirt in sex matters. All the things and activities connected with sex must be cleared up outside the kitchen. Women during menstruation should not touch anything on the platform of the kitchen god. The third category is connected with respect for learning. Any paper with written characters of any kind, even newspapers, should be collected carefully and waste papers should be burnt, never in the kitchen, but on the open ground or in the special furnace in the temple.

The idea of a well organized supernatural kingdom complicates the connection between human actions and supernatural interference. The breaking of any taboo does not automatically provoke certain consequences directed by the supernatural powers. They must come through the supernatural administrative machinery. Therefore if anyone can prevent the inspector, the kitchen god, from seeing or reporting, the taboo can be broken with impunity. The supernatural agents or the spirits are not conceived as absolutely omnipotent and omnipresent. They are actually invisible human beings with very similar human sentiments and desires. Since they are very human, they also commit all human weaknesses and follies. Thus, all the human methods, which can be used towards any human policeman such as cheating, lying, bribing, and even physical bullying, can also be used in dealing with the supernatural inspector.

In the last farewell feast before the kitchen god returns to his heavenly office, the people prepare a kind of cake made of sticky rice. This cake is a favourite of the god. It is believed that when the god eats the cake, his mouth will be stuck together ; and when the heavenly emperor asks for his annual report, which is an oral one, he can only nod his head without saying anything. Therefore no unfavourable report will be possible. But it is not regarded as so certain a remedy as to be an infallible safeguard against any taboo breaking.

The police function of the kitchen god is clear from its mythology. At a certain time, when a foreign power had conquered China, every house was forced to support a foreign soldier as its inspector. This the people found intolerable and at last they made a plot each to murder his soldier at the same time. The sticky cake was prepared and offered to the soldiers, whose mouths were stuck together. They could thus make no noise when being murdered. This plot was successfully carried out at the twenty-fourth of the twelfth month. But the people at once realized the danger of revenge by the spirits of the foreign soldiers. Some sort of compromise was achieved by which from that time on the spirits of the soldiers were to be worshipped in the kitchen as the god of the household and carry on their function of inspectors.

I was told this myth by only a few informants. Most of the people do not know the origin of the god and do not care very much about it. But the myth actually reveals the attitude of the people towards the supernatural inspector. It shows their unwillingness to submit their personal freedom of action to the social restriction which is imposed on them in society. This is slightly different from ancestor worship, which reflects the sentiments of attachment to dead ancestors.

Another god called *luiwan* is worshipped by a larger territorial group which consists of about thirty houses. This territorial group has a special term, *dè*, meaning segment. There are eleven segments in the village :

I. Ch'eng Kioh *yu*	4
II. Liang Kioh *yu*	3
III. Hsi Chang *yu*	2
IV. T'an Chia Têng	2

Each segment has its own idol of the god. Every year households of the same segment, each represented by one member, male or female, will meet twice, in the first and eighth months. At this meeting, the god will be invited to one of the houses, and a big feast is prepared by the host in his honour.

Luiwan, *lui* being the personal name of the god and *wan* meaning king, is a popular god in that region. In my own childhood I was often told about this rather elaborate myth. But all my informants in this village were ignorant of this. They told me honestly that they did not know who *luiwan* was although they had worshipped him for years and years. The purpose of the meeting was said to be related to the harvest. But the link is very vague in the minds of the people. Some confessed that their real interest in the meeting was the feast. As I shall later show, the village is not a self-sufficient religious unit. In case of drought, locusts, or flood, all the religious and magical performances will take place in the district town. The town is not only the economic but also the religious centre. The god, *luiwan*, is the supernatural protector against the locust menace. His myth will be described later (X–3). But it may be interesting to point out here that the lack of independent religious activity in the village on the occasion of agricultural crises is correlated with vagueness and ignorance about the myth connected with the god.

About ten years ago, there used to be a kind of annual meeting for religious and partly for recreative functions. This would be held in the autumn after the harvest. It served as a thanksgiving to the gods responsible for the harvest and at the same time as a request for blessing for the coming year. The images of local gods would be seated among the people and an opera company would be invited to play on the stage constructed specially for the purpose. The village was divided into five groups, called *degi*, meaning " the foundation of the stage." Each group was responsible for the management and expenses of this gathering in turn.

With the deepening of the economic depression in the village, these annual meetings have been suspended and it is difficult for the present to say whether they will be revived when the economic depression is over The interesting fact that there is no tendency to attribute the economic depression to the suspension of the gathering, but, on the contrary, the economic depression was regarded as the cause of the suspension. This shows that the nature of the gathering was less religious or magical than recreative. The economic depression which is due solely to the fall of silk and rice prices is understood in its true nature, and thus the solution resorted to has been the perfectly reasonable one of introducing modern technique and new industries.

The local gods, who were invited to attend the opera in former days, are found in two temples in the village one at the south end and the other at the west end (II-4). Each Chia sends its representative to visit the temple twice a month and make sacrifices individually This is not obligatory and is usually neglected. But persons who continue this observance constantly direct their attentions to one of the two temples, which is determined by the location of their houses. The people living on *Yu* I, III and the north part of II go to the west temple and the rest to the south temple But individuals in the same area do not associate with each other in definite duties and obligations, as we found in the worship of *luiwan*. Their association is only through the temple. We must, in fact, say that there is not a religious group but a religious area.

The two temples are owned by different priests

The owner of the south temple lives in the temple, while that of the east temple is an absentee. The daily work in the temple is managed by a non-religious agent called *san-xo*, meaning " incense and fire." The priest, being himself a buddist, lives on the income of the temple and keeps aloof from secular activities. Nevertheless, he has definite functions in the community. He entertains the visitors and participates in the funeral ceremonies of the people. These services are paid either by an amount of incense, which is kept by the priest for resale, or by cash. But these two temples do not monopolize the religious activities of the people in the village. On important occasions, such as " burning incense " for newly dead relatives and fulfilling certain promises to the god after recovery from illness, people go to the big temples in the town or at the bank of the Lake where the gods are more powerful.

Another important function of the priest is to keep the ancestor records for the people, and this also takes him beyond the village temples. Genealogical records of the families are kept in different temples outside. Since the record keeper is rewarded by the family whose ancestor names are kept, the record book becomes in a way the personal property of the priest. Like other kinds of personal property, it can be bought and sold. Therefore the circulation of wealth among the priests has made the allegiance of the people to the temples more complicated.

The nature of their allegiance, however, has nothing to do with belief or with sects. The priest never preaches any religious doctrine to the people, except possibly to the dead. Even then he preaches in a language alien to the local people. The stranger the accent, the more valuable, in the popular view, is the preaching.

4. THE VILLAGE GOVERNMENT

For various social functions, households are associated together to form larger local groups. These groups do not form a hierarchical series but superimpose on each other. The village, being an aggregate of households in a compact residential area, separated from other similar units by a considerable distance, sets a limitation on the direct extension of territorial ties for various functions. It marks a common boundary for those intimate territorial groups. It synthesizes various social functions and also takes up special functions that cannot be fulfilled by smaller units—all these are performed through the village government by the village headmen.

Village heads are always accessible, because they are known to every villager, and a stranger will be received by them immediately. The visitor will be impressed by their heavy burden of work. They help the people to read and to write letters and other documents, to make the calculations required in the local credit system, to manage marriage ceremonies, to arbitrate in social disputes and to look after public property. They are responsible for the system of self-defence, for the management of public funds, and for the transmission and execution of administrative orders from the higher government. They take an active part in introducing beneficial measures such as industrial reform into the village.

There are two village heads at the present time. The following note gives a short sketch of them.

Mr. Chen is an old man, nearly sixty. He received his order of scholarship—Hsiu Ts'ai—under the late imperial examination system which was abolished at the end of the last dynasty. He had failed to proceed further in his scholastic career and was invited to become a family tutor in the town. At the beginning of the Republic, he came back to the village to start a private school and remained as the only schoolmaster in the village, for more than ten years. From that time on he has assumed the leadership in the village under various formal titles according to the ever-changing administrative system. In 1926, he initiated the silk reform programme with the support of the Provincial Sericultural School and started the experimental station in the village. In 1932, he was formally responsible for the establishment of the co-operative silk factory. He then gave up his job as a schoolmaster and became manager of the factory. When the new administrative system, Pao Chea, was introduced, he found work with the government was not suited to his taste and thus retired from the office, but nevertheless he has remained the *de facto* head of the village, and is still responsible for community affairs.

The other head is Mr. Chou. He is younger, being about forty years of age. He was educated by family tutors but was too late to take the imperial examination. Without scholastic interest he was content to be a simple peasant with his brother. Being literate and honest, he was picked by the reform agent of the silk industry as an assistant. He has from that time on secured the confidence both of the reformers and of the people and gradually shared with Chen leadership in public affairs in the village. When the Pao Chea system was introduced he was, on the recommendation of Chen, formally elected and actually appointed the head of the Hsiang which includes the village.

Headmanship in the village is not hereditary. Chou's father is engaged in the tile trade and his elder brother is still working on the farm. His son is in the town and is not likely to succeed him in the future. There is no kinship relation between Chen and Chou.

Although both Chen and Chou are well-to-do persons, neither is considered the richest person in the village. The richest person is, I believe, a man named Wang, who lives in obscurity and is without any outstanding prestige. It is true that a child of a poor family has less chance of attaining the position since headmanship has no direct economic reward and requires rather long and expensive preparation (to attain the necessary standard of literacy), but wealth alone does not give power or prestige.

Even legal status is not essential for the headmanship. Chen is still the senior head in the village, but he has no position in the formal administrative system. Elder persons tend to avoid the trouble of dealing with the higher government. The basis of the headmanship lies in public recognition and support in the leadership in community affairs, and in being the representative of the community against the outside world. Chen started his career as a schoolmaster and Chou as an assistant in the silk factory. Their service and ability have given them authority and prestige. In the village there are few who are literate and still less who are at the same time willing to take up the responsibility without economic reward. Young men of ambition are not satisfied with the position : it is considered by the two middle school graduates, I met in the

Plate V.

SMALL WOODEN PAVILION KEEPING THE TABLET OF THE NEWLY
DEAD ANCESTOR

The pavilion is presented by the son-in-law of the deceased and
kept in the middle of the front hall for two years and two months
of heavy mourning period.

ABOVE-GROUND BURIAL

The coffin is covered by a shelter built in bricks and tiles; generally
found among mulberry trees.

Plate VI.

SAILING

Surrounded by streams and lakes, the people depend on their boats for any heavy and long-distance traffic. A characteristic scene in this region.

village, as sterile and hopeless. Thus the range for the selection of village heads is not very large.

Although they have no direct economic reward, they enjoy prestige and presents from the persons who have received services from them. For example, they are respected by the people, and can call the generation senior to them, except their own near kin, by their personal names without adding any relationship terms. This cannot be done by an ordinary person. Their leading position in the village also helps them to hold privileged jobs such as schoolmaster and manager of the silk factory.

Headmenship is not connected with any previleged "class." Even seniority in age is not an essential qualification, as is shown in Chou's case. But the sex disqualification has not yet been entirely overcome; women are excluded from public affairs. Only recently women have acquired the same position as men in the silk co-operative society, and a woman teacher has been appointed at the school; but the latter has very little influence in the community except among boys and girls.

5. THE IMPOSED ADMINISTRATIVE SYSTEM, PAO CHEA

As mentioned, the village as such has no legal status because side by side with the functional territorial groups there is an administrative system imposed on the village organization. These two systems, which I have termed *de facto* and *de jure* respectively, do not coincide with each other. In this section, I shall describe the *de jure* system and compare it with the *de facto* system to show the discrepancies.

The new administrative system is called Pao Chea. The term Pao Chea is an old one. The government

E

recently had the idea of reviving an old administrative system which has been proposed by an administrative reformer in the Sung Dynasty (960–1276). How far this old system had actually existed is another question, but for this village it is entirely new. The head of the village explained that the arrangement for the new system had only recently been completed, and it had never within living memory been in existence. He added that the villagers had been summoned by the town head and told to arrange their houses in a manner prescribed by the district government. This had been done. To study this Pao Chea system, therefore, it is necessary to go back to the statute book to see what is the intention and what principle the government followed in its organization.

On June 5th, 1929, the National Government in Nanking promulgated the Law Governing the Organization of the District, based on the principle of local self-government of the late Dr. Sun Yet-sen. According to the law, each district (Hsien) must be divided into several Chu and each Chu into twenty to fifty Hsiang (in rural areas) and Chên (in urban areas). In the rural areas, villages with more than 100 households would be taken as a Hsiang and those with less than this number would be combined with other villages to form a Hsiang. In urban areas, towns with more than that number would be taken as a Chên, and those with less would combine with other villages to form a Hsiang. The Hsiang is again subdivided into Lu (twenty-five households) and Lin (five households). All these units were to be self-governing through their elected headmen and councils. The functions of these local governments are listed in the law as follows : Census taking, population registration, land survey, public works, education, self-defence, physical training, public health, water regulation, forest preservation, industrial and commercial improvement, food storage and regulation, protection and prohibition of plantation and fishery, co-operative organization, improvement of customs, public belief, public enterprise, financial control, etc.

These functions are not altogether new to the local community, most of them having been carried out by various traditional *de facto* groups. The law created new territorial groups with the purpose of facilitating the self-governing administrative functions. But, in fact, there is the danger that it will actually hamper the normal functioning of the *de facto* groups. Thus in the Second National Administrative Conference in 1931 the rigidity in the size of the units was severely criticized. Consequently, an amending bill was introduced in the Legislative Yuen.

While the bill was still in the stage of discussion, another system was instituted which affected the local government. In August, 1932, the Headquarters of the Punitive Campaign Against the Communists, in Central China issued a decree organizing the people in the area of military operation (Hopei, Honan, and Anhwei) into uniform self-defensive units under the system of Pao Chea. According to this sytem, each ten households (Hu) form a Chea and each ten Chea a Pao. The intention of this organization was stated in the decree to be " to organize the people in the devastated area in a more effective way and secure an accurate census in order to increase the power of local self-defence against the communists and to enable the army to discharge its function more efficiently." This system was introduced mainly for military purposes.

Unless the population could be accurately registered, it was very difficult to prevent the communists from mixing with non-communists in the disturbed areas. To counter the active propaganda of the communists, the army introduced the system of mutual responsibility of the individuals in the same Chea and Pao, so that they could act as a check one upon the other.

In 1933, the spread of communist influence drew Fukien into the military area. In Fukien the provincial government had already started the organization of the local self-governing system according to the Law in 1929. The provincial government was ordered by the Headquarters to suspend the local self-governing system and to substitute for it the Pao Chea system. In their conflict between the Law and the Decree, the provincial government submitted to the central government : and the Central Political Council decided to absorb the Pao Chea system in the self-governing system. The Law of 1929 was superseded by a series of laws of 1935. These two systems were compromised in the following six points : (1) the uniform units of Pao and Chea were substituted for the old units Lu and Lin, and the units Chu, Hsiang, and Chên were to be on the same level : in other words, the original status of Chu as an intermediary unit between district and Hsiang or Chên was abolished ; (2) before the completion of the Tutelage period, the method of indirect election was to be substituted for direct election according to the Pao Chea system ; (3) a census was to be taken in the process of arranging the households in the Pao Chea system ; (4) military training in the Pao Chea system was to be extended into a more general civil training ; (5) the system of mutual responsibility was to be applied only in cases of emergency ; and (6) the Pao Chea system was to take up the function of self-government, but local modifications were to be allowed to suit particular conditions.

Obviously, the compromise has not solved the fundamental problem, that is, how far the *ad hoc* self-defensive units with their uniform size could undertake the general administrative functions listed in the Law of 1929. The real issue was not the legal conflict between the law and the decree but whether the traditional functions that have been carried out in the *de facto* territorial groups could be taken over by the arbitrarily created Pao Chea. Since the old units Lin and Lu, of a less rigid kind, had proved to be impracticable it did not seem that a more rigid system was likely to function any better. The effectiveness of the Pao Chea system in self-defence in cases of emergency also did not assure its suitability as a system for administrative self-government. It could indeed be argued that in the process of political integration in China it was desirable to substitute for the heterogenous traditional structure a rational and uniform structure. But it remains to be considered whether such a substitution was necessary and how much it will cost to enforce. Since this new system was only introduced less than a year before my visit to the village, it is too early to draw any conclusions. But an analysis of the working of the system against the background of the traditional structure will obviously throw light on the general problem, and will at least help to stress the importance of this issue in the future administrative policy.

The Pao Chea, as instituted in this village with allowance for local modifications, does not strictly accord with the numerical prescription of the law. The village with its 360 households is divided geographically into four Pao. As I have shown in the village plan, the houses in the village are built along both sides of the streams and are thus distributed in four *yu*. The houses in the same *yu* are grouped into one Pao. According to their positions, counting from east to west and from south to north, the houses are arranged in order, approximately ten in number, to form the units of Chea. These four Pao are combined with another seven Pao in neighbouring villages into one Hsiang, which is called after the name of the village Kaihsienkung Hsiang. Pao and Chea are known by numbers. The four Pao in the village are numbered from eight to eleven. A further discrepancy between practice and law is that the Chu in the old law is still preserved as an intermediary unit between the district and Hsiang, and roughly corresponds to the functional unit of the marketing area of the town (XIV–8). This village can be defined in terms of the administrative system as :

> Kiangsu (province)
> Wukiang (district)
> Chên tsê (Chu)
> Kaihsienkung (Hsiang)
> No. 8–11 (Pao)

To examine the nature of the Hsiang, we must inquire into the problem of inter-village relations. Is there any special bond between the villages that are grouped into the same Hsiang ? What is the functional group that corresponds to this administrative unit ? Economically, villages in this region, as I shall show later (XIV–8), are independent of each other. Every village has its own agent boat which serves as the buying and selling agent of the villagers in the town market. A village, however large it may be, does

not form a sub-marketing centre among its neighbouring villages. In other words, the town as the centre
of the marketing area is able, owing to the ease of
water transport and the institution of the agent boats,
to collect from and distribute to its tributary villages
without any need for intermediate stoppage of the
movement of the goods. Within the area, there are
several dozens of villages dependent on the town but
independent of each other. These villages, which are
occupied in similar work and produce similar goods,
find little need for trade with one another. Thus the
unit of Hsiang, standing between the marketing area
and the village, has no economic basis. The same is
true from the point of view of kinship relations.
Although inter-village marriage is popular, there is
no sign that those villages included in the same Hsiang,
are preferred to those outside.

Linguistically the name Kaihsienkung in daily speech
refers strictly to the village alone. It seems ridiculous
to the local people to say that the neighbouring village
is a part of Kaihsienkung. Their obstinacy in this is
not unreasonable. The change means a great deal to
the people. Some people told me, " If the neighbouring villages are part of Kaihsienkung, then the lake
that belongs to Kaihsienkung people will be shared by
the people of the neighbouring villages. But of course
this cannot be permitted."

At present the increasing prestige and economic
function of the silk reform movement, and the administrative status of the head of the Hsiang, which both
have their head offices in this village, have drawn
together the villages around it. I noticed that people
from other villages, not limited to those of the same
Hsiang, visited the village more frequently than

formerly to order silkworm eggs, to supply cocoons for the factory, and to settle inter-village disputes. But in the last analysis, the head of the Hsiang, Chou, did not work in his legal capacity, but mostly through his own personal influence as the assistant manager of the silk factory, and he did not make any important steps without getting into touch with the *de facto* heads of the village concerned.

Of course, given time and increasing experience of the new administrative functions, there is no reason to say that the new unit will remain on paper for ever.

The unit of Pao, however, is different. To divide the village according to the boundary of streams is not likely to be successful. It is assumed in this case that the stream is a dividing line for social activities. This assumption is not true. As shown, boats are active on the water, and bridges are built to connect those separated pieces of land. They are means, not obstacles, of communication.

Lastly, we come to the Chea. Among the functional groupings, we have seen that there is a type of group called *shanlin*, the neighbourhood, which consists of ten households. But it does not correspond with the Chea. Chea is a fixed local segment while *shanlin* is a chain of overlapping units ; each house taking its location as the centre of reference. The segmentation of Chea is very artificial and contradictory to the idea of the people.

Nevertheless, it will be interesting to study the problem in a future investigation to see how far planned social change can be started from the social structure including the form of the group, formal rules of behaviour, and formal system of thought ; such attempts are evidently becoming more and more popular in a situation where state uniformity is desired.

CHAPTER VII

LIVELIHOOD

Cultural Control on Consumption — Housing — Transportation — Clothing — Nutrition — Recreation — Ceremonial Expenses — Minimum Expenditure

Having made a general survey of the geographical and social background of the village, we are now in a position to study the economic life of the people. I shall begin my description with the system of consumption and attempt to assess the general level of livelihood in the village. This level gives us some idea of the necessary requirements for ordinary living. To satisfy these requirements is the ultimate incentive to production and the impetus to industrial change.

From the point of view of consumption, there is no essential difference among the villagers, but in production, occupational differentiation is found. The present study is mainly limited to the farmers who form the majority. They are engaged in tilling land and in raising silkworms. These are two main sources of their income. Selling sheep and making periodic trading ventures are subsidiary sources. Before describing these activities, I will indicate through the calendar of work how these activities are arranged in a time sequence.

The legal aspect of the problem in relation to agriculture will be discussed in the chapter on land tenure. It would be sufficient to mention here that the traditional forces operating in this institution are strong enough to resist any significant changes. Even in technology, new methods and tools have not yet been successfully introduced. But in the silk industry, it is different.

The most urgent economic problem, from the point of view of the villagers, is industrial reform. The decline of the price of silk is the immediate cause of financial insolvency in the village. During the past ten years, a series of reforms have been introduced and as a result of these efforts both the technology and social organization of the silk industry have been radically changed. Therefore, we are able to analyse the process found in this village as a case study of industrial change in rural economy.

From the analysis of the systems of consumption and production we are led to the system of exchange. Through marketing, the villagers exchange their own produce for those consumed goods which they themselves do not produce. In marketing, we can see how far the village is self-sufficient and how far it is dependent on the outside world.

With the general picture of these economic activities before us, we can now examine the financial conditions in the village. As a result of the decline of domestic industry and the burden of high rent, the villagers are facing an unprecedented economic depression. The difficulty in securing credit and the danger of becoming a victim of usury place the villagers in a dilemma. This will be the end of my descriptive account of the village economy shortly before the bursting of the great storm of the Japanese invasion.

1. CULTURAL CONTROL ON CONSUMPTION

Culture provides means to procure materials for satisfying human needs but at the same time defines and delimits human wants. It recognizes a range of wants as proper and necessary and those lying outside the range as extravagant and luxurious. A standard is thus set up to control the amount and type of consumption. This standard is a measurement for plenty and deficiency by the people themselves. It enables saving when there is plenty, and causes dissatisfaction when there is a deficiency.

To be content with simple living is a part of early education. Extravagance is prevented by sanctions. A child making preferences in food or clothes will be scorned and beaten. On the table, he should not refuse what his elders put in his bowl. If a mother lets her child develop special tastes in food, she will be criticized as indulging her child. Even rich parents will not put good and costly clothes on their children, for doing so would induce the evil spirits to make trouble.

Thrift is encouraged. Throwing away anything which has not been properly used will offend heaven, whose representative is the kitchen god. For instance, no rice should be wasted. Even when the rice becomes sour, the family must try to finish it all. Clothes are used by generations, until they are worn out. Those worn-out clothes will not be thrown away but used for making the bottom of the shoes or exchanged for sweets and porcelain (XIV–7).

In a rural community where production may be threatened by natural disasters, content and thrift have practical value. If a man spends all his income, when he fails to have a good harvest, he will be forced to raise loans which may cause him to lose a part of his right over his land (XV–3). To lose one's inherited estate is against filial obligations and thus will be condemned. Moreover, in the village there are few inducements to extravagance. Display of wealth in daily consumption does not lead to prestige. On the contrary, it may attract kidnappers as seen in the case of Wang several years ago.

But the idea of thrift is absent on ceremonial occasions. Expenses in funeral and marriage ceremonies are not considered as individual consumption but as fulfilment of social obligations. A good son must provide the best possible coffin and grave for his parent. In the marriage ceremony, as mentioned, the parents on both sides will try to provide the best marriage gift and dowry, and offer the richest feasts, as their ability permits.

Thrift only sets an upper limit for the variation of livelihood. It becomes meaningless when one is not able to reach the accepted standard of proper living. It is the idea of generosity and kinship obligation in helping relatives (XV–2), that keeps individuals from sinking too much below the standard. Therefore the unequal distribution of wealth in the village is not expressed in a marked variation in the level of daily livelihood. Only a few persons have special and valuable clothes and there are no essential differences in housing and food.

2. HOUSING

A house, in general, consists of three rooms. The front room is the largest. It is used for working, such as raising silkworms, manufacturing silk, threshing rice, etc. ; for sitting, for dining when the weather is cold or wet, for receiving guests and for storing implements and products. It is also the place where the ancestral shrine is kept.

Behind the front room is the kitchen. It is only about one-fourth the size of the front room. One-third of it is occupied by the stove and the chimney. A small pavilion and a platform is constructed leaning upon the chimney for the kitchen god.

Next is the bedroom. It is sometimes divided by wooden partitions into two rooms if there are two family units in the Chia. Each room contains one or two beds. The married couple and their young child up to seven or eight years old share one bed. When the child grows up, he or she will have a separate bed first in the parents' room. An older but unmarried boy will sleep in the front room, as the employees do. A girl may remain until her marriage in her parents' room or may move to her grandmother's room, but never to the front room because women are not permitted to sleep in the room where the ancestral shrine is kept.

In its broad sense, a house includes an open field in front or behind the building. This open field is, at the same time, used as a public road as well as private ground for work and storage. All the threshed straw is heaped on this ground; it can also be used as a little garden where gourds or cucumbers are planted. Adjacent to the main building, there are little huts for the sheep and sometimes also for storage.

Human manure, being the most important fertilizer in the farm, is preserved in the pits made of earthenware, half buried in the ground at the back of the building. Along the southern bank of the Stream A, the public road is lined up with these manure pits. The government have ordered the villagers to remove these pits for hygienic reasons but nothing has been done about it.

Houses are built by special craftsmen from the town.

Stream

Public road

Front room	
Kitchen	Open yard
Bedroom	Bedroom

Back door

Garden

Sheep hut	Manure pit O O

During the period of raising silkworms, building is suspended, otherwise, according to the local belief, the industry of the whole village will be ruined. Breaking soil is considered as a dangerous action which might provoke supernatural interference. Thus it is necessary to perform certain magical rites which are done by Taoist priests. An ordinary house costs at least five hundred dollars for the total expenses. The length of life of the house is difficult to estimate. It depends on constant mending and oiling. Every two or three years the wooden parts of the house must be oiled once again and the tiles of the roof partially rearranged ; this costs on the average ten dollars a year.

3. TRANSPORTATION

Boats are extensively used for heavy and long-distance traffic. But the villages do not build their boats. They buy them from outside. Each boat costs, on the average, about eighty to a hundred dollars. Nearly every household possesses one or more boats except those who are not engaged in agricultural or fishing work. Both men and women can handle the boat. The art of rowing is acquired in childhood. Once having acquired this skill, one can row for hours without rest. The energy spent on rowing is not in proportion to the weight of the load but to the conditions of the water current and the direction of the wind. Therefore, the cost of this type of transport is reduced as the weight of the load is increased. If the boatman is able to use the wind, distance is a problem of time, not of energy ; cost is thus further reduced. This is an important character of water transport. It makes possible the concentration of houses in one area and determines the position of the house near the stream. It also makes possible the system of scattered farm holding and influences the system of exchange by the part it plays in marketing. All these related aspects will be treated in other appropriate connections.

No animal labour is used in transport. On land, the men have to carry the load themselves.

4. CLOTHING

The domestic industry of weaving in the village has been practically ruined. Although nearly every house has a wooden weaving machine, at the time when I was there, there were only two of them still working. The material for clothing thus largely comes from the outside, mainly linen and cotton. The silk industry works not for self-consumption but mainly for export. Only a few people wear silk dresses on formal occasions.

Owing to the wide variations of climate during the year, the villagers keep at least three sets of clothes : for the hot summer, for the mild spring and autumn, and for the cold winter. In the summer, men wear only shorts, but they will put on a skirt when meeting visitors or when going to town. Village headmen keep their silk gowns at least on their arms, when they leave the village even under the hot sun. Women wear sleeveless jackets and long skirts. Wearing a skirt is a characteristic of the region where women do not work on the farm. In colder weather, distinguished men wear the long gown when they do not work. The ordinary people only wear short jackets.

Clothing is not only for protecting the body but also for making social distinctions. Sex differentiation is clear. Age difference is also expressed ; for instance, girls before maturity will not put on the skirt. Social status is directly indicated in the style. The long gown, for instance, is indispensable for persons of distinction. Two middle school students had changed their style of clothing when they came back from their school. They wore trousers and shirts in the European style but without coats.

Sewing is women's work, except for tailors. Most of the women have skill enough to make ordinary clothes for their husbands and children, because this is a necessary qualification for a bride. At the end of the first month of her wedding, the bride will send an article of her own sewing to each near relative of her husband, whose approval is her pride and a support of her position in the new social group. But for preparing dowries, marriage gifts, and dresses of higher quality for formal use, professional tailors are as a rule called in.

The total expenses for buying clothing materials for an average Chia is estimated as about thirty dollars a year, excluding ceremonial dresses.

5. NUTRITION

Food is the main item of household expenditure. It amounts to 40 per cent. of the total annual current expenses. Furthermore, it is different from the above-mentioned items. Housing does not involve expense every day, and clothing usually is not so urgent as food. The amount of food that is necessary in order to maintain a normal living is more or less constant and consequently represents a relatively constant item in the domestic livelihood.

The staple food is rice. According to my informants' estimate the quantities needed for the annual consumption of different individuals are as follows :

Old man above 50	9 bushels.
Old woman above 40	$7\frac{1}{2}$,,
Adult man	12 ,,
Adult woman	9 ,,
Child above ten	$4\frac{1}{2}$. ,,

For an average household, including an old woman, two adults, and a child, the total amount will be thirty-two bushels. This estimate is fairly exact because the people must know the amount they need before they store the rice. Rice is produced by the people themselves; the surplus is sold in the market to get money for other expenses. The estimate given above is the amount which the people consider to be necessary to reserve in store.

In vegetables, including cabbages, fruits, mushrooms, nuts, potatoes, turnips, etc., the village is only partially self-supporting. The people have only very small gardens adjacent to the houses and limited space under the mulberry trees for growing vegetables. They are largely dependent on the supply of the neighbouring villages along the Lake Tai where vegetable cultivation has become a specialization; and the produce has become one of the important sources of supply for the people in this region.

Oil is produced by villagers themselves from the rapeseeds which are planted in spring before the rice. But owing to the low level of the farms in this part, the crop is very limited and the produce is enough only for domestic use. Fish is supplied by the fishing households in the village. The only kind of meat eaten is pork, which is supplied by the town through retailers in the village. Sugar, salt, and other necessities for cooking are bought daily from the town chiefly through the agent boat (XIV–5).

There are three meals a day: morning, noon, and evening. They are cooked separately. But during the period when men are busy on the farm they will prepare their lunch in the morning with the breakfast. The woman is the first to get up. She cleans the stove and warms the water and then prepares the meals. Breakfast consists of rice porridge and some preserved salty cabbage. Porridge is made by boiling the dried rice crust in the water. Lunch is the big meal of the day, but during the time when men have to work on the farm, they carry with them their prepared lunch. They do not come back until evening. Women and children who are left in·the house also take the prepared lunch which is rather light.

In the evening when the men come back, the whole household take dinner together, in the front room. But in the hot weather the table is arranged in the front of the house ; it is very impressive to walk in the street on a summer evening. The street is lined by a row of tables. Neighbours talk with each other while they are eating at their own table. All the members of the household sit around the same table, except the woman who is busy in the kitchen and serves the table.

At the table they have definite positions, following the kinship order of the family. The head of the family sits at the " upper side," facing south. The left side, facing west, comes next and then the right side. The women, especially the daughter-in-law, take the lower side, or they do not appear at the table but take their food in the kitchen.

The commensalism of the evening meal is important in domestic life, especially for the father and child to see each other. The father is absent the whole day and the child may not be able to see him until that time. At the table they are together. The disciplinary function of the father operates at this time. Relevant to this context is the manner of eating. The child must not complain about the food or show special preference for certain dishes. If he does so, he will be at once scorned and sometimes beaten by his father. At the table the child is usually silent and obedient.

During the period of agricultural work, the dinner is comparatively rich. They have meat and fish. But in ordinary times meat is not very often served. Pure vegetarianism is rare except for a few widows. Ordinary women take vegetarian meals twice a month, the first and the fifteenth day : this is because of the religious teaching that heavenly gods do not like killing animate creatures. Thus vegetarian practice will help one to have a better after-life.

Food prepared in the kitchen should not be set aside for individual members. But occasionally the family unit may have some special dish for themselves out of their own expenses and eat in their own room. This is considered to be bad behaviour and offensive to the other members. Cakes and sweets bought with one's own pocket money are private.

6. RECREATION

Relaxation from muscular and nervous stress after hard work is a physiological necessity. In so far as recreation needs collective action, social institutions develop for this function. The collective action in recreation reinforces the social ties among the participants. Thus its function goes beyond pure physiological relaxation.

In the household the period for domestic gatherings is in the evening when the daily work is over. In this gathering the family bonds are strengthened and an intimate feeling develops.

Work in agriculture and in the silk industry affords periodical intervals. The people after having been busy for a week or ten days may have a pause. The period of recreation is inserted into the time-table of work. During the intervals, rich dinners are prepared and visits among relatives take place.

Men will use this pause to enjoy themselves in the teashops. Teashops are in the town. They bring together the people from different villages. Business bargainings, marital negotiations and arbitration of disputes take place. But they are, primarily, men's clubs. Only occasionally some women will appear with their men in the shop. Women spend their intervals of work in visiting relatives, especially their own parents and brothers. Most of the children go with their mothers.

The evening gathering of the domestic group, the gatherings in the teashops and frequent visiting among relatives during the rest periods are informal and not obligatory. In this respect, they are different from the festivals and formal communal gatherings. The time-table for social activities, given in Chapter IX, summarizes all the occasions of festivals in relation to other chronological activities.

It is fairly clear that festivals come always in between periods of industrial activity. The " New Year," celebrated in February by fifteen days for rejoicing and obligatory visiting of relatives, comes at a time of few agricultural activities. Wedding ceremonies also come in that period, which is regarded as a proper time for marriage. Shortly before the active period in the silk industry, is the festival of Ch'ing Ming for ancestral worship and visiting tombs. At the third exuviæ of silkworms, a rejoicing feast is prepared at Li Hsia. After the silk reeling work and before the transplantation of young shoots of the rice to the main field, the festival of Tuan Yang comes in. Full moon in the eighth month, Chung Ch'iu, is celebrated at the time when the rice bears fruit and in the middle of the first long interval of agricultural work. At the end of that interval another festival of Ch'ung Yang is on the schedule. When the agricultural work is completed it is the festival of Tung Chih. All these festivals are obligatory and usually connected with religious worship of ancestors and of the kitchen god. Celebration of such festivals is limited to domestic groups and intimate relatives.

Occasions for periodical obligatory gatherings of larger local groups, such as *luiwanwe* of the *de*, the annual meeting of the village (VI–3), and the inter-village parade every ten years along Lake Tai, *sanyanwe*, are also connected with religious ideas. For more than ten years all these occasions, except *luiwanwe*, have been suspended. The immediate reason for the suspension is the disapproval of the government. According to the government these activities are superstitious and luxurious, and it is one of the duties of the magistrate to prohibit them.[1] But the ultimate and more effective cause is the economic depression of the rural district. When immediate needs such as food and clothes have become a burden to the people, there is no surplus money to finance such less urgent social activities.

How far the suspension of community gatherings has weakened the local ties among the people is difficult to ascertain from my present material. But when I sat among the people and listened to their narrations of the past exciting events of the inter-village parade, their feeling of loss and disappointment at the present situation was very clear to me. I am not going to try

[1] Decree governing District Administration, Article 7, June, 1928.

to reconstruct the grand occasion and estimate the social value involved in it, but the memory of the past forms an important element in the present attitude towards the existing situation. The suspension of these festivities is a direct indication, in the mind of the people, of deterioration of social life. In so far as they are looking forward for a return of the happy days, they will not reject any possible measure which they are convinced as making for improvement. This psychology has its significance in the lack of strong resistance to social change, as I shall show later (XII–2).

7. CEREMONIAL EXPENSES

Ceremonial expenses connected with the crises of life—birth, marriage, and death—looked at from the economic point of view are indispensable items of liability to the domestic economy. Marriage gifts and dowries are the necessary provisions of the new family unit. Funeral arrangements are necessary measures of disposing of the dead. The sentiments arising from these crises of the individual life and of the related social groups cause the ceremonies to be more elaborate and to involve considerable cost. When the ceremonial procedure has been generally accepted, one cannot pass these crises except through this costly channel.

The economic depression has, however, affected the ceremonies. For instance, the institution of *siaosiv* has been adopted to modify the expensive marriage procedure (III–8). It is adopted for economic expedience but has far-reaching consequences in kinship organization. The total or partial reduction of affinal relationships has influenced the social position of women and children. The cancelling of marriage gifts and dowry prolongs the economic dependence of the young. All these illustrate the fact that the ceremonial expenses are not altogether waste or luxury. They perform essential functions in social life.

Again, the marriage feast provides an opportunity for the gathering of relatives for recognizing newly established kinship ties and reinforcing the old. The kinship tie is not a matter of sentimental relation only. It regulates various types of social relation. From the economic point of view, it prescribes the mutual obligation to join the financial aid society (XV–2), and the periodical offering of gifts. In the modified marriage ceremony, the list of guests invited is usually shortened. This loosens the wider kinship ties and thus closes, in the long run, a possible channel of financial help. These consequences may not be immediate and apparent but will be felt eventually. This is why the people reject the institution of *siaosiv* and revert to the normal course as soon as economic conditions allow. Many even, in order to maintain the traditional procedure, delay marriage or borrow money to stage the ceremony in an unimpaired form.

In view of the importance of ceremonial occasions in the life of the people, it is not surprising to find the high percentage of ceremonial expenses in the domestic budget. For an average family of four members, assuming the average length of life to be fifty years, there will be one ceremonial occasion every five years. The minimum expenses for these ceremonies are estimated as follows : birth 30 dollars, marriage 500 dollars, and funeral 250 dollars. The average annual expense will be 50 dollars. It amounts to one-seventh of the whole annual expenditure.

To this sum we must also add the gift presented by
he house to their relatives who are passing through
hese life crises. Their presents vary according to the
earness of kinship and of friendship, from 5 dollars
) 20 cents. The average amount per year per Chia
s about 10 dollars at least.

These estimates seem to be rather high as compared
ith other rural communities in China. According
) J. L. Buck's study, the average amount for a wedding
er family is 114·83 dollars and for a funeral 62·07
ollars, in East Central China.[1] The difference may
e due to local characters or to the number of items of
xpenditure included in this heading. The expenses
n the wedding day in Kaihsienkung lies between 250
) 100 dollars. There was a notorious case, quoted
y my informants as exceptional, of a ceremonial
1anager who could conduct a wedding for less than
)0 dollars. The estimate here given includes also
1e marriage gifts. So it is reasonable that it should
e higher.

The funeral expenses vary greatly according to the
)cial status of the deceased. As observed in Peiping,
)r children " the funerals cost a little more than
1e-eighth of the family's monthly income. The
1nerals of older people are naturally more expensive.
he total varies from 1·25 to 1·3 months' income.
one of these included a funeral feast. Funerals for
1sbands, wives, older brothers, mothers, cost their
milies from 2·5, 3, 5, and 5·5 months' income."[2]
1ck's average is derived from 2·8 per cent. of all the
milies that had funeral expenses to pay during the
ar. It may be a little lower than the amount

[1] *Chinese Farm Economy*, pp. 416–417.
[2] S. D. Gamble, *How Chinese Families Live in Peiping*, 1933, p. 200.

regarded as proper expenditure for the funeral of an adult member of the family, as given by my informants.

These periodical expenses demand saving during the interval. It may take the form of payment of loans, but usually, of subscriptions to a financial aid society, which is a local institution of saving (XV–2). Thus we can check the estimate of ceremonial expenses with the average annual amount of subscription per Chia. In general, as I found, each Chia joins two societies at the same time with a total annual subscription of 40 dollars. It tends to support the reliability of these estimates.

8. MINIMUM EXPENDITURE

All the quantitative assessments given in the above sections represent only the recognized minimum requirement of a proper living in the village. To secure these estimates, I consulted a number of informants. Differences between individual estimates were very small. It shows a high comformity of such estimates. The average Chia under consideration consists of four individuals: an old woman, an adult man, an adult woman, and a child, who are full owners of a holding of nine *mow* of land.

These estimates are useful for several reasons. (1) A single-handed field investigator finds it practically impossible to adopt the account-book method, especially in a village where keeping accounts is not habit of the people, unless he devotes his whole time to investigating this problem. (2) These estimates can give a certain general idea of the livelihood of the villagers because they represent the minimum requirement of a normal living which cannot be very far from the actual average. (3) The lack of striking differential

tion in the standard of living in the village allows such
a simple approach. (4) As mentioned, these estimates
form a standard in the minds of the people as a measurement of sufficiency of material well-being in the community, and consequently an actual social force in
controlling consumption.

Moreover, in studying the problem of the standard
of living in a rural community, the account-book
method has its limitations. The rural community is
partially self-supporting. The livelihood will not be
comprehended in full in the daily accounts which are
usually limited to money transactions. The account-
book only reveals the extent to which the villagers
depend on outside supplies of goods. The degree of
dependence does not always indicate the standard of
living. For instance, under normal conditions, the
villagers will not buy rice because they have their own
reserves. Only when the reserves have been sold
under financial distress, will they buy rice to feed
themselves. In this case the increased amount of
money transactions is related to the decline of livelihood
and not the reverse, as might appear from the accounts
only.

It is clear that in a study of the standard of living
of a rural community it will not be enough simply to
give a summary of the family budget in terms of
money income and expenditure. The investigator
must prepare a double entry for the goods consumed
to assess those bought from the market and those
produced by the consumers themselves. The former
should be expressed in terms of money value. The
sum of this category represents the amount of money
needed to finance the life of the people. It determines
the amount of produce sold by them in order to get

that amout of money. Those goods produced by the consumers do not enter into the market. Their money value is unknown because the price would be affected if they entered the market. To express them in terms of market price is theoretically unsound. Indeed, without reducing them to a money value, it would not be possible to give a general index of the standard of living of the people. But such a general index is unreal and has little value in an empirical analysis. To keep these two categories apart will help us to investigate the relation between them, and this relation is very important in the study of rural economy. For instance, one of the important problems in the present Chinese rural economy is the decline of the price of the rural produce. For a given necessary requirement of living, the villagers are forced to sell more of their produce to the market. It thus reduces the degree of self-sufficiency of the villagers. On the other hand, the process of de-industrialization in the rural districts has reduced the amount and type of rural produce and increased the need of money for buying manufactured goods. To approach these problems, it is important to analyse the relation of these two categories of consumers' goods.

This " double-entry " method demands much more work from the field investigator. It may be impractical for him to make statistical observations. Thus I suggest the method of consulting estimates. If possible, it could be supplemented by sampling observation— selecting a few representative cases and systematically assessing the amount of consumption for a period. But the present work is not able to provide this type of data. The following table gives only the money value of those items that the villagers have to buy from the market, and the obligatory payment of tax and rent. It is useful as an estimate of the minimum amount of money needed for the livelihood of the villagers. Those goods produced by the consumers themselves include the foodstuffs, such as rice, oil, wheat, and vegetable, and a part of the clothing materials. The most important part of the self-sufficient economy is labour and service. As mentioned, only a few households employ labourers on the farm. Further analysis of this category will be given in connection with the process of production.

I. Things bought from the market :			
Foodstuffs		47	
Vegetables and miscellaneous	30		
Sugar.	5		
Salt	12		
Clothing materials . . .		30	
Presents		10	
Fuel, light, etc. . . .		36	
House and boat oiling . .		20	
Tools and fertilizer . . .		10	
Expenses in silk industry . .		50	203
II. Land tax			10
III. Periodic expenses (expressed in saving)			50
TOTAL			$263

CHAPTER VIII

OCCUPATIONAL DIFFEREN-TIATION

Agriculture as the Basic Occupation — Special Occupations — Fishing

1. AGRICULTURE AS THE BASIC OCCUPATION

In the process of consumption there are no essential classifications into which the villagers must be divided, but in the process of production occupational differentiation is found. According to the census, occupations are classified under four headings : (1) agriculture, (2) special occupations, (3) fishing, and (4) non-occupied.

These classes are not mutually exclusive. Persons not classified as agricultural may nevertheless be partly engaged in agricultural activities. Agriculture is the fundamental occupation common to nearly all the villagers except among the landless outsiders. The difference is only a matter of emphasis. Those who are classified under the heading of agriculture do not depend on land exclusively but are also engaged in raising silk-worms and sheep, and in trade ventures. The fourth category includes households whose adult male members have died and where the widows or the children are living on the rent of the leased land but not through their own productive effort.

The occupation of a Chia is recorded in the census

according to the occupation of its head. Members of the Chia may be engaged in different occupations—for example, the children of the store-keeper may be engaged in agriculture and the farmer's daughter engaged in industrial work in the town. This, however, is not indicated. The number of Chia in each category is given in the following table :

I. Agricultural	.	.	.	274
II. Special occupations	.	.	.	59
III. Fishing	.	.	.	14
IV. Non-occupied	.	.	.	13
TOTAL .	.	.	.	360

The above table shows clearly that more than two-thirds, or 76 per cent., of the total population are mainly engaged in agriculture. Owing to the limited time of my field work, my investigations were chiefly concerned with this group. A fuller analysis of the productive activities of the group will be given in the following chapters. Other occupational groups I can only describe briefly.

2. SPECIAL OCCUPATIONS

A further analysis of the second category is given in the following table :

The first heading includes only those Chia whose heads are living in the town engaged in trade or in other occupations. The girls working in the silk factories outside are not included.

Silk spinners represent a special occupation. They work for the silk houses in the town, which collect the native raw silk from the villagers. The quality of the silk is irregular, and it must be sorted out by means of spinning before it can be exported or sold

to the weaving factories. This sorting work is done
by the villagers. The collectors distribute the raw
material to the spinner and collect the silk again.
Wages are paid according to the amount of work done.

I.	Engaged in special occupations in town .	14
II.	Silk spinners	6
III.	Retail traders	10
IV.	Agent boats	4
V.	Crafts and Professional Services . . .	25

Carpenters	4
Tailors	3
Staff Members of the Co-operative factory	3
Basket makers	2
Barbers	2
Millers	2
Operators of modern pumping machines	2
Mason	1
Midwife	1
Priest	1
Shoemaker	1
Silversmith	1
Weaver	1

TOTAL 59

A description of the retail traders and of the agent
boats is given in the chapter on marketing (XIV–4–6).

The whole group of craftsmen and professional men
includes only 7 per cent. of the total households in
the village. This low percentage is striking. It is
due firstly to the fact that such work is not exclusively
specialized. Tailoring, shoemaking, and milling are
common work in all households. Wood, bamboo, and
mason's work of a crude type requires very little
knowledge and skill and the necessary tools are found
in most houses. The modern pumping machines are
not in wide use, and are used mainly in time of
emergency. Childbirth does not always need expert
help. In the above list, besides the work of the

Plate VII.

A VILLAGE WOMAN IN SUMMER DRESS

A TYPICAL FRONT VIEW OF A HOUSE

[*face p.* 140

Plate VIII.

SHEEP HUT

Raising sheep has recently become an important supplementary industry. Sheep are kept in huts, and grass is gathered by children from outside to feed them. (Chapter XIII.)

CARPENTER'S HOUSE

operators of the modern pumping machines, perhaps only the work of the barbers, the temple keeper, the priest, and the staff members of the co-operative factory is so specialized as not to be more usually undertaken by the farmers themselves.

Moreover, when the people need goods or services, they do not necessarily depend on the supply available in the village.   Wood, bamboo, and metal articles of better quality can be bought from the town.   Even the barber once complained to me that the villagers were gradually tending to have their heads shaved in the town.   In the case of funeral ceremonies priests are sent for from distant temples.   Serious cases of child-birth cannot be trusted to the village midwife.

All the outsiders living in the village are traders and craftsmen and form, in fact, one-third of the total number of that group (II–5).   I have no information showing whether the trades and crafts were originally novel occupations introduced from outside, but there is good reason to suspect that new crafts are often introduced by their agents from outside.   Since technical knowledge is usually transmitted through the kinship line, it is often not easily assimilated by the indigenous population.   Moreover, even when the crafts are open for apprenticeship, parents who are able to provide their children with the opportunity of tilling and like to keep them on the farm.   Land in the village is insufficient to support an increase of popula-tion.   It is, therefore, difficult for an outsider to acquire land, and land in any case seldom comes into the market.   Thus, as mentioned above, at present all the outsiders are landless and the only means for them to find a living is to engage in certain new crafts or in trades.

F

3. FISHING

There are two groups of fishing households, differing in methods of fishing and in their residential areas. The first group, living at the west end of the village on *Yu* I and II, only follow fishing as a supplementary occupation. Their method is by nets and hooks. Their heavy work is in the winter. At that time, when agricultural work is at a pause, they start their large scale " circle fishing." Several boats co-operate together to form a team. Small hooks are hung close to each other on a strong and long rope, to which are added several heavy weights. The fishing team distribute themselves in a circle, letting the hooks sink into the bottom of the lake. In cold weather, especially when snow has fallen, the lake does not freeze, but the fish are all half-hibernated in the mud, and, as the hooks drag through the mud, the fish are easily gathered. This " circle fishing " is sometimes continued for several weeks and yields a large return. On ordinary days the fishermen spread their large nets in the water and collect fish from them several times a day. This kind of fishing can be done only by those whose houses are near the lake. That is the reason for the localization of this group in the area at the west end.

Shrimps are collected from the lake by a kind of trap, made of basketry. Shrimp trapping is a common occupation of those households which live near the lake. According to reports I gathered in the summer of 1935, there were forty-three boats engaged in this work. The traps are connected by cords to a long line and put into the water. Every four hours they are cleared, because the shrimps will die if they are allowed to remain too long in the traps, and dead shrimps are of less value on the market. The average income is one dollar per boat per day worked by two persons.

The other group of fishing households are found along the middle course of Stream B, on *Yu* II. These raise fishing birds, which will dive into water to catch fish. Raising and training these birds requires special knowledge which is transmitted in the family, and thus this occupation is hereditary. These families form a special group and co-operate with their fellow professional men even in other villages. Since they may need to go very far from the home village and the birds must be carefully sheltered at night, they form a super-residential group based on their common professional interest. All the fishermen engaged in the same profession are obliged to extend their hospitality to their fellows.

CHAPTER IX

CALENDAR OF WORK

Systems of Time-Reckoning — Three Calendars — Time-Table of Economic and Other Social Activities

1. SYSTEMS OF TIME-RECKONING

To study the productive system of a community, it is necessary to investigate how their activities are regulated in time sequence. It is especially so in analysing a rural economy because crops are usually directly dependent on climatic conditions.

The knowledge of the seasonal cycle of the organic world is of practical importance to the people. Their activities in production are not individualistic and spontaneous. They need collective actions and preparations. They must know when the seeds can be germinated in order to determine the date of sowing. They must know how long it will take for the bud to develop into the young shoot, so that they can determine when they should prepare the soil and transplant the shoot into the main field. The knowledge of the right time for certain actions cannot be secured without a system of time-reckoning.

Recognition of time is not a result of philosophical contemplation or of astronomical curiosity. As Professor B. Malinowski has clearly pointed out, " a system of reckoning time is a practical, as well as sentimental, necessity in every culture, however simple

Members of every human group have the need of co-ordinating various activities of fixing dates for the future, of placing reminiscences in the past, of gauging the length of bygone periods and of those to come." [1]

The functional approach to the problem of time-reckoning leads us to examine the calendar in detail in order to see how the system regulates and is defined by the social activities.

The traditional calendar used in the village is based on the lunar system. The principle of the lunar system is as follows : the full moon is taken as the night of the fifteenth day of a month. Thus the number of days in each month is either twenty-nine or thirty. (The synodic lunar month consists of 29·53 days.) Twelve months will be counted as a year which contains 354·36 days. The total number of days fails to make the required total of 365·14 days a year for the solar system. An intercalary month is added every two or three years to make good the annual deficiency. But the seasonal cycle of the organic world is due more to the relation between the earth and the sun than to the relation between the earth and the moon. Although the two systems are adjusted in the long run by the intercalary month, the date of one system can never regularly correspond with that of the other.

The date in the lunar system does not indicate consistently the position of the earth with reference to the sun and consequently the seasonal climatic changes. For example, supposing the people catch the right time for sowing at the seventeenth day of the fourth month this year, they will, owing to the intercalary month, be too late if they sow at the same date next

[1] " Lunar and Seasonal Calendar in the Trobriands," *Journal of the Royal Anthropological Institute*, Vol. LVII, pp. 203–215.

year. The discrepancy between the lunar system and the seasonal cycle renders the former ineffective as a guide in time-reckoning in agricultural activities. This theoretical consideration leads to a further examination of the traditional calendar.

In the traditional calendar, in fact, there is an underlying solar system. It indicates the exact position of the earth in its solar orbit at various periods. The unit in this system is Chieh, meaning section or joint. The whole solar year is divided into twenty-four Chieh. The total number of days of the twenty-four Chieh in 1936 was 364·75. It shows that there is still a slight difference of 0·59 day with the synodic solar year. The principle in determining the Chieh system is not known to me. But in the old-type calendar book, one can always find that the exact time for the commencement of each Chieh is defined in terms of Shih (two-hour) K'ê (quarter-hour) and Fen (minute). The intercalation takes place in the slight variation between the lengths of different Chieh in different years. It therefore needs no special indication for it. The following table gives the name and the time of commencement of each Chieh in the year 1936.

Name of the Chieh	Traditional Calendar and Time	Western Calendar and Time
Li Ch'un (Beginning of Spring) [1]	13th of 1st month Ch'en Ch'u 3 K'ê	Feb. 5—7.45 a.m.
Yü Shui (Rain Water)	28th of 1st month Yin Ch'u 2 K'ê 10 Fen	Feb. 20—3.30 a.m.
Ching Che (Waking of Insects)	13th of 2nd month Ch'ou Ch'u 3 K'ê 12 Fen	March 6—1.57 a.m.

[1] The translations follow Derk Bodde, *Annual Customs and Festivals in Peking*, 1935, p. 107.

Name of the Chieh	Traditional Calendar and Time	Western Calendar and Time
Ch'un Fen (Spring Equinox)	28th of 2nd month Yin Ch'u 3 Fen	March 21—3.3 a.m.
Ch'ing Ming (Pure Brightness)	14th of 3rd month Ch'en Ch'u 1 K'ê 2 Fen	April 5—7.17 a.m.
Ku Yü (Corn Rain)	29th of 3rd month Wei Chêng 1 K'ê 14 Fen	April 20—2.44 p.m.
Li Hsia (Beginning of Summer)	16th of 3rd (intercalary) month Ch'ou Ch'u 14 Fen	May 6—1.14 p.m.
Hsiao Man (Grain Full)	1st of 4th month Wei Chêng 1 K'ê 13 Fen	May 21—2.28 p.m.
Mang Chung (Grain in the Ear)	17th of 4th month Mao Ch'u 3 K'ê 10 Fen	June 6—5.55 a.m.
Hsia Chih (Summer Solstice)	3rd of 5th month Hai Chêng 3 K'ê 4 Fen	June 21—10.49 p.m.
Hsiao Shu (Slight Heat)	19th of 5th month Shen Chêng 1 K'ê 11 Fen	July 7—4.26 p.m.
Ta Shu (Great Heat)	6th of 6th month Ssŭ Ch'u 3 K'ê 9 Fen	July 23—9.54 a.m.
Li Ch'iu (Beginning of Autumn)	22nd of 6th month Ch'ou Chêng 1 K'ê 5 Fen	Aug. 8—2.20 a.m.
Ch'u Shu (Stopping of Heat)	7th of 7th month Yu Ch'u	Aug. 23—5.0 p.m.
Pai Lu (White Dew)	23rd of 7th month Mao Ch'u 13 Fen	Sept. 8—5.13 a.m.
Ch'iu Fen (Autumn Equinox)	8th of 8th month Wei Chêng 2 K'ê	Sept. 23—2.30 p.m.
Han Lu (Cold Dew)	23rd of 8th month Hsü Chêng 2 K'ê 8 Fen	Oct. 8—8.38 p.m.
Shuang Chiang (Frost's Descent)	9th of 9th month Tzŭ Ch'u 2 K'ê	Oct. 23—11.30 p.m.
Li Tung (Beginning of Winter)	24th of 9th month Tzŭ Ch'u 1 K'ê 4 Fen	Nov. 7—11.19 p.m.

Name of the Chieh	Traditional Calendar and Time	Western Calendar and Time
Hsiao Hsüeh (Slight Snow)	9th of 10th month Hsü Chêng 2 K'ê	Nov. 22—8.30 p.m.
Ta Hsüeh (Great Snow)	24th of 10th month Shen Ch'u 2 K'ê 3 Fen	Dec. 7—3.33 p.m.
Tung Chih (Winter Solstice)	9th of 11th month Ssü Ch'u 11 Fen	Dec. 22—9.11 a.m.
Hsiao Han (Slight Cold)	24th of 11th month Ch'ou Chêng 10 Fen	Jan. 6—2.10 a.m.
Ta Han (Great Cold)	8th of 12th month Hsü Ch'u 1 K'ê 7 Fen	Jan. 20—7.22 p.m.
Li Ch'un (Beginning of Spring)	23rd of 12th month Wei Ch'u 2 K'ê 4 Fen	Feb. 4—1.34 p.m.

The western solar calendar has been also introduced into the village since it has been adopted as the legal system. It differs again from the traditional solar system because it takes a round day as a unit and consequently has a regular intercalary system. Thus they cannot have exact corresponding dates in different years.

2. THREE CALENDARS

These three calendars are all used by the villagers. But each has its own function and is used in its own particular context. The western system is used in connection with those newly introduced institutions such as the school, the co-operative factory, and the administrative office. These institutions have to adjust their work with the outside world where the western system is employed.

The traditional lunar system has its widest use in such situations as remembering sentimental events and making practical engagements. It serves as a system of names for the dates in the traditional social activities

In the sphere of religious activities, the lunar system is largely used. Regular sacrifices are offered to the kitchen god on the first and fifteenth day of each month. The people visit temples and observe vegetarian ritual also on these dates. Ceremonies of ancestral worship are carried out on the dates of birth and death of the ancestors and on regular festivals ; though among the festivals some of them are regulated according to the traditional solar system.

The traditional solar system is used not as a system of dates but of climatic changes. With this general system, each locality can adjust its calendar of work according to its local conditions.

This system is used chiefly in reference to productive work. Beside daily conversations, the following folk song will document this statement :

Balou ba mimi	.	Pai Lu white indistinctly (referring to the blossoms of the rice).
Tchiu fen da shiou tchi	.	Ch'iu Fen rice bears fruit completely.
Tson gian gjien tzao da	.	Shuang Chiang reap early rice.
Li dong i tchi dao	.	Li Tung all completely fall.

A part of a letter from my informant can also be quoted :

> People in the village have two periods of leisure every year. The first period is in the autumn from Ch'u Shu to Han Lu and lasts about two months. . . . The second period is in the winter from Ta Hsüeh to the end of the year, also covering two months. During this leisure time, we go out for trade ventures.

The villagers remember and predict their sequence of work in terms of the traditional solar system. But this system cannot stand alone because it is very difficult to understand without a system of dating. The system of date in the village is the lunar calendar.

F *

The people have to learn what is the corresponding date for each section in different years. For instance in the above table, the first Li Ch'un is on the 13th of the 1st month and the second is on the 23rd of the 12th month. Therefore it is also correct to say that the lunar calendar regulates the sequence of work of the people through the Chieh system.

The villagers do not arrange their calendar themselves. They simply follow the published calendar in the form of a little red booklet bought from the town. The principle of these systems is not understood by them. They even do not know where the calendar is issued and who is the authority. Since the government prohibited the traditional calendar, publication of these booklets has been illegal. I was not able to find out who was the publisher responsible.

The government's action had not in any sense affected the popularity and prestige of the booklet. It is to be found in any house and in most cases it is the only book in the house. It is usually put on the stove before the kitchen god, and regarded as a kind of amulet. It is consulted not only for arranging work but also for various social activities and personal affairs. In the booklet, each day has a column indicating those things which are lucky or unlucky. For illustration I give a few columns below :

March 1st (1936), Sunday ; 8th of 2nd month.
   Birthday of Chang Ta Ti (God of flood).
   Good for : Offering sacrifice, praying, asking for posterity, making petitions, visiting relatives, trading, accepting office, arranging marriage, offering marriage gifts, weddings, entering new houses, changing lodging, tailoring, mending buildings, laying foundations, fixing beams, mending storerooms, opening market, making contracts, opening storerooms, planting, breaking soil, burying dead.

Bad for :   Thatching roof, introducing water to the field, hunting.

March 2nd, Monday ; 9th of 2nd month.
   Good for : Visiting relatives and friends, catching animals.
   Bad for :   Making accusations in court, curing diseases, taking medicine.   (Plants begin to bud.)

March 16th, Monday ; 23rd of 2nd month.
   Good for nothing.
   Bad for everything.

March 27th, Friday ; 5th of 3rd month.
   Good for : Taking a bath, fishing, catching animals, clearing houses.
   Bad for :   Fixing a bed, buying land and other properties.
                                    (Beginning of thunder.)

It is not true that people always follow the advice of the column. But they actually consult the booklet in such activities as building houses, arranging marriages, starting long trips, etc. They generally distinguish " good day " and " bad day " according to the length of the column of " good for." They avoid taking any important and adventurous activities on these bad days, especially those which are explicitly stated as " good for nothing." At the end of the column every few days, there is an item, given in parentheses, indicating certain recurrent natural phenomena such as " Plants begin to bud " and " Beginning of thunder," etc. It is an additional system of reckoning time by recurrent natural phenomena.

3. TIME-TABLE OF ECONOMIC AND OTHER SOCIAL ACTIVITIES

With these systems of time reckoning, we are now able to tabulate the time-table of various economic and social activities in the village. It will serve as a system of reference for the further analysis. Explanations for specific items will be given elsewhere in their appropriate connections.

Other Social and Religious Activities According to Lunar System	Lunar System	Western Solar System	Climate (in Shanghai) Temp. (F.)	Climate (in Shanghai) Rain (mm.)	Section System	Silk Industry	Agriculture	Other Social and Religious Activities According to Section System
1st: New Year, Sacrifice to Buddha, Reception of new kitchen god, Visiting temples. 1st–8th: Men visiting relatives. 8th–15th: Women visiting relatives. 5th: Sacrifice to god of wealth 10th–30th: Good for wedding.	I	Feb.	39°	57	Li Ch'un		Rapeseed	Sacrifice to kitchen god
					Yü Shui		Wheat	
	II	March	46°	70	Ching Che			
					Ch'un Fen			Sacrifice to kitchen god
	III	April	56°	90	Ch'ing Ming	Hatching eggs		Sacrifice to ancestors and god of silkworms Visiting tombs Sacrifice to kitchen god
					Ku Yü	Third exuviæ		Rejoicing feast Visiting relatives' silkworms
Funeral preparation for old people in the intercalary month.	III (Intercalary)	May	65°	90	Li Hsia	Cocoons (Main crop)	Sowing seeds Young shoot in nursery farm Preparation in main farm	Prohibition of house building
					Hsiao Man	Domestic reeling		
	IV	June	73°	166	Mang Chung		Transplantation	
5th: Tuan Yang, rejoicing feast, sacrifice to kitchen god.	V				Hsia Chih	Second crop	1st busy agriculture period	

Month (lunar)	VI	VII	VIII	IX	X	XI	XII
Month (solar)	August	Sept.	Oct.	Nov.	Dec.	Jan.	
	148	118	73	46	29	54	
Temperature	80°	73°	63°	52°	42°	38°	

Festivals and sacrifices:

- 3rd: Birthday of kitchen god, sacrifice.
- 15th: Chung Ch'iu, full moon, rejoicing feast. 24th: Birthday of kitchen goddess, sacrifice.
- 9th: Ch'ung Yang, rejoicing feast, sacrifice to kitchen god.
- 1st: Sacrifice to ancestors' new rice.
- 24th: Farewell sacrifice to kitchen god. 30th: Sacrifice to ancestors

Solar terms: Li Ch'iu, Ch'u Shu, Pai Lu, Ch'iu Fen, Han Lu, Shuang Chiang, Li Tung, Hsiao Hsüeh, Ta Hsüeh, Tung Chih, Hsiao Han, Ta Han

Agricultural work:

- Rice in blossom — Rice bears fruit — Agricultural interval
- Reaping, Husking, Storing, Selling — Wheat — Second period of busy work in agriculture
- Sacrifice to ancestors

Trading:

- First trading venture
- Second trading venture

CHAPTER X

AGRICULTURE

Lay-out of the Farm — Rice Cultivation — Science and Magic — Organization of Labour

The importance of agriculture in the village economy has been shown in the above pages. More than two-thirds of the households are engaged mainly in this occupation. Nearly eight months are spent in work on the land. And for foodstuffs the people are entirely dependent on the produce of their own farms. Thus in a study of the problem of production, agriculture must come first in view.

The term agriculture is used here only in a narrow sense, and refers to the use of the land for cultivating desirable crops. The study of how the land is used must start with an analysis of the land itself. The chemical composition of the soil, the topography of the land and the climate—all these are conditions governing agriculture. It is also necessary to know the biological nature of the crop. But these analyses, essential as they are, demand special knowledge which an anthropologist does not usually possess. However, the land that enters into agriculture is more than a natural entity. It has been transformed by culture into farms. Moreover, what immediately directs human labour in agriculture is the knowledge about

the land and the crop possessed by the people themselves as expressed in their technology and beliefs.

To start our analysis from the material substratum
we will first attempt a description of the farm.   The
lay-out of the farm, based on technical considerations,
has far-reaching effects on the organization of labour,
on land tenure, and on the kinship organization.   The
study of it will be the best introduction to these more
intricate aspects of the relation between man and land.

1. LAY-OUT OF THE FARM

The lay-out of the farm depends on what kind of
crop the people select for cultivation.   In this village
the chief crops cultivated are rice, rapeseeds and
wheat.   Rice starts in June and ends at the beginning
of December.   It is the main crop.   After this crop a
part of the higher land can be used for cultivating wheat
and rapeseeds.   But these two crops are only supplementary.   The produce is only enough for domestic
consumption.

More than 90 per cent. of the land is used for
these crops.   Along the margin of each *yu*, ten to
thirty metres of land is left for plantation of mulberry
trees and a wider space for house building.   This land
on the margin is higher.   It also serves as a dyke for
the farm.

The land used for the growing of crops is divided
into farms.   Rice cultivation requires a regular supply
of water.   Thus the lay-out of the farm depends on
the measures for water regulation.

My informant said : " Water is the most important
thing in the farm.   The rice will die if the soil begins
to break due to dryness and it will also die if water

covers its ' eye '.'' The " eye " of the rice is the upper joint of the leaf with the stalk. When this point is covered by water, according to local opinion, the rice will wither within six or seven days. It may not perhaps be strictly true that this point in the rice plant is so vulnerable ; nevertheless the " eye " is used as a mark for the proper level of water in the farm. This level must be adjusted to the growth of the rice and effort must be made to irrigate the farm when the level is too low and to drain it when the level is too high. Water regulation is one of the main tasks in agriculture and dictates the topography of the farm.

The land is divided up by streams into tiny pieces which are called *yu*. Each *yu* is surrounded by water. The accessibility to water of each particular farm depends on its location in the *yu*. The farther one goes into the centre of the *yu*, the more difficult is it to get supplies of water from the stream. In order to make it possible for the centre part to obtain water, the levels of the *yu* must be graded like a dish. But this dish-shaped surface creates a difficulty in the storage of water. The water tends to find its level and, instead of there being an equal distribution of water over the farm, there will be a pool in the centre with the marginal land left dry. Dykes, therefore, have to be constructed, parallel to the margin. Another difficulty is that water must be brought in from the lower level of the stream. Pumps must be used to carry the water up to the higher level. To fix the pump, a spot must be selected along the bank and a ditch is dug out leading to the interior parts. Each strip of land, depending on water supplies from the same pumping spot, is marked out by dykes perpendicular to the margin. These two kinds of dykes, crossing each other, divide the farm into small pieces which are called *be* or plots.

Within each plot, the level must be even in order that there should be an equal distribution of water. This is a frequent cause of dispute among cultivators of the same plot when it is not owned by the same Chia.

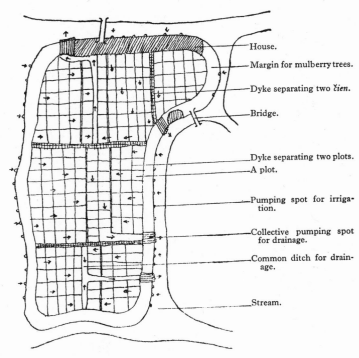

— House.

— Margin for mulberry trees.

— Dyke separating two *tien*.

— Bridge.

— Dyke separating two plots.
— A plot.

— Pumping spot for irrigation.

— Collective pumping spot for drainage.

— Common ditch for drainage.

— Stream.

MAP IV.—Lay-out of the Farms in Hsi Chang Yu.

There is a common ditch running through each strip, and each plot in a strip has an outlet to it. When the farmers introduce water to the plots, they start from the marginal plot. They close the ditch just below the outlet of the particular plot so that the water runs onto it. When it is sufficiently irrigated, they close the outlet and open the ditch to irrigate the next plot in the same way. They go on until the last. Thus the strip is the unit of irrigation (Map V).

When there is too much water on the farm, due to over-abundance of rainfall, the system used for irrigation cannot be used for drainage because the water does not flow from the lower centre to the higher margin. A big trench has therefore to be constructed

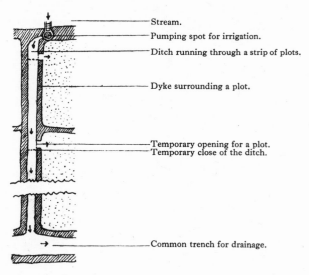

———————————————— Stream.
———————————————— Pumping spot for irrigation.
———————————————— Ditch running through a strip of plots.

———————————————— Dyke surrounding a plot.

———————————————— Temporary opening for a plot.
———————————————— Temporary close of the ditch.

———————————————— Common trench for drainage.

MAP V.—System of Dykes and Ditches in the Farm.

in the lowest part of the whole dish-shaped *yu*. This collects the surplus water from all the strips and pumps are fixed at the end of the trench for draining it away. The different system in irrigation and drainage calls for different organization of work, as we shall show presently.

The difficulty involved in the problem of drainage, purely from the technical point of view, is the size of the *yu*. The size is determined by the natural distribution of streams. It varies enormously. For instance, in the village we are describing there are eleven *yu* which vary from eight *mow* to more than nine hundred *mow* (II–2). The bigger the size, the more difficult it becomes to fit it into the process of collective drainage. To meet the need of urgent and efficient work, the big *yu* must be divided into smaller drainage units, which are called *čien*. Larger dykes are constructed to separate *čien* from one another. These dykes are also used as the main roads in the farm.

The plan of the lay-out of the farm is illustrated in Map IV. It is much simplified but sufficient to show the principles just described.

2. RICE CULTIVATION

The land is mainly, not exclusively, used for the cultivation of rice. The present study will be restricted to this aspect.

Rice cultivation starts in June. A small piece of ground is prepared as a nursery for the young shoots. Seeds are sown in the nursery. In about one month the rice has grown to about thirty centimetres in length. During this period the young shoots do not need much space but require more care in water regulation. It is thus convenient and economical to keep them in a small space while the main field is under preparation.

Before the young shoots can be transplanted into the main field, the soil must be prepared. Preparation consists of breaking, refining and levelling the soil, and then of irrigation. All the work is done by human labour. One characteristic of the agricultural work in this region is the absence of animal labour. As we shall see later, the size of the farm is small and the holding of each household is scattered in such widely separated places, that animal labour cannot be used. The farmers use only the implement called *tid'a*, which is an iron hoe with four teeth, fixed on a wooden stick about a man's height. These form a slight acute angle. Holding the implement by the end of the stick, the workman swings the hoe behind his back and over his head. The teeth strike with a considerable momentum and penetrate into the soil at a sharp angle. By pulling the hoe backwards, he is able to break the soil pressing on the teeth. Ploughs are not used in the village.

The surface of the soil, after having been broken, is rough and uneven. The second step is to refine the soil and to level the surface. The same implement is used in these processes. It takes about four days for the preliminary preparation of each *mow* of land by one man.

At this stage water is introduced onto the land. Dykes and ditches must be first examined and repaired if necessary. The water is introduced from the stream by a pump. A pump consists of a long, rectangular, box-like three-sided wooden tube in which there is a series of valves, made of small wooden plates connected by a chain of movable sections and forming a circle. The small valves touch the three sides of the tube and thus form a series of small empty squares in the tube. The chain is connected by a pivot to the wheel. When the farmer tramps on the projections of the wheel, the chain of valves revolve in a circle. The lower end of the tube is fixed in the water and the upper end opens towards a little pool leading to the ditches. The small squares, formed by the valves and the sides of the tube, will be filled with water at

he lower end. The revolving of the chain of valves
n the tube carries the water contained in the small
squares up to the upper end. As soon as a valve
reaches the upper end, the direction of its movements
turn upwards and the water falls into the pool. The
water is brought up to the pool not through the
differential air pressure but through the movement of
the valves.

The implement is not very efficient in carrying water
to the upper level. The squares formed by the valves
and the sides of the tube can never be very tight and the
friction is high. It takes about one day to fill one *mow*
with ten or more centimetres above the land surface.
The inefficiency of irrigation creates a difference in the
value of the successive plots in each strip. As I have
shown above, the water flows from the margin to the
centre passing through successive plots. When water
is needed, the central plot must wait until the marginal
plot has been irrigated : and when there is too much
water, the central plot must remain longer under
water while the margin is drained. The length of
time spent in waiting for irrigation and for drainage
depends on the efficiency of the pump. The unsatisfactory system of irrigation and drainage is certainly a factor in reducing the amount of produce. It
is also responsible for a difference in land value. The
difference between the marginal plot and the central
plot sometimes amounts to ten dollars or one-fifth of
the average value of the land.

In the past two years, two air pumps, run by motor
engines, have been introduced into the village. One
is owned by an individual and the other by the co-
operative factory. A fee is charged per *mow* for the
regulation of water during the whole year. This

collectivizes the irrigation process and specializes the work. However, these machines have not yet been widely used, mainly because the labour saved by the machine has not yet found any productive use. From the point of view of the villagers, they still prefer working on the old pump to paying a fee and being themselves idle for months. Some told me that some-one who was lazy and relied on the air pump had ruined himself in the gambling house in the town because he had nothing to do. It is still too early to see the effect of this labour-saving machine, and the process of collectivization in irrigation, on the social organization as well as the lay-out of the farm.

After water has been brought on to the land, it takes another day for each *mow* of land to be levelled. The total amount of time spent on the land for preparation can thus now be estimated. If there are seven *mow* for one person to work, it will take about thirty-five days, approximately equal to the amount of time needed for the growth of the rice in the nursery.

There is no ritual ceremony at the beginning of the agricultural work and every household is free to deter-mine its own time for starting. The difference in time covers a range of two weeks.

Transplantation of the young shoots from the nursery farm to the main field is a major part of rice cultivation. The people describe this period as " busy in farm." The farmers start in the early morning for the nursery, which sometimes is far from the main field ; they must transport the young shoots by boat. Children are brought to help in the work, but not women. The young shoots are planted in the main field in bunches of six or seven stalks. Children make themselves useful by handing the young shoots to the leaders while they are planting. One person will plant six or seven bunches in one row within his reach without stepping sideways. Finishing one row he will take one step backwards and start another row. Finishing one strip he will start another from the beginning. If there are several persons at work on the same farm, they will form a row and move backwards at the same time. The rhythmatic movement of the workers is very impressive. To maintain the rhythm, which is helpful in this monotonous work, they often sing rhythmic songs. Special songs have grown up under the name of *yengo*—" Young shoot song." But since in this region women do not participate in the work, the development of such songs is less than in the neighbouring areas.

Each person can plant about half a *mow* a day. To plant seven *mow* well thus takes about two weeks.

In July it is already summer. In hot weather (80° F.) rice grows very fast. During this period rain is plentiful (5·5 inches); heaven helps people to supply water to the young rice shoot. But nature cannot always be relied on. If there are two or three days without rain, the delicate young shoots will need to be watered by pumping, which calls for human labour. If it rains for three or four days continuously, the people will, on the other hand, be busy in pumping out the surplus water.

The wild grass mixed in the rice grows sometimes still faster. Only one week after the people have finished their work of transplantation, they must again be busy in weeding. A special instrument is used. This is a plate which has many nails on one side and is fixed to a long bamboo pole. The workman handles the pole by drawing the nails through the mud to uproot the wild grass.

When the field is weeded, the next task is to supply fertilizer for the soil. Fertilizer consists of human and animal manures and bean cakes. Bean cakes are made of the sediment of the soya beans after the oil has been pressed out. The cake is minced into small pieces and is evenly distributed over the farm.

Human manure is preserved in special pits behind the house. Sheep manure is collected from the hut. After long exposure in the air, and after being mixed with grasses, it is distributed over the field. Fresh manure is not used.

When the rice has reached a considerable height, and before it blossoms, the farmer must weed it thoroughly. This time the nailed plate cannot be used, because it might damage the root of the rice. The farmer has therefore to use his hands. To avoid damaging the rice, a saddle-like bamboo basket is attached to the upper leg. This brushes the rice away as the farmer walks in the mud.

Weeding and watering take all the farmer's time from July to September with several short intervals. The amount of work varies according to the amount of rain. In the early part of September the rice blossoms, and at the end of that month it bears fruit. No special work is necessary during that period. This is the long interval in agricultural work. During the latter part of October some of the early rice can be reaped. The instrument for reaping is a long curved sickle. The rice is cut near the root of the stalk, and is carried in bundles to the open space in front of the house. Threshing is done in the open space or in the front room, by striking the ears of the grain against the side of a big box. Grains are thus separated from the stalk and collected at the bottom of the box. Threshed stalks are heaped on the ground beside the public road.

Grains are hulled in a wooden mill. Husks are separated from the seeds by a whirling machine. The hulled seeds of rice can be sold but cannot be cooked without another process of refined husking. The last process has been entirely taken over by the modern machines. The old instruments of mortar and pestle are not used any more.

3. SCIENCE AND MAGIC

The knowledge embodied in the lay-out of the farm, in irrigation, in drainage, in breaking the soil, in trans-plantation, in weeding, etc., is accumulated from the long experience of the population, transmitted from generation to generation and learned by practical demonstration. It is an empirical knowledge that enables the people to control the natural forces in order to attain human ends. A detailed investigation would show how highly developed is the science of agriculture in this region. The above account has already indicated that the people understood definite general principles of biology concerning the process of growth of the rice, the quantity of water needed during different periods, the function of leaves and roots in plant physiology, and of physics concerning the level of surface and the movement of water.

Their empirical approach to their enterprise is again seen in the way in which they adopt new technique and implements. The selection of implements is solely based on the principle of efficiency and economy. For instance, the air pump is used when there is urgent need of water regulation, but not when it proves to be expensive.

Science, however, only rules in so far that the natural factors can be successfully controlled by human effort. There are uncontrollable factors in nature. For instance, the primary need of a water supply can only be partially controlled by human means through irrigation, drainage, and the construction of dykes and ditches. It still largely depends on the rainfall. If there is too much or too little rainfall, rice will die regardless of how hard the people work on their pumps. Locusts may come unexpectedly. In this fateful sphere, and in this only, we find magical beliefs and practices.

It does not mean that the people conceive rain and locusts as supernatural manifestations. They have scientific meteorological knowledge. " When it is too hot, the lake will evaporate too much and when the temperature changes there will be rain." But these natural phenomena are beyond human control. They might be a great menace in practical life and turn all effort to nothing. At this vital point, the people say, " We depend on heaven." The recognition of human limitations gives birth to magic. But magic is not a substitute for science. It is only one means for combatting natural disasters. It does not rule out other means. Science and magic go hand-in-hand to attain a practical end.[1]

Magic is not a spontaneous and individual action. It is an organized institution. There is a definite person who is charged with the function and possesses magical powers. Secondly, there is a traditional ritual

[1] Theory of magic and science: see Professor B. Malinowski, " Culture," *Encyclopædia of Social Sciences.*

o call in the supernatural intervention. Lastly, there re myths to justify the ritual and the ability of the magician.

The occasions for magical performances are threats f flood, drought and locust plagues. Whenever the ccasion arises, the people go to the district government nd appeal for magical help. By ancient tradition the district magistrate was the magician of the people. n case of flood, he would go to the river or lake to demand the receding of the water by throwing his fficial belongings into the water. In case of drought ie would issue an order to stop killing pigs and would rganize a parade with all the paraphernalia suggesting ain, such as umbrellas and long boots. In case f locust plagues he would parade with the idol of *uiwan*.

The obligation of the magistrate to act as the district magician and his efficiency in this rôle, is explained by he following myth. About a mile outside the north ate of the city of Wukiang, the headquarters of the district, there is a temple worshipping the god called Chang Ta Ti (Chang the Big Emperor), whose birth-day is on the 8th of the 2nd month (IX–2). According o the belief of the people he was a magistrate of the district at a remote historical period. During his term f office there was a threat of flood from continuous ieavy rain and the overflow of the water in the lake. Going to the lake, he commanded the water to recede t once, and threw his shoes, his clothes, and his official ade girdle one after another into the water. But the vater still overflowed, and rain continued to fall. At ast, he threw himself into the water. The menace vas conquered. At the present time, it is said that vhenever there is a threat of flood in the district

the gown of the idol will be always very wet becaus
he still performs his function invisibly.

The myth connected with *luiwan* and his functio
in locust magic is not known in this village, so far a
I could find out. But it is very popular in the neigh
bouring city of Wukiang. *Luiwan* was a historic
person. He had been maltreated by his step-moth
throughout his life. He was a very mischievous bc
and possessed magical power. One night he invite
all his friends to a big feast and killed all the cows c
his family. In the morning he arranged the heads an
tails of the cows in such a way that they looked ha
buried underground. But before he had finished th
arrangement the day began to break. He ordered th
sun to wait a minute. The sun went down under th
horizon. Even at the present time, it is said, the su
will recede for a minute in the morning. When h
step-mother found the cows half buried undergroun
the cows, owing to the magical power of the boy, lowe
towards their master and moved their tails. As th
result of his tormenting his step-mother, she treate
him outrageously and he at last died. After his dea
his spirit has been believed to be continuously powerf
in magic and able to drive away locusts. This my
testifies to the magical ability of the mischief-makir
boy and is the charter for the present belief and practi
in locust magic of the people.

The magical function of the magistrate runs count
to the modern concept of civil office. Furthermor
the present government regards superstitious belie
among the people as a great obstacle to social improv
ment. Various orders have been issued for the pr
hibition of magical performances of any sort. Th
present magistrate, therefore, not only denies h

aditional function to be the people's magician, but is
ipposed to enforce the law against magic. But the
atural menaces of flood, drought, and locusts continue
) threaten the people. Their scientific knowledge
nd equipment are still not sufficient to control many
f the disasters of nature, and the need for magic
emains unchanged.

An ex-magistrate told me how the problem was
olved. " Under the pressure of popular demand to
o something against the drought, I had to issue an
rder to stop killing pigs. I considered it to be very
seful since epidemics always go together with drought,
nd vegetable food helps to check an epidemic. This
; the real function of the belief. The parade was
rganized in my absence. It was no good to force the
eople to do nothing against the drought."

Magic exists in spite of government orders and
arious justifications, so long as it plays a useful part
n the life of the people. A change in theory from
onceiving magic as a kind of pseudo-science and
bstacle to technological development to recognizing
ts practical function will throw light on practical
neasures for dealing with this problem. It is not a
hing to be prohibited by order, but to be eliminated by
roviding more effective human control over nature.
Since complete control is inconceivable at present, it
s difficult to rule out magic in human culture.

4. ORGANIZATION OF LABOUR

Who are working on the land ? On what occasions
lo the farmers need to co-operate ? Who will co-
pperate ? What kind of organization has resulted ?
Let us examine these questions—still from the technical

point of view and leaving the legal problem to the next chapter.

I have said that the household is the basic economic unit. But the members of a household do not all participate in agricultural work; children go to the farm only occasionally and women are entirely free from it. Agriculture is chiefly men's occupation. This division of labour between men and women is characteristic of the silk-producing area. It suggests that the development of the silk industry is a factor responsible for the practice. During the period when domestic reeling was prosperous, women were busy in reeling while men were busy in preparing the soil. On the other hand, the income secured from the silk industry was comparable to the income secured from agriculture. It enabled the people to live on small farms. The size of farms therefore remains limited and the amount of labour required in agriculture is correspondingly restricted.

To show how well adjusted are labour and land in the village, some statistics may be cited. The total number of adult men, the real or potential workers on the land, between 15 to 55, is 450. The total area of land, including a small percentage of non-cultivated land, is 3,065 *mow*. If the land is equally distributed among the workers, each will get 6·6 *mow*. In the above section, I showed the rate of work and the length of time needed for the growth of the rice, and came to the conclusion that the amount of land that can be cultivated by a single man is about seven *mow*. From the point of view of technology, I have also shown that the use of the hoe in cultivation has made most of the work very individualistic. Group work yields no more than the sum total of individual efforts. It also does not increase the efficiency very much. Present technology has fixed the amount of labour required by the size of the land. Thus we have approximately identical figures for the amount of land which can be cultivated by each worker. This fact has far-reaching influence on land tenure, on the scattered system of farms, on the frequency of family division, and on the small size of the household.

The present decline of the silk industry has dislocated the traditional adjustment of economic activities. The size of farms has remained the same while the silk industry has been taken over by modern factories. The small farm cannot absorb the female labour that has been set free by the industrial change. The maladjustment is seen in the leisure enjoyed by the women in the village and the higher mobility of female population from the village to the town. In the neighbouring villages where farms are comparatively large, in the process of adaptation to the new situation female labour has been introduced into agriculture. This shows that the traditional division of labour, orginating as a part of economic adjustment, is a practical arrangement and is not due to any non-empirical cause. So far as men work by themselves and so long as the farm cannot be extended, female labour is not needed in agriculture. The only occasion for female labour is during the urgent period of irrigation and drainage. Water regulation sometimes requires prompt action. Women will not hesitate to work on the pump when they are needed.

The male members of a household work together on the same farm. But they have no special division of work. Everybody does the same work, except that in transplantation the children do not take part in actual planting but supply the young shoots to the adults. Thus the work is largely individualistic.

The need of co-operative work is in water regulation. In the process of irrigation, the members of the household, including women and children, always work on the same pump. In the process of drainage, the water is pumped out from the common trench of a *čien*. The people who work in the same *čien* share a common fate. Hence develops a well organized system of collective drainage. To describe this system, I will take a concrete example of the North *čien* of the Hsi Chang *Yu*.

This *čien* consists of 336 *mow* of land. The common trench opens on to the stream A at the north margin. At the opening there are fifteen pumping spots. This means that there can be fifteen pumps working at the same time. Each pump requires three workers. The amount of labour contributed by each member of the *čien*, taking the household as a unit, is proportional to the size of his holding. The system of apportionment is calculated in terms of labour units. A unit is 1/3366 of the total amount of labour in four days. Each of the fifteen pumps shares 22·4 units. Each person working for four days counts as 6 units and the contributor of the pump and manager of the team counts as 4·4 units. This system of counting is called " six *mow* starting." It means that each holder of six *mow* in the *čien* should contribute a person to work every day, each holder of three *mow* should contribute a person every alternate day, and so on. Every *čien* owing to varying size, has its particular system of calculation.

The members of the *čien* are organized into fifteen teams corresponding to fifteen pumps. Each year one

Plate IX.

DIVING BIRDS FOR FISHING

SHRIMP TRAPS

These traps are spread in the lake during the night to collect
shrimps every four hours.

Plate X.

RICH RICE-FIELDS

of a group will be charged with contributing the pump
and managing the team. This position is taken in
turn by the members of the group. Among the
fifteen groups, there is a chief manager. This position
is also taken in turn. At the beginning of the year,
the chief manager calls the fourteen other managers to
a meeting. A feast is prepared as a formal inauguration.
The chief manager has authority to determine when
the drainage should begin and stop.

Whenever drainage is needed, the chief manager will
give orders to the managers. Early in the morning
these managers will inform the workers on duty by
beating a bronze brace. If anyone on duty does not
show himself at the pump half an hour after the signal,
the other two charged to work on the same pump will
stop their work, take the pivot of the pump to the
nearest grocery and bring back to the spot fifty-three
pounds of wine and some fruit and cakes, the cost of
which will be charged to the absentee as a fine. But
if the manager has not informed the absentee he himself must bear the responsibility.

The collective responsibility of drainage has made
the introduction of the modern pumping machine
difficult, because it requires the unanimous consent
of the whole *čien*. It still remains to be seen how this
type of organization will adjust itself to the technological
change.

G

CHAPTER XI

LAND TENURE

Lakes, Streams, and Roads — Ownership of Farm-Land —
Farm Labourers and Land Leasing — Absentee Landlordship —
— Full Ownership — Inheritance and Agriculture

Land tenure is commonly conceived as the customary
or legal system of titles over land. " But," as Professor
Malinowski has pointed out, " this system grows out
of the uses to which the soil is put, out of the economic
values which surround it. Therefore land tenure is an
economic fact as well as a legal system.

" We could lay down at once the rule that any attempt
to study land tenure merely from the legal point of
view must lead to unsatisfactory results. Land tenure
cannot be defined or described without an exhaustive
knowledge of the economic life of the natives." [1]

" The maxim that you cannot understand the rules
of the game without a knowledge of the game itself
describes the essence of this method. You must know
first how man used his soil, how he waves round it his
traditional legends, his beliefs and mystical values,
how he fights for it and defends it ; then and then
only will you be able to grasp the system of legal and
customary rights which define the relationship between
man and soil." [2]

[1] *Coral Gardens and their Magic*, 1935, p. 318.
[2] *Ibid.*, p. 320.

We have, in the last chapter, studied how the villagers use their land and water. We are now prepared to go into the problem of land tenure.

1. LAKES, STREAMS, AND ROADS

In so far as the water is used for communications, it is not exclusively for anybody. But when one enters the village, one sees rails constructed at the entrance of the stream. These are closed during the night. In this way the use of the stream as a means of communication is restricted. The reason is to prevent the communication route being used in such a way as to threaten the life or property of the villagers.

On the other hand, since the communication route is not the exclusive right of anyone, nobody is allowed to interfere with the general convenience by stopping boats in the middle of the stream. The same restriction is found in the use of water for drinking and cleaning. The silk factory had to be built at the lower course of the stream, otherwise the sewage would have dirtied the water and prevented others from using it for drinking purposes.

Regulation of water for irrigation is much more complicated. People are not allowed to build dykes in the stream in order to monopolize the water supply. This is a common issue of dispute between villagers especially during drought. The water introduced on to the farm by human effort belongs exclusively to the person who has effected this by labour. The dykes are not allowed to be opened in order to " steal " water from the higher plot. But a single plot may be owned by several persons. Each has a part in it. Since there is no dyke to separate the parts owned by different persons, the water is shared by all. In such a case, the labour spent in irrigation is equally distributed between the owners according to the size of the land in the plot. Most important of all, the level of the plot is maintained evenly in order that there should be a fair distribution of water. This is another cause of dispute, because, as I witnessed on several occasions, each farmer tries to lower his own part in order to receive a favourable reserve of water.

The natural products of water—consisting of fish, shrimps, and weeds which are used for fertilizing the farm—are the common property of the village. This means that the inhabitants of the village have equal rights to these products, and that people from other villages are excluded. To illustrate the implication the following case can be cited.

The fishing right in a lake west of the village, was in 1925 leased by the village head, Chou, to people who came from Hunan Province. This was because at that time the village needed money to repair the rails on the stream for self-defence. When the contract was made, Chou announced to the villagers that henceforth no one would go to fish in the lake. The villagers kept this agreement. When I was in the village, there was a dispute. The Hunanese arrested a boat engaged in shrimp trapping and took the fishermen to the police office in the town, accusing them of theft. Chou protested that it was not the lake that had been leased to the Hunanese but the fishing rights which did not include the right of shrimp trapping. Eventually the arrested persons were released.

The villagers also prevent outsiders from gathering weeds in the streams.

The right of collecting natural products in the water surrounding and inside the village is shared by the villagers, but those fish and weeds that have been collected are the exclusive property of the collectors.

The public road and dykes on the farm, so far as they are used for communications, are not the exclusive property of anyone, like the water route. No one can stop any other person walking on the public roads or dykes. But the roads and dykes are also used for growing vegetables. The right to use them for this purpose is exclusive to a group which have special claims—the Chia. The problem is complicated because the public road passes across the open space in front of houses, which is used for heaping straws, for fixing silk machines and manure pits, for arranging dining-tables, and for drying laundries. Each house has the exclusive right to the use of the road for these purposes.

2. OWNERSHIP OF FARM-LAND

All the farms are divided between Chia for cultivation. Before we come to the owners, the idea of ownership of the farm-land must be clearly defined.

According to the native theory of land tenure, land is divided into two layers : namely, the surface and the subsoil. The possessor of the subsoil is the title holder of the land. His name will be registered with the government because he pays the taxes on the land. But he may possess only the subsoil without the surface, that is, he has no right to use the land directly for cultivation. Such a person is called an absentee land-lord. The person possessing both the surface and the subsoil is termed the full owner. The one possessing only the surface without the subsoil is termed tenant. I shall use these terms only in the meanings defined above.

The owners of the surface, whether full owners or tenants, can cultivate the land themselves ; this distinguishes them from absentee landlords. They also can lease the land to others, or employ labourers to work for them. The lessee who possesses the right of using the land temporarily can also employ labourers. In these cases, the person who owns the surface rights, may not be the actual cultivator of the land. Thus we must distinguish between the actual cultivator, the surface owners, and the owner of the subsoil. They may be the same persons and they may be different persons with reference to the same piece of land.

All of them have definite claims on the produce of the land. The owner of the subsoil can demand rent from the tenant. The surface owner can demand rent from the lessee. The employee can, in return for labour, obtain wage from the employer. The absentee landlord, the lessor, the employee receive fixed shares in terms of rent and wage irrespective of the actual return from the land. Therefore the risk involved is born by the full-owner, the tenant, and the lessee. The latter, except sometimes the employees, are also the owners of the implements used in cultivation. The following table summarizes these points.

3. FARM LABOURERS AND LAND LEASING

Ownership of the land surface is always held by the Chia group, which supplies male members to work on the farm. But sometimes the group may not be able to supply enough labour and the institution of farm labourers comes into being. The persons thus introduced are long-term employees. They live in the house and are provided with food and shelter. They are paid a yearly wage of eighty dollars with two

Title	Legal Right	Reward	Obligation	Owner of implements
Employee (a) Short-term.		Daily wage	Cultivation	No or yes.
(b) Long-term.		Yearly wage, food and shelter	Cultivation	No or yes.
Lessee	Temporary use of the land surface	Produce	Cultivation, rent to lessor	Yes.
Tenant	Permanent ownership of the land sur-face	Produce	Rent to ab-sentee landlord, cultiva-tion	Yes.
Absentee landlord	Ownership of subsoil	Rent from tenant	Taxes to govern-ment	No.
Full-owner	Ownership of land surface and subsoil	Produce	Taxes to govern-ment	Yes.

months' holidays at the new year when agricultural
activities are suspended. Short-term employees are
taken on when there is a short-period need for labour.
They live in their own houses and provide their own
food. They usually have their own land and are employed only when they have completed their own work.

The long-term employees sell their labour and do
not possess means of production except sometimes the
hoe. They come from those Chia whose land holding
is too small to absorb their labour. Especially those in
need of money to enable them to obtain a wife will seek
employment for a few years. I did not meet anyone

who had been landless all his life. The total number of employees in this village is only seventeen (VI–1). This shows that this institution does not play an important part in the village economy, and if we examine the population statistics this phenomenon can be explained. As mentioned (III–3), any Chia which has a land holding above the average is likely to raise more children. When the children grow up, the estate is divided. In other words, the chance of labour in the Chia proving insufficient is considerably reduced by the population pressure and the ideology of kinship. Moreover, there is no sign of people leaving their land in search of other occupations and meanwhile employing labourers to cultivate the land. This is due, first to the low degree of occupational differentiation (VIII–1), secondly to the special value attached to land (next section), and lastly to the under-development of industry in the town.

The institution of land leasing is also very limited. It occurs in most cases when the male members of a Chia are dead and the widows and children are unable to work on the land. Leasing of land is quite different from tenancy. The lessor preserves the right of ownership. There is a definite period for the contract. He is free to choose his lessee and to make changes when the contract expires.

It is interesting to compare this with the situation in South China, where both the hired labourers and landless peasants are numerous and the system of land leasing is far more elaborate.[1] This seems to be chiefly due to the presence of the system of " permanent tenancy " as a character of the absentee landlordship

[1] Chen Han-seng, *Agrarian Problem in Southernmost China*, Lingnan University, Canton, 1936, p. 4, and Chapter III.

in Eastern China, while it has died out in South China. This leads us to an examination of the system of absentee landlordship.

4. ABSENTEE LANDLORDSHIP

To study the institution of absentee landlordship, it is necessary to examine first the values attached to land. The primary function of land is to yield a food supply. But land is not only a means for producing food.

The productivity of land fluctuates according to the amount of attention and labour devoted to it. Furthermore, it is only partially controllable. There are unexpected risks. Thus land acquires its individuality through its variability in reacting to human expectation. Fear, anxiety, expectation, comfort, and love complicate the relation between man and land. People can never be certain what will come from the land. Land provides the means for self-assertion, for conquering the unknown and for the pleasures of accomplishment.

Although the productivity of the land can be only partially controlled, this partial control supplies an empirical measurement of workmanship. Honour, ambition, devotion, social approval are all thus linked up with the land. The villagers judge a person as good or bad according to his industry in working on the land. A badly weeded farm, for instance, will give a bad reputation to the owner. The incentive to work is thus deeper than the fear of hunger.

The relative inexhaustibility of the land gives the people a relative security. Although there are bad years, the land never disillusions the people completely, since hope for plenty in the future always remains and is not infrequently realized. If we take the other

G*

kinds of productive work, we shall see that the risks involved in them are much greater. The sense of security is expressed in the following statement made to me by one of the villagers :

"Land is there. You can see it every day. Robbers cannot take it away. Thieves cannot steal it. Men die but land remains."

The incentive to hold land is directly related to the sense of security. The farmer says, " The best thing to give to one's son is land. It is living property. Money will be used up but land never."

It is true that there are many ways of getting food. But the people will not exchange their land for other means, even if more productive. They do take up other occupations, such as the silk industry and fishing, but agriculture remains the principal occupation in the village.

The deeper we analyse the situation, the more it appears, not only that land in general has a particular value to the people, but that the property inherited by a Chia has for it a particular value. Land is transmitted according to fixed rules (N–3). People inherit their land from their fathers. The sentiment originating in the kinship relation and reinforced by ancestor worship is manifested also in this personal attachment to the particular plots of land. Religious belief in the importance of the continuity of descendants finds its concrete expression in the continuous holding of land. To sell a piece of land inherited from one's father offends the ethical sense. " No good son will do that. It is against filial piety." This comment sums up the traditional outlook.

Personal familiarity with a particular piece of land as the result of continuous work on it is also a cause of personal attachment to the land. It is very common for people to work on the same piece of land from early adulthood to death. To say that their land is an integral part of their personality is scarcely an exaggeration.

The non-economic value of the land complicates the transactions in land. Although land has its non-economic value, it does not in any sense lose its economic value. The sentimental and ethical reactions to the selling of land do not rule out completely the possibility of land transactions. People sometimes need money urgently. Economic strain compels them to treat the land as an economic commodity. But I found no case of alienation except under real pressure. Even then the process usually takes a roundabout form.

A person needing money urgently, either for taxes or rent payment, is forced to borrow from the money-lender. After a definite period, if the borrower cannot pay back the capital as well as the interest, he is forced to transfer his title over the land, limited to the subsoil, to the lender.[1] This transaction in practice means very little to the borrower, since the borrower under the ever-increasing burden of interest can hardly hope to repay his debt. To pay high interest is more unbearable than to pay a definite rent.

[1] It is also observed in South China that the land right is transferred through the intermediary step of mortgage. Chen Han-seng says, " Sometimes one-half of the peasant families have mortgaged their lands, as in many villages of Wung-yuen and Mei-hsien, where the percentage of land owning peasants is relatively high. The mortgaged piece is from 50 to 60 per cent. of the land price, very rarely 80 or 90 per cent. Of course, only a very few peasants would like to sell their lands, most of them prefer to mortgage in the hope of recovering them. But once the peasants have stepped into the sepulchre of usury, they are led to descend down the inescapable staircase with only a remote chance of coming out again. At least 70 or 80 per cent. of the landless peasants in Kwangtung have lost some of their land possessions through mortgage." . . . " According to the statistics of ten representative villages in the district of Pan-yu, the peasants there have mortgaged and sold 5 per cent. of their land area within five years." Op. cit. p. 96.

In fact the conversion from annual payment of interest to rent does not make a great difference to the debtor. I found one case where the person concerned did not even understand the meaning of the change. "I borrow his money, and he takes my land. I have no hope of redeeming my pledge. What does it matter whether the money I pay is rent or interest?"

The difference is again obscured by the existence of the native theory of land tenure. The tenant preserves his title to the land surface. This right cannot be interfered with by the owner of the subsoil. By this custom the tenant is protected from any direct intervention by the owner of the subsoil.[1] His only obligation is to pay the rent. According to law, if the tenant is unable to pay his rent for two years, the landlord can give him notice to quit, but the law does not apply to those places where custom is paramount.[2]

---

[1] Code Nos. 846 and 847.

[2] The system of permanent tenancy seems to be a protection of the peasant against a quick process of losing land rights owing to the financial needs of the rural industry. It should be studied not as a historical survival but as an adjustment of the interests of cultivator and financier, an integral part of the absentee landlord system. This can be illustrated also by observation in South China. "It is a remarkable fact," says Chen Hanseng, "that nothing is ever heard of permanent tenancy in the south-western part of Kwangtung, just the sort of region where one would expect some such reminder of the old economy, because here, so far, the influence of modern commerce has been comparatively little felt. On the other hand, the custom does obtain, where it would least be expected, namely, in the extreme eastern part of the province, up and down the Han River where not only junks and barges but also modern steamers and a local railway ply a lively trade, emerging the modernizing influence of the Swatow business world far into the interior. Indeed, in the region there are not merely remnants of a system of permanent tenancy but a considerable part of the cultivated area is actually under this form of lease," op. cit. p. 52. Chen tends to solve the system by an historical explanation, p. 51, although, as the above quotation shows, the present fact does not fit in with his expectation. To me the historical explanation may be interesting by itself but is not important if we are trying to understand the function of the system in the institution of land tenure. Without his ungrounded expectation, Chen may be able to realize the importance of the financial problem in relation to the land problem which he has very rightly pointed out on several occasions in his analysis but not been able to em hasize.

The practical difficulty of ejecting a tenant is to find a substitute. Absentee landlords do not cultivate the land themselves. Outsiders from the villages will not be welcomed into the community if they come at the expense of old members. Villagers are not willing to cut the throat of their fellow members who for any good reason cannot pay their rent. In these circumstances it is in the interest of the landlord to tolerate the default in the hope of getting rent in the future. This situation does not really challenge the status of the landlord, since there are positive sanctions to enforce payment of rent whenever this is possible.

By this analysis several important points in the problem of land tenure are cleared up. The actual cultivators of the land in the village—except labourers—continue unchanged even in the event of a change of ownership of the subsoil. Since the practice of usury is regarded as morally wrong, it is not possible for neighbours to squeeze each other. The institution of absentee landlord arises only in the relation between village and town. The ownership of the land surface remains in the hands of the villagers ; even the outsiders who live in the village do not find it easy to become owners of land surface, *i.e.* cultivators of the soil (II–5).

The institution of absentee landlord, thus described, has acquired a new significance as the result of the close financial relation between the town and the village. Professor R. H. Tawney has rightly put it, " What appears to be occurring, in some regions at least, is the emergence . . . of a class of absentee owners whose connection with agriculture is purely financial." [1] Again he said, " Nor must it be forgotten

[1] *Land and Labour in China*, p. 67–68.

that the nominal owner is often little more than the tenant of a money-lender." [1]

The change in ownership of the subsoil actually means the investment of town capital in the village. Thus the value of the land in the town market is quite different from the real value of the land. From the point of view of the landlords the value of the land resides in the ability of the tenant to pay rent. The price of land fluctuates according to the amount of capital available for investment in land and the security of rent collection. Thus the market price of land does not include the price of the land surface. As my informant told me, if his landlord likes to cultivate his land, he must buy the land surface from him. Since such a case has never been known, the price of the land surface cannot be calculated.

The ownership of the subsoil implies only a claim to rent and can be sold on the market in the same way as bonds and stocks. It may belong to any legal person,

---

[1] *Op. cit.* p. 36. The present material seems to confirm the general point suggested by Professor Tawney that the problem of tenancy is a function of the financial relation between village and city. " Occupying ownership," says he, " is least prevalent in the proximity of great cities where urban capital flows into agriculture—in the Canton delta 85 per cent. of the farmers, and in the neighbourhood of Shanghai 95 per cent., are said to be tenants—and most generally in the regions but little affected by modern economic developments. The provinces of Shensi, Shansi, Hopei, Shangtung, and Honan, where some two-thirds of the farmers are stated to be owners, are the original home of Chinese agriculture. They have been little touched as yet by commerce and industry. The yield of the soil is too low to make it an attractive investment to the capitalist, while the farmer has not the resource to rent additional land. In the south, where the soil is more productive, agriculture yields a surplus, the commercialization of economic relations has proceeded further and both the inducement and the ability to invest capital in land are accordingly greater. It is reasonable to expect that, with the expansion of modern industry and financial methods into regions as yet unaffected by them, similar conditions will tend to establish themselves in other parts of the country. In that case, the struggle which has so often taken place in Europe between the customary rights of the peasant, farming largely for subsistence, and the interest of the absentee owner in making the most of his speculation is likely, it may be anticipated, to be repeated in China. In parts of the country, it is being repeated already," *op. cit.* pp. 37–38.

whether an individual, a clan, or the government. It can be private or public. But we cannot here go into details, since this would require an investigation beyond our present scope.[1]

The security for rent payment, an important condition for the development of the instituion of absentee landlordship, leads to an examination of the method of rent collection and the attitude of tenants towards this obligation. Owing to the free market for land (*i.e.* the subsoil) in the town, the personal relation between the owners and the land they own has been reduced to the minimum. Most of the absentee landlords know nothing about the location of the land, the crop raised upon it, and even the men who pay the rent. Their sole interest is the rent itself.

Rent is collected in various ways. The simplest system is the direct one ; the landlord comes in person to the village. But this is not a very efficient way. It takes time and pains for the landlord to visit each tenant in different villages. Most of the landlords are unwilling to burden themselves with this. Moreover, direct and personal contact sometimes handicaps the process of collecting. The tenants may be poor and always ready to ask for exemptions or reductions. The landlord, on the other hand, is not infrequently inspired by humanitarian teachings, especially if he belongs to the old literati. On several occasions I knew that they were reluctant to squeeze their tenants. The conflict between traditional ethics and the practice of living as parasites sometimes leads these gentlemen landlords to derive only moral satisfaction from their trip but not enough money to pay the tax. But this direct system is limited to a small group of petty

[1] *Cf.* Chen Han-seng, *op. cit.* Chapter II, 24–41.

landlords. The majority collect their rent through agents.

Landlords of big estates establish their own rent-collecting bureaux and petty landlords pool their claims with them. The bureau is called Chü. The tenants do not know and do not care who is their landlord, and know only to which bureau they belong.

Names of the tenants and the amount of land held by each are kept in the bureau records. At the end of October, the bureau will inform each tenant of the amount of rent that should be paid that year. The information is forwarded by special agents. These agents are employed by the bureau and have been entrusted with police power by the district government. The bureau is thus in fact a semi-political organ.

Before deciding the amount of rent to be collected the landlords will hold a meeting in their union to decide what exemptions are to be made on account of flood or drought and also to decide the rate of exchange for converting rice rent to money. (The rent is regulated in terms of quantity of rice but payment is made in money.) The rate of exchange is not the market one, but is arbitrarily determined by the union of landlords. The peasants must sell their rice in order to get money for the payment of rent, and at the time when this is due the market price is usually low. Thus the combination of rent in kind and rent in money considerably increases the burden of the rent payer.

Nine grades are made in rent for different qualities of land. The average is about eight pints (2·4 bushels) of rice per *mow*. This amounts to 40 per cent. of the total rice produce of the land.

In the village, rent is paid into the hands of agents

of the bureau. This is a peculiar practice different from that of other parts of the same district. The actual amount of payment is not necessarily equal to the amount written on the demand notice. As an old agent told me, " The villagers are illiterate. They don't know how to calculate from rice to money. There is no receipt or anything like that." If the tenant refuses to pay, the agent has power to arrest him and put him into the prison of the district government. But if the tenant is really unable to pay, he will be released at the end of the year. It is no use keeping him in prison and leaving the farms uncultivated.

A more detailed description of the system of rent collecting would be beyond the scope of the present study. But it is interesting to notice the different attitudes of the tenants towards their obligations.

By the old people, rent payment is regarded as a moral duty. As some of them said : " We are good people. We never refuse to pay our rent. We cannot steal even when we are poor. How then can we refuse to pay rent ? "—" Why do you pay your rent ? "—" The landlord owns the land. We cultivate his land. We only have the land surface. The surface cannot exist without the subsoil." These positive sanctions are adequate to maintain the institution. It is not only the fear of imprisonment that makes the tenants discharge their obligation. Where the tenant does not pay the rent, it is on account of distress for which he has no responsibility such as famine, illness, etc. A good landlord will then allow exemptions and deductions.

Recently the situation has been changing. The economic depression in the rural district has made rent a heavy burden on the peasant, and the income derived from the rent much more vulnerable for the landlord. The peasants are more susceptible to new ideas offered to the institution. " Those who till the land should have the land " is a principle laid down by the late Dr. Sun Yat-sen and accepted, at least theoretically, by the present government.[1] A more extreme view is spreading among the communists and other left groups. All these ideas have affected the sanctions described above. Peasants unable to pay rent now feel justified in neglecting to do so, and those who are able to pay will wait and see if they are compelled to do so. On the side of the landlords, strong measures must be taken to maintain their privileges and their available capital tends to be no longer in agricultural land. The result is an intensification of

[1] In the Preface to the *Annual* of the land Bureau of Chung-shan Hsien a follower of Dr. Sun Yat-sen wrote, " The agrarian problem is fundamental to our national livelihood. If this problem were to be rightly solved, naturally there would be a proper way out for our national livelihood. Only by the solution of this problem can mankind gradually get rid of war. Equality in land ownership has been the principle advocated by the Kuomintang. Our chief purpose is to prevent the monopoly by a few, and to provide equal rights and equal opportunity of land utilization for all the people." Quoted in Chen Han-seng, *op cit.* p. 23.

Declaration of the First National Congress of the Kuomintang, 1924 contains the following statements : " The principle of the People's livelihood—This principle of the Kuomintang contains two fundamental aspects. The first is the equalization of land and the second is the control of capital. In as much as the greatest cause of the inequality of economic organization lies in the fact that the right of land is controlled by the few, the Kuomintang proposes that the State shall prescribe the law of land, the law for the utilization of land, the law of the taxation of land, the law for the taxation of the value of land. Private landowners shall declare its value to the government which shall tax it according to the value so declared with the option of buying it at the price in case of necessity. This is the essence of the equalization of land. . . .

" China is an agricultural country, and the peasants are the class that have suffered most. The Kuomintang stands for the policy that those peasant that have no land and consequently have fallen into the status of mere tenants should be given land by the State for their cultivation. The State shall also undertake the work of irrigation and of opening up the waste land so as to increase the power of production of land. Those of the peasants that have no capital and are compelled to borrow at high rates of interest and are in debt for life should be supplied by the State with credit by the establishment of rural banks. Only then will the peasants be able to enjoy the happiness of life." T. C. Woo, *The Kuomintang and the Future of the Chinese Revolution*, Appendices C, pp. 255–6.

conflict between tenants and landlords, and a financial crisis in rural economy. The district jail has been repeatedly crowded with default cases. Organized action of the peasants in refusing rent payment has provoked serious conflict with the landlords who are backed by government force. In this part of China, a peasant revolt took place in 1935 and led to the death of many peasants in villages near Soochow. The value of land has depreciated rapidly, and the whole financial organization of the village is at stake. This situation is general in China. The gravest part is found in central China, where the issue has taken the form of a political struggle between Chinese Soviets and the Central government. But in the village which we are now describing the problem is less acute. The better natural endowment and the partial success of reforming rural industry have been effective palliatives. The positive sanction in favour of rent payment is still functioning.

5. FULL-OWNERSHIP

Absentee landlordship is only found when there is close financial relation between village and town. Corresponding to the investment of town capital in the countryside, the ownership of the subsoil of the farm land passes into the hands of the townspeople. At the present time, about two-thirds of the subsoil of the village is owned by absentee landlords. The other third is still in the hands of the villagers. (I am not able to give accurate statistics on this point. The estimate was given to me by my informants.) The villagers themselves may lease their land, may employ labourers, but never acquire the title to the subsoil only.

The full-owners, lessees and tenants do not form clear-cut or water-tight classes. The same Chia may possess all rights to some part of its land, may lease another part from or to others, and a part may belong to absentee landlords. The amount of land actually cultivated by each Chia is determined by the amount of labour available. Since the number of male adult members of each Chia does not vary much, the amount of land cultivated by each is much the same. But if we inquire how far a Chia is cultivating its own land, or how much land is fully owned by each Chia we find a considerable variation. The administration office of the village gave me the following estimate :

Amount of land (*mows*).	Percentage of Chia.
50–70	0·6
30–49	0·7
15–29	0·9
10–14	4·0
5–9	18·0
0–4	75·8

According to this estimate, about 90 per cent. of the population in the village have less than ten *mow* or 1·5 acres of their own land. They have surplus labour but not enough land. Therefore they become lessees and tenants.

Theoretically the tenants are free from the obligation to pay taxes. Land tax falls on the owner of the subsoil. But the practice is somewhat different. The system of tax collecting in the region is a peculiar one, and differs from that of other parts of the same district.

From the ex-magistrate, I received the following explanation. At the end of the last imperial dynasty the government tried to register the tax payers. But this was never completed. The tax in the region has been divided yearly between the cultivators of each *yu* ; a definite amount is assigned to them. One of the cultivators who owns more than twenty *mow* in the *yu* will be responsible for collecting the sum. This job is taken in turn by all the qualified persons in the *yu*. The government will not interfere with the way in which the collector distributes the tax.

The amount of tax to be paid by each *yu* is determined by its size. But since the land was only recently surveyed, and the land register has not yet been completed, the size is determined according to the estimate of the local collectors. The estimate is thus made not strictly according to the actual size of the land but according to the ability of the people to pay taxes. The collector is obliged to hand over the assessed amount to the government regardless of how much he has actually collected. To avoid the danger of having to pay a deficiency himself, he will submit a low estimate on the pretext that land has been deserted. In case of flood or drought, he will request the government to make reductions. (This request was formerly made in connection with petitions for magical help.)

Thus the actual distribution of the burden of tax is not rigid. The collector is able to use common sense in distributing the burden according to the ability of the people. Honesty and the sense of equality checks the abuses possible under such an informal practice.

Under the present system, tenants are not actually exempted from the obligation to pay taxes. I have no definite material on this point to show how the actual allocation is made.

The government will try to collect taxes according to the actual size of the land of each individual owner

when the land survey and registration are completed.
By this action the traditional system is likely to be
changed. It may relieve the burden of the tenants
but it will certainly increase the total sum of taxes if
the rate is not reduced because the reported size is
always smaller than the surveyed size. The villagers
realize the possibility and frequently try to sabotage
the government action. At present, the problem is far
from settled.

6. INHERITANCE AND AGRICULTURE

In Chapter III, I postponed the problem of how
the land is actually divided in the process of transmission of property, because it required a prior knowledge of the system of land tenure. On the other hand,
some points of land tenure and of agricultural technology still remain obscure unless the factor of kinship
is taken into account. In this section, I intend to
link the land tenure and agriculture with kinship.

Let us take the example, given in the previous
chapter, of the division of a Chia among a father and
two sons. The land is divided in this case into three
unequal parts. Let us suppose that before division
the Chia possesses a strip of farms consisting of four
successive plots : A, B, C, and D. These four plots
are different in value because their distances from the
streams are different. In principle the father can
choose his own share. Suppose he takes plot A and
half plot B, which may be divided parallel to the margin.
The rest of plot B is assigned to the first son as his extra
portion. The remaining two plots are equally divided
among the two brothers. To ensure equality of division, they must be divided perpendicularly to the
margin. Each son takes one belt. If, on the death

of the father, the share reserved to him is divided
again, it would be divided in the same way. This is
illustrated in the following diagram.

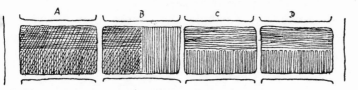

▦	For the first son when the Chia is divided.
▤	For the second son when the Chia is divided.
▦	For the first son after the further division of their father's reserve.
▤	For the second son after the further division of their father's reserve.

These lines of division, or the boundaries of holdings,
do not necessarily coincide with the dykes constructed
for the regulation of water. They are immaterial
demarcations, and are marked by planting two trees
at each end of the plot on the dykes. The boundaries
of individual holdings become very complex as the
result of successive divisions upon inheritance. The
farms are divided into narrow belts, with a width of a
few tens of metres.

Non-contiguity of farms is widely observed in China.
It is found in the village. Although the frequency
of land division cannot be taken as the origin of this,
it definitely intensifies the scattering of holdings.
Each Chia possesses several belts of lands widely apart.
It sometimes takes twenty minutes for the boat to go
from one belt to another. According to the estimate
of my informants, few belts are above six *mow* in size.
Most of them are not more than one or two *mow*.
Each Chia, at the present time, has three to seven belts.

The narrow belt and the scattered holdings hamper the use of animal labour or other collective methods of farming. They are the chief causes of the technical backwardness of farming in China.

Moreover, in a single plot there may be several owners, each of whom is responsible for his own belt. We have seen how this gives rise frequently to disputes on water regulations.

The small size of holding of the Chia limits the number of children who can be raised. On the other hand, the relatively large landholders will raise more children and consequently the size of their holding will be reduced within a few generations.   Under these conditions, the ratio between land and population is adjusted.

CHAPTER XII

THE SILK INDUSTRY

Scheme of the Process of Change — Conditions Working for Industrial Change — Agents of Change and Their Intentions — Local Support for Change — Programme of Change in Raising Silkworms — The Co-operative Factory — Government Support — Difficulties in Change — Effects on Kinship Relations

The silk industry is the second main source of income of the villagers. This is characteristic of the villagers around Lake Tai. The domestic silk industry has been carried on by the people for more than a thousand years. But during the last decade, for the reasons mentioned above (II–3), it has been declining. A new factory system of silk manufacturing has been introduced. The industrial change has deeply affected the life of the people in the villages. It has also called forth various attempts on the part of the government and other institutions to control the change in order to reduce or eliminate its disastrous consequences. The village we are studying, being one of the centres of the industry, provides a typical case for analysing the process ; and also, owing to the fact that an experiment has been made by the Sericultural School to reform the industry, it is specially interesting to see the possibilities and difficulties involved in such a deliberate effort of economic change.

I. SCHEME OF THE PROCESS OF CHANGE

The present analysis will take into view the different forces effecting the situation.   They are classified into outside forces working for the change and traditional forces bearing on the change.   The interplay of these forces results in a changing situation.   Thus the process can be schematically represented by three columns as follows.[1]   The items listed in the scheme will be discussed in the following sections.

A Outside Forces Making for a Change	*B*. Changing Situation	*C*. Traditional Forces Bearing on Change
I. World economic depression ; and world-wide development of silk industry on scientific lines and by factory methods.	I. Decline of the price of raw silk. Decay of domestic silk industry. Resulting economic poverty in the Chinese village as seen in : (A) Deficiency in family budget and shortage of food. (B) Suspension of recreative meetings and postponement of marriage. (C) Usury.	I. Minimum standard of living. Domestic silk industry as an indispensable supplement to farming in Chinese village. On which rest : (A) Daily necessities. (B) Ceremonial expenses. (C) Capital for productive work.
II. The Sericulture School as an active agent for industrial changes.	II. Readiness of the people for change. Support of the local leaders : (A) Assuming leadership in the reform. Increase of personal influence through participating in the reform.	II. Lack of sufficient knowledge for industrial change on the part of the villagers. Social position and function of local leaders : (A) Source of influence not hereditary, not by wealth but by strategic position in cultural contacts.

[1] The method of three-column analysis is devised by Professor B. Malinowski to study cultural contact.   The theorical basis of this method is expounded in his " Introductory Essay on The Anthropology of Changing African Cultures," *Memorandum XV of the International Institute of African Languages and Cultures,* 1938.

A. Outside Forces Making for a Change	B. Changing Situation	C. Traditional Forces Bearing on Change
	New leader created by the reform. (B) Economic benefit of the reform to the leaders.	(B) No direct economic reward for the position of the village head as such.
II. Intentions of the agent of change : (A) To apply scientific knowledge of the silk industry in order to :	III. Programme of Reform : (A) Initiating, organizing, and directing the reform programme by the staff and students of the School in :	III. Traditional method subject to change : (A) Technical defects of the traditional method :
(1) Prevent disease germs carried by the egg of the worm.	(1) Dependence on the specialists for egg supply.	(1) Infected eggs produced by individual families or by local hatcheries caused widespread disease.
(2) Increase the quantity and improve the quality of the cocoons.	(2) Raising worms under the supervision of the teaching centre.	(2) Customary method leaves the process of growth of the worm unregulated, causing high reduction in production and poor quality of the cocoons.
(3) Produce raw silk up to the export standard.	(3) Establishment of factory equipped with modern machines.	(3) Irregular fineness and frequency of break of the silk fibre reeled by the old type of machine.
(B) Organize the industry on the principle of co-operation.	(B) In the reform programme.	(B) Individualistic nature of the domestic industry.
	(1) Co-operative aspects : (a) Common house for raising young worms. (b) Co - operative factory. (i) Ownership belonging to members. (ii) Raw material supplied by members. (iii) Profit distributed among members.	(1) Confirmation of the new idea from the tradition : In classical teaching, and In practice in collective drainage and credit system.

A. Outside Forces Making for a Change	B. Changing Situation	C. Traditional Forces Bearing on Change
	(2) Non - co-operative aspects : (a) Labour is paid by wage system. (b) Management is in the hand of reformers and local leaders. (c) Members have no practical control over the management. (d) Lack of initiation of the members and of auditing.	(2) Lack of education in practising the system of popular control and in exercising the new right.
	(3) Counter - co - operative aspects : (a) Members refuse to subscribe their shares in full after the factory has failed to distribute annual profit. (b) Members reluctant to fulfil their obligation in supplying raw material.	(3) Interested only in practical benefits
(C) To improve the economic condition of the village.	(C) Improved economic condition in the village. (1) Success : (a) Reduction of cost in the process of raising worms. Production of cocoons increased. (b) Wage as a new source of family income. (2) Failure : (a) Profits have not reached the expected amount. (b) Waste of female labour in the household owing to the labour-saving of machine work.	(C) Expectation of economic recovery. (1) (a) High cost of production of the traditional method. (b) Labour did not form a commodity. (2) Survival of traditional reeling. (a) Small profit in domestic industry. (b) Division of labour between sexes, small size of farm and no other work to absorb female labour,

A. Outside Forces Making for a Change	*B.* Changing Situation	*C.* Traditional Forces Bearing on Change
	(*c*) Delayed payment of the full value of raw material supplied to the factory.	(*c*) Need of raw material for domestic reeling which is still partially preserved in the village.
V. Government as change agent with the intentions : (A) Balance of international trade.	(IV. Government supports the reform programme. (A) Subsidizing silk export and giving high price for the production of the factory in 1935.	IV. Local autonomy and suspicion of the government by the people. (A) Importance of raw silk in Chinese export.
(B) Rural reconstruction policies concerning rural industry. (1) Encouraging technical improvement.	(B) Governmental participation in the reform. (1) Inspection of egg production and taking over the work in supervising the raising of worms.	(B) Economic obligation towards the government. (1) Inferior production affecting export.
(2) Encouraging the co-operative movement.	(2) Dependence on governmental loans of the factory.	(2) Lack of financial ability of the people to maintain the new enterprise.

. CONDITIONS WORKING FOR INDUSTRIAL CHANGE

Several facts already mentioned in the above chapters must be noticed once more in order that a proper estimate may be made of the relative importance of agriculture in the domestic economy. The average holding of land is about $8\frac{1}{2}$ *mow* (IV-4). Under normal conditions each *mow* can produce six bushels of rice every year. The total produce will then be 51 bushels for that average holding of land. The amount of rice needed for direct consumption by members of the household is 42 bushels (VII-5). Therefore there is a surplus of 9 bushels. At the time when the new rice comes to market the price of rice is about $2\frac{1}{2}$

dollars per bushel. If the surplus is sold the return
will be about 22 dollars. But for current expenses
alone a Chia needs at least 200 dollars (VII–8). It
is thus evident that life cannot be supported by
agriculture alone. The deficiency amounts to 175
dollars a year. The situation is much worse with
the tenants, and these are the majority of the villagers
(XI–4). Tenant farmers with an average holding have
to pay 20 bushels of rice as rent to the landlord.
This amounts to 40 per cent. of the total produce.
The remaining 30 bushels are barely enough for the
consumption of the household.

Thus it becomes clear that a supplementary industry is indispensable for maintaining a normal
livelihood, which must be sufficient to cover daily
necessities, ceremonial expenses, tax and rent and
capital for future production (Col. C. I). When the
silk industry was prosperous the production of raw
silk could yield an average household about 300
dollars with a surplus (profit and wages) of 250 dollars.
(The highest price of native silk exceeded 1 dollar per
Liang (1/14 lbs.) and the total production for an
average household is 280 Liang. The cost of production, excluding wages, is about 50 dollars.) Under
these conditions the standard of living was much higher
than the minimum expected standard given above
(VII–8). The villagers had then sufficient money to
finance the various recreative and ceremonial activities
which have been suspended for more than ten years.

The price of native silk has fallen. In 1935 the price
was 1 dollar for 3 Liang. Without any decrease in
the amount of production, an average household
could then only obtain a profit of 45 dollars. In
such conditions and with the traditional system of

production, it is difficult to balance the domestic budget. In the next chapter, I shall show how a new industry has been introduced and how the villagers have also attempted to increase their income by expanding their trading activities. But in many cases they have sold their rice reserves in the winter and borrowed rice from the shop in the summer XV–3). In case of urgent need they have appealed to usurers (XV–4). On the other side they have tried o cut down expenses which are not immediately necessary, such as those for recreative meetings and marriage (Col. B, I).

The fall of income of the villagers is not due to a deterioration of quality or decrease of quantity of their production. Villagers produce the same type and the same amount of silk but it does not command the same amount of money from the market. The factors affecting price lie, of course, outside the village, and here I will only note two of the most important of them, namely, the post-war depression of world economy and the uneven quality of the domestic silk which renders it unsuitable to the highly mechanized weaving industry (Col. A, I).

3. AGENTS OF CHANGE AND THEIR INTENTIONS

The relation between the decline of silk prices and he increase of poverty was clear to the people. At irst they tried to discover what changes in the industry were necessary in order to restore the former conditions. But with their limited knowledge they were by themselves not able to take any definite action. Initiative and direction in the process of change come from outside.

The initiating party in this case was the Sericulture

School for Girls, in Houshukuan, near Soochow. This has had a profound influence on subsequent development but has of course been a factor outside the village.

A technical school in China is one of the centres for spreading modern technique in industry. Modern technique has been chiefly introduced from foreign countries, in the case of the silk industry chiefly from Japan. It is the result of the meeting of Chinese and Western civilizations—a typical contact situation. The difficulty of the technical school in fulfilling its function is that unless the new technique is accepted by the people, it cannot by itself serve progress. A failure in this respect is reflected in unemployment of the trained students. The situation there is most acute in the silk industry. The silk industry, especially the process of raising silkworms, is a kind of domestic work in the villages. In order to make the improved technique acceptable to the people and to find jobs for the students, industrial reform in villages has become an urgent problem for the technical schools. They cannot remain as purely educational institutions. Therefore, the Sericulture School has established a special department responsible for spreading in rural districts a knowledge of the new methods.

The nature of the change agent is important because it determines the change programme. The measure introduced to cope with the situation is formulated and actions are organized by the agent whose understanding of the situation is the premise. But the definition of situation influenced by the social setting of the agents is usually a partial representation of the reality.[1] To come back to our village, the causes of

[1] *Cf.* Karl Mannheim, *Ideology and Utopia, and Introduction to the Sociology of Knowledge,* 1936.

COLLECTIVE DRAINAGE

Drainage is the only collective activity in farming, and also one of the sensational
occasions in the village.

Plate XII.

THE CO-OPERATIVE SILK FACTORY

he fall in silk prices are multiple. The capitalistic
tructure of world economy, the struggle among im-
erialistic countries, the control of world finance by a
pecial " racial group," the political status of oppressed
ations as well as the modern girls' newly acquired
esthetic valuation of bare feet—all these might directly
r indirectly be responsible for the decline of the price
f the silk produced in Chinese rural districts, but not
ll of them came under the consideration of the change
gent. Since the change agent in this case is the
echnical school, the situation is defined in terms of
echnical factors. The person responsible for initiating
he reform programme in the village gave me the
ollowing account.

In the worst years, by means of the traditional
method only about 30 per cent. of the total silkworms
reached the final stage and produced cocoons. The
amount of silk given by the worms was small. This
unsatisfactory state of affairs was due to the lack of
preventive measures against the spread of disease
among the worms. The micro-organism responsible
for the disease was carried by the mother moth to
the eggs through physical contact between them.
Thus disease was handed down from generation to
generation, and there was no way of stopping it.
The house and the implements were not disinfected
before they were used for raising new worms.
Once a house was infected by disease, it would
suffer for years and years. The diseased or dead
worms were cast under the mulberry trees. People
thought that these dead worms were fertilizer for
the trees. But actually they spread the germs,
which were brought back with the mulberry leaves
to the house. (Col. C. III. A. 1.)

H

The temperature and humidity, which are very important conditions in the process of the growth of the worms, were left unregulated. According to custom, after the third exuviæ, fire was put out regardless of the actual fluctuation of the climate. In the village there were not enough mulberry trees The people had to buy mulberry leaves from neighbouring villages. Owing to the difficulties of transport they usually fed the worm with leaves already withered. The quantity and frequency of feeding were irregular. Even those worms unaffected by disease were unhealthy and not able to produce good cocoons. (Col. C. III. A. 2.)

The fundamental principle in silk reeling is to draw the silk fibre from the cocoon and to combine several fibres into one thread that can be used in weaving. The old type machine used for reeling consisted of three parts, namely, a furnace to boil water, a wheel to collect the thread after the fibre had been combined into one thread, and a rotating axle connected to a plate for treading by foot Warmed water was used for dissolving the sticky matter of the cocoon. But the temperature was not constant. Thus the degree of dissolution was uneven. This affected not only the lustre of the silk thread but the frequency with which the fibre broke.

Several cocoons are drawn at the same time by the movement of the wheel. The fineness of the thread depends on the number of fibres combined. The fibres from different layers of the cocoon are not of the same fineness. To maintain regular fineness of the thread, it is essential to keep a constant number of fibres and adjust the fibres from different layer of the cocoon. This was not easy to attain by hand reeling, because first, the frequency of breakage was high, secondly the movement of the wheel was not even, and thirdly the workers were not specially trained. (Col. C. III. A. 3.)

Silk is the raw material for the weaving industry. Since the silk produced in the village is mostly exported, it must be adjusted to the technical development in the weaving industry in western countries. The highly mechanized weaving industry has imposed a new standard on the raw silk. The degree of fineness should be uniform and accurately defined. Breaks should be reduced to a minimum. Such requirements cannot possibly be fulfilled by traditional hand reeling. The result is that the silk produced by the villagers is unsuitable for the improved weaving industry. The decline of demand for such crude silk leads to a decline of price. That is the reason why we must introduce the scientific method to the village. (Col. A. III. A.)

But technical change cannot be produced without corresponding changes in social organization. For instance, the smooth movement of the wheel can be attained only through the regular mechanical movement of a central power. Introduction of the steam engine for technical purposes leads to a change from individual domestic work to collective factory work. The use of electric power, which might again decentralize the productive process, requires a much more complicated co-ordination among industries. Under a system of collective enterprise, the relation between the means of production and labour also become more complicated. To introduce new social organizations for production, the agent must also teach new social principles. The selection of the social principle in organizing the new industry is also related to the interest of the agent. The technical school is not interested in making a profit for itself because it is not an economic institution. Who would therefore gain from industrial reform ? The agent's answer is the people. The organization of the new industry is on the principle of " co-operation." (Col. A. III. B.) The agent justified this change as follows :

Machines should be used to increase human happiness. Unfortunately, they have been used for the contrary purpose. But I still believe that it is the duty of the reformer who is trying to introduce these types of tool into China to find a way of using them properly. To me, the most important thing is that men should not be the slaves of machines. In other words, machines should be owned by those who use them as a means of production. That is why I insist on the principle of co-operation. It would be much easier to organize the new factory on capitalistic lines, but why should I do it ? Should I work for the interests of the capitalists and intensify the sufferings of the people ? The profit secured from the improved technique should go to the people who share in the production.

My other conviction is that the silk industry has been, and should remain, a rural industry. My reason is that if we attract the industry away from the village, as has been done by many industrialists and is so easy to accomplish, the villagers will in fact starve. On the other hand, I know very well how the workers are living in the cities. Village girls have been attracted by the opportunity to work in the city factories for a small wage, on which they can hardly support themselves. They have left their own homes. This process has ruined both the city workers and the village families. If Chinese industry can only develop at the expense of the poor villagers, I personally think we have paid too much for it.

The aim of my work is to rehabilitate the rural economy through the introduction of scientific methods of production and the organization of the new industry on the principle of co-operation.

The socialistic ideas of the reformers represent a part of the current ideology of the present literate class in China. In their new version they are introduced from the West, side by side with the modern technology and capitalistic system of industry. The position of the Chinese people in the world economy and the repeated struggle with the western powers have created a situation favourable for the spreading of socialist ideas. A reaction against capitalism, as understood by the Chinese people, prevails among the general public. Even those who stand for capitalism do not dare openly to justify its principles. This attitude was explicitly stated in the " Three people's principles " of the late Dr. Sun Yat-sen, which have been accepted, theoretically, by the present government as the guiding principle of its national policies.

On the other hand, socialist ideas are nothing new in China. The basic political idea of Dr. Sun Yat-sen was to realize the traditional teaching such as, " Under the heaven every thing is public," or " Those who till the land should have the land." (Col. C. III. B. 1.)

4. LOCAL SUPPORT FOR CHANGE

As we have seen, the Sericulture School, being outside the village, was only a potential agent. To turn
the potential agent into an active one there was needed
another factor. There was no direct social relationship
between the School and the villagers. The group
which possessed the new knowledge had no direct use
for it and the group which needed the knowledge had
no opportunity of acquiring it. A bridge by which
the agent of change could be made to function in the
village was essential. It was found in the local leaders.
According to the published report of the co-operative
factory the initiative was due to the local leaders. The
following passage written by Chen may be quoted.

> Kiangsu is known as a silk-producing area. But
> the industry depended more on natural factors than
> upon human effort. The result was the failure of
> the villagers in the industry. This had frequently
> ruined the people. In view of such conditions
> I (Chen) and Mr. Sen (a local leader in the town,
> Chên Tsê), proposed to the town council, in the
> regular summer meeting in 1923, that a teaching
> centre should be established to reform the method
> of raising silkworms. The proposal was passed
> and 600 dollars were allotted for the purpose.
>
> It happened that the president of the Sericulture
> School had, also as a result of the fall of silk prices,
> started a department for extension work for reform-
> ing the traditional methods of the silk industry. In
> the winter of that year, he came to Kaihsienkung,
> accompanied by Misses Fei and Hu and gave a
> series of public lectures. The people were greatly
> interested. Then the chairman of the town council,

in accordance with the resolution, authorized the president to organize the proposed teaching centre. The president consented to co-operate with the town council and subsidize the plan, and it was decided to start the work also in Kaihsienkung.

In addition to my own family, I called together twenty other families which had suffered very much in the past from continuous failure in the industry. The reform work was started in the spring of 1924.[1]

I have mentioned that the village headmanship is not a hereditary office. He has no other ground for his authority than the usefulness of his services to the community (VI–4). One of his most important functions is to interpret local needs and to assume leadership in taking necessary measures. The village head receives no economic reward for his position. But through introducing special work in the village, he can derive economic benefit from it. These were the intentions of Chen in supporting the programme of industrial reform. (Col. B. II. A. and B.)

The strengthening of the social position of the local leaders by industrial reform appears still clearer in the case of Chou. Chou had had no social influence before the industrial reform was introduced. Owing to his literacy and ability, he became an assistant in the work and gained prestige from it. Finally he was appointed by the higher administration to be the head of the Hsiang (VI–5). His social position has been acquired wholly through his participating in the reform programme.

This analysis is important in explaining why the village heads did not prove, on the contrary, a force resisting social change. Active resistance against the

[1] *Past Three Years of the Co-operative Factory*, 1931, in Chinese.

reform was not experienced at the initial stage. There was promise of improved condition on the side of the Sericulture School, and hope on the side of the people.

The rapid fall in prices had forced the people to accept certain changes in the traditional industry. But they lacked sufficient knowledge to define the situation or to formulate a definite programme of change. (Col. C. II.) They were also not properly equipped to judge the desirability of the proposed programme. The suspicion of novelty went hand-in-hand with the readiness to accept reforms when, by demonstration, the new technique could be proved useful. That is why at the beginning there were only twenty-one households in the programme, and, as the report specifically stated, these had suffered from hopeless failure when working by traditional methods. But it took only two years to draw the whole village under the supervision of the teaching centre.

5. PROGRAMME OF CHANGE IN RAISING SILKWORMS

The primary aim of the reformers, as I have explained, is the technical improvement of rural industry, but change in one aspect of culture automatically calls forth a series of changes in other aspects. Such a process once started tends to go on until a complete re-organization of the whole system has been affected. The sequence of change is of special interest for studying the functional relations between social institutions.

The reform programme has proceeded along the line of the natural process of the silk industry. This starts from the production of eggs through the breeding of moths and continues with the hatching of the eggs and raising of the silkworms, and collection of cocoons ;

it ends, as far as the village is concerned, with the reeling of the silk thread. The problem of marketing I shall deal with in the chapter after next.

Scientific knowledge in egg production consists of two parts, namely, the breeding of superior species through experimental crossing, and the separation of infected eggs through microscopic examination. Formerly the people produced eggs through pure line breeding of their own worms. They would also allow the germs to be handed down to the second generation. To reform the system of egg production, it was not practical to teach each villager the principles of genetics and the use of the microscope. It is much cheaper to employ a specialist to produce the eggs for the use of the villagers. The school therefore took over this work at first and supplied the villagers. It is interesting to note that in this respect the reformers were inconsistent in their aims. They decided to keep industry in the village, but egg production has been removed from the village into the hands of specialists. But egg production is economically unimportant, because the cost of the eggs is only 3 per cent. of the total cost of the production of raw silk.

The demand for disinfected eggs increased rapidly as the silk reform gradually spread over the whole region of the lower Yangtze valley. The School could not meet the demand and thus many private egg producers seized the chance to make a profit. The quality of eggs could not be maintained and the bad effects on the reform programme became evident. This situation led to government interference. A bureau for censoring the eggs was established by the provincial government with authority over the private producers and prices were also controlled. (Col. B. IV. B. 1.)

H*

The people receive their eggs only a short time before the period for hatching. Eggs are treated by the producers with special care. From hatching up to the collection of cocoons, the whole process of work is comprised in the term " raising silkworms." This process is carried out in the village under a special organization. At the beginning of the reform, directors were sent from the teaching centre to teach the villagers how to make use of scientific knowledge, especially in the prevention of disease of the worm and in the regulation of temperature, and humidity. To facilitate management and supervision, the young worms of different owners are concentrated in a common house, on the principle of co-operation. Expense and labour are shared by the owners in proportion to the amount of worms put in the common house. At present there are eight common houses in the village, containing practically all the young worms raised in the village. A special building with eight big rooms was built for this purpose. The money for the building was collected by adding 20 cents to each sheet of eggs during the years 1923 to 1925. (Col. B. III. B. 1. a.)

The collective process of raising silkworms can be effective only when the worms are young and small. Within six weeks they grow from a tiny size to two and a half inches at the time of maturity. After the third exuviæ the present common houses are not large enough to accommodate the worms. The collective system has then to be discontinued unless big buildings are available. The construction of such buildings is economically not worth while, because the period during which a large space is required is short, and it is much more convenient to use private houses. For the last

wo weeks all the rooms in the house, except the kitchen
ınd half of the bedrooms, are occupied by the worms.
This fact alone means that, unless the material sub-
.tratum of the village is radically changed, silkworm
·aising must remain mainly a domestic industry.

After the third exuviæ, the worms are removed to the
ɔrivate houses and each household raises its own worms
·eparately. Before the removal, the private houses
ıre disinfected under instructions given by the teaching
:entre. Constant supervision is maintained during
his process. Diseased worms are removed at once
ο prevent the disease spreading. Temperature and
ıumidity are regulated according to the need of the
vorms. (Col. B. III. A. 2.) The result of these
neasures is that the loss of worms due to disease has
ɔeen kept under 20 per cent., and the total production
ɔf cocoons has increased at least 40 per cent. as com-
ɔared with that under the traditional method.

When the teaching centre had proved its success in
he villaɔe, the provincial government extended its
vork to the whole silk-producing area. We will
lescribe this more fully in another section.

Before we go into the process of reeling, an estimate
·f the production and cost in this part of the process
nay be attempted. The total amount of silkworms
hat can be raised by a Chia depends on the size of the
ıouse and the labour available. Silkworms are raised
n rectangular and shallow containers about 1½ by 1
netre in size. They are put on the shelves of a stand.
:ach stand has eight containers. Each house has
:nough room for five stands. The silkworms hatched
rom a sheet of eggs (which is of standard size),
·equire in the final stage of development a whole stand
or accommodation. One person can manage two or

three stands. Each stand will yield 34 pounds o
cocoons which can be reeled into 48 Liang (or 3·4
pounds) of raw silk. Under reformed conditions, the
total amount of cocoons produced by an average Chia
is about 200 pounds, which can be sold at a price o
60 to 70 dollars per 100 pounds (according to the
reports mentioned above).

Each stand of silkworms needs about 400 pounds o
mulberry leaves. The price of mulberry leaves fluc-
tuated very much during the period of silkworm
raising. The highest price for a 100 pounds sometimes exceeds $3\frac{1}{2}$ dollars, and at the lowest is under
$1\frac{1}{2}$ dollars. The total expense for feeding worms lie
between 30 to 40 dollars. In addition to othe
expenses, the cost of cocoon production, excluding
labour, is about 50 dollars per Chia. If the cocoon
are sold, this will give an income of 70 to 90 dollar
for an average Chia.

The reform programme has also included the intro
duction of multiple crops. In this region three crop
can be grown. But owing to the climate, more equip
ment and precautions are needed in summer and
autumn crops. At present, these two crops are stil
very limited.

6. THE CO-OPERATIVE FACTORY

We now come to the process of reeling, that is, the
transformation of cocoons into the final stage of raw
silk. Reform in this process is directed to producing
a better quality of raw silk. Quality is judged by uni
formity in fineness and reduction of frequency o
breaks in the thread. According to the expert of the
Sericulture School, the weakness of the traditiona
method lies in (1) the irregular temperature of wate

used in dissolving the sticky matter of the cocoon, (2) the indefinite number of fibres forming a thread, (3) lack of regard for the different fineness of the fibres from different layers of the cocoon, and (4) the irregular movement of the wheel. To improve the quality of the silk, the reformers have tried several methods. The following statement made by the agent will explain the situation.

At the beginning, we had no idea of introducing the factory system. We tried to keep the work in the household. As a substitute for the old type of machine, we introduced a better wooden machine which is only a modification of the old. The wheel was turned by foot and everyone could work separately in her own house. Chemicals were used in dissolving the sticky matter, but the temperature of the solution could not be strictly controlled. Skill in maintaining a constant number of fibres and in adjusting the combination of different layers of the cocoons was taught in training classes lasting three months, organized by the School in the town. In 1924, there were only ten machines of this type in the village. But in 1927, the total number had increased to more than one hundred. More than seventy young women were trained in the special class. But owing to the irregular movement of the wheel, the quality of the produce was still below the requisite standard for export. On the other hand, the depression of the market was more acute. In 1928, the price for this type of " reformed silk " had dropped to sixty dollars per hundred Liang. Although it was better than the native silk, we were not satisfied with its condition. We knew very well from the experiment that unless we could have a central power equipped with a steam engine, the quality could not be raised to the export standard. But the introduction of the steam engine must go hand-in-hand with the collective factory system. In other words the domestic system of production could not be retained if we were to improve the quality of the produce. We decided therefore to test out what is the smallest size of silk factory in which all the advantages of applying modern technique of production can be realized but which at the same time is not too large to be maintained in the village and to use local labour and local supplies of raw material. This experiment has a wider significance. If we can produce, with lower labour costs, silk equal in quality to that of the larger scale factories, we can extend this system without fearing competition from factories in the cities. Through this small scale factory, rural industry can get a firm basis and the rural economy can be rehabilitated. We started the experiment in 1929. Our experiment proved to be successful only after the re-equipment in 1935, with the new machine which is a modified form of the latest Japanese type. With this we are able to produce the best silk in China. In 1935 the produce of this factory was ranked by the export bureau as of the highest grade.

From this account it is very clear that the substitution of the collective factory for the domestic system was dictated by technical considerations. The steam engine which makes possible a controlled and smooth movement of the wheel, and consequently speed and evenness in drawing the fibres from the cocoons, leads inevitably to a centralized system. Whether the introduction of electric power might again change the centralized system is a matter for future experiment. (Col. B. III. A. 3.)

A factory system of production requires a building suitable for equipment with machinery. To construct the factory needs technical knowledge and money. Technical knowledge was supplied by the School, but where did the money come from? This question led to the problem of ownership and the problem of distribution. According to the intentions of the reformers, the basic principles on which these were regulated had been laid down before the factory was established. The principle was that the factory should be owned by the people. But how can the people own it and who are the people?

Ownership is vested in the group of people who are members of the co-operative society. Their liability towards the factory is limited to the share they contribute. Membership is voluntary and is not limited to the people of this village. Anyone who observes the obligations of membership can be admitted as a member of the society. The obligation of a member is to hold a share in the factory and to supply a definite amount of raw material, cocoons, every year. There are 429 members of the society, including practically all the households in the village, and more than fifty members from neighbouring villages.

Final control of the factory is, according to the regulation, vested in the general meeting of the members. At the general meeting an executive council is elected, which is in theory responsible to the general meeting. In practice, it works the other way round. The people work according to the instructions of the local leaders, the executive council, and the local leaders work according to the instruction of the reformers, the School. The members have nothing to say, since the whole work is under the direction of the reformers, and the people have not sufficient knowledge to run the factory by themselves. A high percentage of illiteracy and the lack of educational opportunity on the part of the villagers have made it very difficult for the reformers to carry out their plan of training the villagers, the real masters of the factory. (Col. C. III. B. 2.) There has been no attempt by the members to exercise their right of vote to control the factory, since the ballot system is entirely new to them. The members do not understand more of the factory than that its practical benefit in terms of profit are distributed among them. (Col. C. III. B. 3.) They do not know on what basis they have a claim to the profit, just as they do not know on what basis they should pay rent to the landlord. Ownership then actually means to them only a grant for the distribution of profit. This will be still clearer when we examine the financial side of the factory.

There was of course no surplus capital in the village to finance the factory (Section 2). The total expense of its establishment was 49,848 dollars (about £3,000). This amounted to 114 dollars, or £27, from each member. In fact, of the total amount, the share contributed by the members in the first year, was only 2,848 dollars, about £180, *i.e.* 5·7 per cent. of the total.

Nominally, the " capital," or the contribution of the owners of the factory or the limits of the liability of the owners, is fixed at 10,000 dollars (£625). This is divided into a thousand shares of 10 dollars each. Each member subscribes at least one share. In the first year, 700 shares were taken up. These shares were payable over five years. At present only half of the amount has been collected. (Col. B. III. B. 3. a.) It is clear, therefore, that the finance of the factory depends on other sources than the owners.

The steam engine and the machines (of older type) were borrowed from the School. Their value was assessed as 4,000 dollars or £250. It was agreed that the factory would pay back that amount, out of profits, to the School within five years. But, owing to financial conditions, the factory has not yet fulfilled the promise. For the building and other expenses the factory had secured a long-term loan from the Provincial Peasant Bank of 15,000 dollars (or £800). This loan was not granted by the bank for strictly commercial reasons. It is clear that the liability is limited by the " capital," 10,000 dollars, and in case of bankruptcy the buildings and other immobile property could not be put up to auction since it is located in the village. But it was the government's policy to finance rural industry and this made it possible to raise the loan. (Col. B. IV. B. 2.) Another short-term loan of 3,000 dollars, or £190 (with land and building as mortgage) was secured from a local bank in Chên Tsê, the nearest town. From this examination of the financial basis of the factory, it is clear that the factory is actually based on government credit, not on the investment of the people.

The raw material is supplied by the members. Fresh cocoons are collected every year. Members receive a payment of 70 per cent. of the value of the cocoon supply at delivery. The money for this is borrowed yearly from the Provincial Bank, cocoons being accepted as mortgage.

As 30 per cent. of the payment is delayed, the members do not take much interest in supplying more than the lowest limit, especially since 1930,

which was the last year that profit was distributed
among the members. The following statistics supplied by the factory can be quoted.

Year	Members' Supply	Bought from Outside	Silk Reeled	Silk Reeled for Others	Days of Working
1929	527·07	—	41·31	—	175
1930	591·55	—	43·18	—	204
1931	415·73	—	32·21	—	145
1932	202·92	92·10	22·21	25·63	107
1933	307·87	45·37	40·46	5·00	186
1934	255·35	330·00	57·84	—	187
1935	375·80	301·08	64·21	—	199
1936 (incompleted)	424·80	—	—	—	—
			(units in piculs)		

The above table shows the gradual decline of the
supply of cocoons by members from 1930 to 1935
(Col. B. III. 3. *b*.)   In 1932, the total supply was too
small to keep the factory working more than a hundred
days.   For the machines to stand idle is not economical
Thus cocoons had to be bought from the market.   In
1934, the amount bought from outside was more than
the amount supplied by members.   On the other hand
the factory received orders from other factories to ree
for them, using the latter's supply of raw material
This system is called *teza*, reeling for others.   In
1932, the amount of silk reeled for other factories
exceeded twenty-five piculs, which was practically equal
to the amount of silk reeled from the raw material
supplied by the village.   After the factory had been
re-equipped in 1935, the total production of silk was
increased one-third over the average of preceding
years.   But the supply of cocoons from members did
not keep step although it increased a little in 1935

For raw material the factory was half dependent on outside supply.

Labour is recruited from members. By introducing the factory system, the labour needed in production is much reduced as compared with that needed under the domestic system. In the reeling process thirty labourers are sufficient. These are all young women varying from sixteen to thirty years of age. Ten to fifteen unskilled labourers are enough for the selecting and cleaning of the cocoons. After the silk has been reeled it must be re-wheeled and wrapped in a standard form for export. Six to eight skilled labourers are employed in this. The total number of labourers is about fifty. In addition there are two managers, one technical director, one treasurer, one engine keeper, and two servants.

In reeling and re-wheeling special training is needed. Thus employment and membership must be differentiated. Those who work in reeling and re-wheeling are paid in terms of a daily wage, forty to sixty cents a day. Those who work in selecting and cleaning cocoons are paid by piece-work. They receive about twenty to thirty cents a day. (Col. B. III. B. 2. a.)

The technical director is recommended by the School and the treasurer is recommended by the local bank. General business management is in the hands of local leaders, Chen and Chou. But the final authority is the Extension Department of the School. The staff are all paid fixed salaries. The total amount of wages and salaries, in 1929, was 7,557 dollars, or 57 per cent. of the total current expenses. Each common labourer can get roughly 70 dollars a year from 150 days of work.

From the above analysis, we can see that the factory is (1) owned by the members, (2) financed largely by the Provincial Peasant Bank, (3) managed by the School through the local leaders, and (4) worked by a part of the members. The so-called co-operative principle is significant chiefly in the problem of distribution.

The profit made by the factory in 1929, the first year, was 10,807.934 dollars. It was distributed according to the following principle :

" To encourage the members and to expand the organization, we decided to fix a high percentage for dividends. It should amount to seventy per cent. of our total profit. We will ask the members to lend half of their dividend to the factory to clear the loans. Fifteen per cent. of the profit will be our reserve fund. The rest will be divided into (1) reserve for improvement, (2) allowance for next year's current expenses, and (3) bonus for the staff, in the proportion of 4 : 3 : 3." [1]

In that year the amount of dividend actually received by the members was double the share they had contributed. But since that year, the price of silk had dropped to such a degree that no profit was made. The balance sheets since 1931 have not been published. I can only give the figures of the first three years.

Year	Net Profit	Net Loss
1929	$10,807·934	—
1930	—	$3,010·330
1931	—	4,183·655

From 1931, the factory has tried to pay back the loan. For instance, in 1929, as shown in the balance sheet, the loan amounted to 135,663·763 but in 1931 it was reduced to 77,271·544. The interest of the

[1] *Past Three Years of the Co-operative Factory.*

large loan was also a cause for the loss. In 1929 it was 5,060, in 1930, 5,500, and in 1931, 4,121. In 1935, the factory was re-equipped with modern machinery. It is expected to gain some profit after 1936. They want to revise the principle of distribution. Both the change agent and the local leaders told me that to give a high dividend in the beginning was a mistake. The members took it as a matter of course. But when the factory failed to distribute profit, they complained and were disillusioned. They realized that it would be better in the future to distribute a constant but small dividend every year instead of high dividends periodically.

7. GOVERNMENT SUPPORT

I have indicated above how the government had entered into the change situation. In the very beginning, the local government in the town, the town council, co-operated with the School to start the reform programme. But at that time, 1923, the Provincial government was in the hands of a war lord who had no interest in any measure of that kind. Only after the establishment of the Nationalist Government in Nanking in 1927 had rural reconstruction gradually become one of the main policies of the government. Special attention has been paid to the rural silk industry as well as to the co-operative movement. The co-operative factory in this village was therefore able to secure its financial support from the government. Moreover, the experiment in the village was the forerunner of the big programme of change in this rural industry in China ; it will be interesting to review how the government took up the trend and spread the programme to many silk-producing areas in China.

The following quotations from *The Chinese Year Book* are selected to represent the governmental programme in this connection.

(1) *Sericulture Reform*

" One of the most important of China's rural industries is sericulture, but of recent years it has been hard to stand up against Japanese competition, largely because of the superiority of the silkworms bred in that country.

" In all the provinces where the production of silk is extensive, the local authorities are either acting in co-operation with the National Government, or taking special measures to improve the condition of those engaged in sericultures. What is being done in Kiangsu and Chekiang may be cited as typical of the measures being taken all over the country to revive the silk industry. The raising of the silkworms was formerly left in the hands of the farmers, whose conservative attitude and lack of resources precluded the possibility of introducing reforms to improve the industry. . . . The Kiangsu and Chekiang officials, as a preliminary step towards improvement, organized a Commission for controlling the silk industry. At the outset the Commission contented itself with preventing competition among cocoon merchants by suggesting an official price for fresh cocoons. In the autumn season the Commission's attention was directed to stock improvement, which it tried to accomplish by replacing inferior indigenous varieties of silkworms with improved breeds. The egg-cards used by the Chekiang farmers were issued by the government sericultural experimental stations, the production of egg-cards by private hatcheries being prohibited. In

Kiangsu similar control was exercised during 1934, though the measure, being tentative, was not so thorough-going as in Chekiang. . . . In addition to stock improvement, the Commission also fixed an official price for fresh cocoons and limited the number of collecting agencies in each locality.

" A three-year plan for the improvement of the silk industry in the provinces of Kiangsu, Chekiang, Shantung, Szechwan, and Kwangtung has also been drawn up by the Sericulture Improvement Commission of the National Economic Council. The scheme calls for the expenditure of $1,500,000 for the realization of the first year's plan in 1935.

" For the financial year, July 1934, to June 1935, the National Economic Council has allotted $400,000 for the use of the Sericulture Improvement Committee." [1]

(2) *Co-operative Movement*

" Since the introduction of the Co-operative Movement in China in 1919 it had enjoyed only a slow development ; but with the success of the Northern Expedition and the unification of the country, the Co-operative Movement began to occupy an important place in the programme of the Kuomintang, which was dedicated to developing China on a basis of equality with foreign nations. Since then, the Co-operative Movement has enjoyed a very rapid growth. The Kuomintang began to be interested in the Co-operative Movement as early as 1919. In his lecture on local government, Dr. Sun Yat-sen once suggested the promotion of co-operative enterprises among workers and farmers. . . . At the second National Congress of the Kuomintang, it was resolved to organize farmers'

[1] " Reconstruction in China," Ed. Tang Leang-Li, reprinted in *The Chinese Year Book*, 1935–6, p. 859.

banks and to promote co-operative enterprises among the Chinese peasants. During the Plenary Session of the Central Executive Council of the Kuomintang in August 1936, it was resolved that the government should push the organization of co-operative societies among farmers. . . .

" With the establishment of the Nationalist Government in Nanking many provinces began seriously to push the Co-operative Movement. At the fourth Plenary Session of the Central Executive Council of the Kuomintang in February 1928, General Chiang Kai-shek and Chen Ko-fu jointly proposed the organization of a special Committee on Co-operation. In October of that year, the Central Executive Council of the Kuomintang issued an order to all the branches in the country, asking them to include co-operative work as a part of their political activities.

" In addition, the Kiangsu Provincial Government promulgated a set of Provisional Regulations regarding Co-operative Societies and organized the Kiangsu Agricultural Bank on July 16, 1928, with a view to developing rural economy, and to offering credit facilities to the farmers at low costs." [1]

8. DIFFICULTIES IN CHANGE

The intention of the people to accept the reform is due to its practical benefit as expressed in increase of family income. Now we can examine how far the reform programme has met this expectation.

The disinfection of silkworm eggs, the organization of a common room for raising young worms and the supervision given by visiting instructors in the later

[1] " The Co-operative Movement," Wang Chih-hsien, *The Chinese Year Book*, 1935–6, p. 881–2.

tages have reduced the cost and increased the production of cocoons. This part of the reform has
enabled the people to get an income roughly twice as
much as they had before. (Col. B. III. C. 1. *a*.)
The result of the reform in reeling is not so promising.
In 1929, the members had received as dividend about
ten dollars per share. But ever since that year, they
have got nothing of that sort from the factory. On
the other hand, they were under obligation to supply
raw materials with a delayed payment of 30 per cent.
Up to the present, those whose income has actually
been increased by the introduction of this factory are
the labourers and the staff in the form of wages and
salaries. They are the minority of the community.
(Col. B. III. C. 1. *b*.)

The inability of the factory to distribute yearly
profit among the members is due to two fundamental
factors. First of all the reformers are not able to control
the price level. They have succeeded in producing
silk of high quality, but between the quality and the
price the ratio is hardly proportionate. It is true that
better silk can be sold at a higher price, but the price
of silk in general fluctuates at different times. So long
as the reformers cannot control the market, mere
improvement in the quality of production cannot
necessarily bring back higher returns and is not able to
increase the income of the villagers.

A more immediate factor responsible for the present
state of affairs is the financial problem. It is not true
that the factory has not made profit during the years
1930 to 1936, because the total amount of loans has
been reduced every year. In other words, the factory
saved from its own profit in production so as to buy over
the means of production which was so far borrowed.

The people do not account for this. They only know the concrete income of the family. As soon as their expectations could not be realized they began to be disillusioned. The direct reaction was discontinuance of further payments of their subscriptions. Up to the present time, only about one-half of the amount subscribed has been paid in.

Of course, according to the regulation, the members have the right to audit the account themselves and demand explanations from the manager. But the people are satisfied on the level of suspicion and occasional gossip without taking any definite steps to investigate. They are mostly illiterate. They do not understand what is written on the balance sheet. Their rôle given in the regulation is new to them. The reformers have only taught the girls how to reel silk but not the members how to be the masters of the factory. They have no knowledge of their own responsibility. As long as the educational work cannot keep pace with the industrial reform, the co-operative factory can be only run for the people and can partially belong to the people but can never be really controlled by them.

Introduction of modern machinery into the village economy, as we have seen in the case of water pumping in agriculture, has created a new labour problem under the domestic system where every household had its own reeling machine. In other words, there were at least three hundred and fifty women in this village engaged in the work of reeling silk. Now under the factory system, the same amount of work can be done easily by less than seventy persons. The amount of labour needed in production has been reduced. For instance, by the present reeling machines, each worker

can look after twenty spindles at the same time while
with the older machines one could only handle four
or five. From the technical point of view it is a great
improvement. But what does this improvement mean
to the rural economy ? Nearly three hundred women
have lost their opportunities to work. (Col. B. III. C.
2. b.) The problem of " unemployment " has its
wider repercussions—the traditional division of work
according to sex remains unchanged, but the size of the
farm is so small that introduction of female labour to
the land is impossible ; and no new industry has been
introduced to absorb the surplus of female labour.
(Col. C. III. C. 2. b.)

The reformers have tried to solve the problem by the
system of distribution of profit. But it has not been
successful, as we have shown above. The results are
(1) for those who cannot go to town for various reasons,
survival, or, to a certain extent, revival of the traditional
domestic industry which becomes a kind of resistence
of the reform programme through competition in
securing raw material, (2) movement of the female
population to the towns, which is contradictory to the
original intention of the reformers, and (3) creation of
a special wage-earning class in the village.

The survival of the traditional domestic industry can
be quantitatively estimated. The total amount of
cocoons produced in this village is about 72,000 lbs.
The decrease of members' supply to the factory indicated the increase of domestic reserve, taking the total
production as constant and the amount of cocoons
directly sold to the town as insignificant. In 1929
the reserve was about one-sixth of the total production
but in 1932 it increased to two-thirds. In 1936, before
I left the village, the reserve was about one-third.

How much more one can get by selling native silk instead of selling cocoons, it is difficult to say, because the prices of cocoon and that of silk fluctuate and villagers do not know how to forecast them. As we can see under the lowest price of native silk, one dollar for three Liang, the producer can get little more than the value of the raw material, if the price of the latter is about fifty dollars per picul. But the price of native silk is not known when the market for cocoon is open. It is not the real calculation of the prices of silk and cocoon that makes the people reserve their raw material for domestic reeling but the belief that they can get more money if they reel silk instead of selling the raw material.

The substitution of the factory for the domestic system in the silk industry is a general process which is not limited to the village. The development of silk filature in the nearby cities in the last twenty year has been rapid.[1] The urban industry attracts rural labour. This movement of population undoubtedly is a disruptive force in the traditional social structure of the rural community. To counter this process was one of the original intentions of the reformers. But the small-scale factory in the village, as limited by its local supply of raw material, cannot fully utilize the available labour in the village. On the contrary, has not been able to check the outflow of rural population. I have shown above that in 1935 there were thirty-two girls between the ages of sixteen to twenty-five who lived outside the village (VI–1). They were engaged in silk factories in Wuhsi. At the time when I was in the village another silk factory was established in Chên Tsê. More girls were recruited from the

[1] D. K. Lieu, The Silk Industry in Shanghai.

illage. The total number of girls between the age
of sixteen to twenty-five is one hundred and six in this
illage. More than 80 per cent. of them are now
engaged in factories outside of the village or in the
co-operative factory. They are new wage-earners.

A wage-earning class is not traditional in the village.
The employees in agriculture are few. Labour enters
into the realm of commodity in a very limited sense.
Only by the decline of domestic industry, female
labour has created a labour market in the village. To
this problem we shall devote our discussion in the
next section.

9. EFFECTS ON KINSHIP RELATIONS

Wage-earning is now regarded as a privilege, because
it makes an immediate contribution to the domestic
budget. Those who have no adult daughters begin
to regret it. The woman's position in society has
undergone a gradual change. For instance, a girl
who was working in the village factory actually cursed
her husband because he forgot to send her an umbrella
when it rained. It is interesting because this little
incident indicates changes in the relation between
husband and wife. According to the traditional conception, the husband is not supposed to serve his wife,
at least he cannot do so in public. Moreover, the
husband cannot accept his wife's curse without any
protest or counter-curse.

The traditional economic status of a girl is subordinate to her father or to her husband. She has no
opportunity to possess any large amount of money
(IV–2). The financial power of the Chia is in the
hands of the head. It is correlated with the traditional
system of collective production. The men who work

on the farm are dependent upon their women for the supply of their food. The mulberry leaves needed in feeding the silkworms are carried from a distance by the man. The private sense of the production is overshadowed by the collective aspect. But the wage-earning is essentially individualistic. The earner feels that the wage is the result of her own effort. This sense is shared by both parties, the owner herself and the head of the Chia. Furthermore, the wage is paid by the factory to the earner herself. At least during that moment, she is able to spend a part of her earnings in accordance with her own wishes. Therefore, the economic relation in the Chia is gradually modified. For instance, if the girl spends her wage within reasonable limits and for proper purposes such as buying clothes, it will be accepted without interference. But she is not allowed to spend all her wage ; a large portion of it must be handed over to the head to go into the common budget. To maintain the collective and centralized system of economy under the new situation, the head of the Chia, even at the expense of his authority, will be forced to be considerate towards fellow members of the Chia. Complications come again in the problem of to whom she will hand over her earnings. When the girl is not married and has a mother, but when the head of the Chia is her grandfather, her mother may hold up a part of her earning for future use in her marriage. If the economic condition is not favourable for saving, the amount will be absorbed in the general budget. A married woman will keep a part of her earnings as her own savings. These facts show the increasing differentiation of the individual family from the compound group Chia.

The physical separation of the wage-earner from

he members of her family may also produce essential
hanges in the kinship relations. The separation of a
laughter-in-law from her mother-in-law will reduce
he possibility of daily conflict. But the separation of
vife from husband will loosen the marital tie. One
xtreme case can be cited for illustration. A girl left
er husband about one year after she had married.
She stayed in a factory in Wuhsi and fell in love with a
vorkman in the same factory. They were both dis-
harged by the factory when the illegal union was dis-
overed. Having lived together for two months, but
being pressed for money, they separated. The girl
eturned to the village and was greatly disgraced. Her
parents-in-law refused to admit her, but afterwards
ccepted her because they planned to arrange a re-
narriage for her in order that they could get a sum of
noney for compensation. Later, in view of her earn-
ng capacity in the silk factory in the village, her
parents-in-law cancelled their plan and treated her as
isual. Her husband took a passive attitude towards
he entire affair.

The separation of the child from its mother re-
rranges the intimate relation in the Chia. The suck-
ing period is shortened. The grandmother will take
ip the mother's obligation in further nursing and care
of the child. This also establishes new relations
between the daughter-in-law and mother-in-law.
Similarly, with those women who work in the village
actory and cannot bring their children with them, the
ame situation is found.

All these facts point to the re-organization of the
kinship relations in a new pattern which will find
djustment with the industrial changes. My present
naterial is only sufficient to suggest the problem for
urther investigations.

CHAPTER XIII

SHEEP RAISING AND TRADE VENTURES

The reform of the silk industry is only one of the attempts being made in the village to increase income and thus to counteract the decline in silk prices. But my present material does not allow me to give such a detailed analysis of the other measures which are being taken.

The most important of the new enterprises is sheep raising. This was introduced about ten years ago but only recently became an important industry. Its development was not due to the initiative of any one agent. People in the village learned from their neighbours that in the town there was a new shop collecting sheep fœtus, or newly born sheep. The demand in the market called forth the new industry in the village. Even now the people have no exact knowledge of what is the use of the sheep fœtus, and they often asked me about this. Some supposed that the mother sheep was killed in order to get the fœtus, the skin of which is valuable. This idea does not accord very well with traditional ethics, although the people themselves practise infanticide.

The main difficulty in sheep raising is the problem of feeding. 90 per cent. of the land is used for farming (X–2). Except for a few plots of ground occu-

ied by tombs belonging to the people of the town,
here is practically no pasture land available for sheep.
The farms are open ; there are no fences to prevent
possible damage by wandering animals. In such circumstances it is impossible to raise sheep in the open.
Therefore special huts have been built, and the sheep
re kept enclosed. As I mentioned above, the sheep
hut has become a common appendage of a house.

To feed the sheep, grass must be collected ; in
winter dried mulberry leaves are used. A new division
of labour in the household has been developed in this
connection. Collecting grass is left to the children.
Walking through the village you will see children even
below ten scattered everywhere in small groups, collecting grass under the mulberry trees, along the
streams, and on the open tomb ground. The children's
labour is thus incorporated into the domestic economy.
This has created a new problem for the public school.
Literary education seems to the people less valuable
than the immediate contribution which children can
make to the family income. The list of absentees in
the classes is correlated with the number of sheep
raised in the village. Chen remarked with regret that
the school curriculum is too rigid to be adjusted to
present economic conditions (III–5). This leads to
interesting questions on the relation between economics
and education, but this I cannot deal with at present.

Another advantage of keeping the sheep enclosed in
the hut, is that the sheep manure can easily be collected. This is a valuable fertilizer. There are more
than three hundred small huts in the village. The
number of sheep in each hut varies from one to five.
A rough estimate of the total number of sheep raised
in the village is about five hundred.

I

For starting sheep raising, a certain amount of capit is necessary, at least enough to buy the ewe. Ram can be borrowed from relatives or hired for breeding Payment for this service is not fixed and is mad mostly by means of gifts. If a farmer cannot himse raise the money to buy an ewe, he can raise she belonging to other people. A special system is th developed, which the villagers call *fenyan*, literal " dividing sheep." The person raising the sheep responsible for their feeding and gets half the youn sheep as well as the manure in the hut. Chou's fath is the biggest owner of sheep. He owns forty shee of which only four are kept in his own hut.

The ewe can be sold shortly before the fœtuses a fully developed. The price for each fœtus is three five dollars. The owner can also sell new-born she and keep the mother. In this case the price is lowe But a mother sheep may bear young ones once twice a year, while to raise a young sheep to maturi takes more than a year. People therefore prefer to s young sheep instead of the fœtus. The traditic against killing pregnant animals reinforces this prefe ence. On the average a mother sheep produce tv to four young ones every year, which will yield t owner an income of twenty to thirty dollars.

Another source of income to the people is tra ventures, which are embarked on in the lengtl intervals in the agricultural activities (IX–3). T people go to the neighbouring province, Chekiang, transport goods—not those produced by themselves by their own boats, and from there to some towns alor the coast. This is a kind of interlocality trade. B from the point of view of the villagers, it is really selli their services as trading agents or as transport hand

My informants stated that each boat engaged in this venture can yield forty dollars a year. Of course, this depends on the type of goods transported and sold and the fluctuation of their price. I had no chance of following their route because their activity in this line takes place from the end of August to the middle of October, and from the middle of December to the end of January, when I had already left the village. These ventures are regulated by the solar calendar. I cannot go into details here, except to mention that this is an important source of income. According to my informants, the number of boats thus engaged has increased in recent years.

CHAPTER XIV

MARKETING

Types of Exchange — Internal and External Marketing — Pedlars — Retail Stores — Agent Boats as Consumers' Buying Agent — Agent Boats as Producers' Selling Agent — Other Types of Collecting — Marketing Areas and the Town — Marketing and Production

I. TYPES OF EXCHANGE

Exchange is a process of reciprocal transfer of goods or services between individuals or groups of individuals on the basis of some sort of equivalence. Exchange is necessary wherever there is specialization of production. Specialization of production takes place even between the members of a family. But the process of exchange within a family takes a form different from that found in the market. For in the first place the processes of distribution and exchange in a collective economy are not easily differentiated. The husband who works on the farm depends on his wife for the cooking of his food. In so far as the wife has contributed to the process of production, her claim on the farm produce comes under the head of distribution of the product. But when she consumes more than her share, exchange actually takes place. Secondly, the element of exchange is obscure where property is held in common by the members of a group. Where there is division of labour, the members contribute by their different occupations to the common source from which each derives his living. What exchange actually takes place between the members is thus not apparent.

This does not mean that the ideas of reciprocity in privilege and obligation, and of equivalence in contribution and share do not exist in the intimate social groups. On the contrary, they are among the most frequent causes of disputes and dissatisfactions in domestic life and are jealously upheld. Quantitative assessment of these economic relations in the domestic group requires a very refined field technique, but is not impossible.

The less apparent and less immediate forms of exchange are made possible by positive sanctions inherent in the institutions of the group. For example, parental obligation towards the child is balanced by the support given later by the young to the old, by the obligation to the next generation, or both. The longer the time involved and the more roundabout the transfer of goods and services, the stronger are the social ties in the group. The exchange of goods or services is a concrete expression of social ties. Where obligations can be fulfilled only over a long period of time the individuals involved tend to feel more strongly their social relationship. This is in consequence one of the cohesive forces of the group. From this angle generosity can be viewed as the advance from one person to another of services or goods, bringing in consequence the persons closer to one another.

A similar type of exchange is found in larger social groups such as extended kinship groups and neighbourhood groups. Neighbours in the village are often allowed to take things from each other for consumption or other use in case of need. Within certain limits a man is glad to be useful to his neighbour. If the borrower makes repayment immediately and states the equation of exchange explicitly, the lender will be offended. " We are not outsiders to each other," they will say. In case extra labour is needed on the farm, relatives living nearby will come to help without payment ; so will neighbours on ceremonial occasions (VI–2). Mutual accommodation and services between relatives and neighbours are balanced out in the long run. Exchange on the basis of definite and calculated equivalence tends to diminish in proportion to the intimacy of social relationships.

The making of gifts may be considered as another type of exchange. This is not a result of specialization of production. Even relatives who are engaged in different occupations do not present their special produce as gifts. The type of objects used for formal gifts is prescribed by customs and consists mostly of food, besides offerings of cash on ceremonial occasions. The food offered as gifts is either bought from the market, such as ham and sweets sent at the end of the year, or produced by the people themselves such as special kinds of triangular-shaped rice pudding sent at the festival of Tuan Yang (IX–3). The receiver makes the same type of pudding and buys similar objects to offer to his relatives in return. This type of transfer of goods is significant not in making up mutual deficiency but in strengthening social ties.

From the foregoing analysis, it will be seen that social obligations, mutual accommodations and gift-making are not sufficient to enable a household in the village to secure all the daily necessities which it does not itself produce. Of goods consumed, those produced by the consumers are less than one-third of the

otal (VII–8).   On the other hand, of the goods pro-
uced in the household, many are not consumed by the
·roducers.   The actual use of the young sheep and
·heep fœtus does not even seem to be known to the
·eople who raise the sheep (XIII).   In the silk-pro-
ucing area, silk clothes are rare.   Even the rice is
·nly partly consumed by the people themselves.
'hus it is clear that there must be an extensive exchange
·ystem.   The predominant type of exchange in the
·illage is marketing.

. INTERNAL AND EXTERNAL MARKETING

By marketing is meant the type of exchange in which
·quivalence in value is explicitly expressed in the trans-
·ction and immediately given or promised.   In simple
·anguage, it is the process of buying and selling.   In
·he village it is carried out, with a few exceptions,
·hrough money.

We can distinguish two types of marketing : internal
·nd external.   Internal marketing is the exchange of
·oods and services within the village community, and
·xternal marketing is that between the village and the
·utside world.   They are interdependent.

The internal market of the village is bound up with
·he occupational differentiation in the community
·VIII–1).   As we have seen, more than two-thirds of
·he total population in the village are engaged in pro-
·ucing rice, silk, and sheep.   These do not sell their
·roduce in the village but to the town.   Those engaged
·n fishing sell only a small portion of their produce to
·heir fellow villagers.   Those who produce special
·oods and render special services to the villagers are
·imited to a small group which is only 7 per cent.
·f the total population (VIII–2).   Most of their work

is not exclusively specialized but is supplementary to common household work. Carpenters, basket makers and masons are engaged mostly in repair work. They keep a working place in their own house but they also work in the houses of their clients. Tailors work mostly in clients' houses.

The small degree of occupational differentiation in the community has made the internal market very narrow. People depend on the outside world for the supply of goods and services. This raises a general problem : how do the goods flow into the village. Goods may be bought by the villagers directly in the outside market and brought back to the village. Or they may be carried to the village by different kinds of middlemen. Among these three general types can be distinguished :

(1) Pedlars who visit the village periodically and sell goods at the house of the buyer.

(2) Retail stores which keep a permanent place in the village to store imported goods and attract buyers to their places.

(3) Agent boats which buy goods from the town on behalf of the consumers and transport the goods to the village.

3. PEDLARS

Pedlars may be regular or irregular. This depends on the type of goods they sell. Goods may be produced by the pedlars themselves or may be retailed from the market. Most of the irregular pedlars sell their own produce and do not come from the town but from other villages. This is a type of decentralized inter-village marketing outside the town. The extent of such markets is limited by the fact that the local

BARGAINING WITH SELLERS ON THE STREAM

The village depends on outside supply for vegetables and fruits, which are sold by the pedlars on the boats. Hot bargains are frequently found between the village women and the sellers on the stream.

Plate XIV.

A VILLAGE STORE

Village stores are generally very small, because the villagers have
their agent boats to supply their daily necessities.

AN AGENT BOAT ON ITS WAY TO THE TOWN

Agent boats are the key of the marketing system of this region.
They act as selling, buying and credit agents of the villagers, and
render free service for the transport between the villages and the
town.

ifferentiation of production within the nearby villages
. not very far developed. The only differentiation,
s mentioned (VII–5), is in vegetable cultivation. In
ie village gardens are too small to grow an amount
ifficient for the consumption of the villagers. But
ie villagers near Lake Tai can produce large quantities
f vegetables, and find their market among the nearby
illages. Similarly seasonal fruits which are not grown
i the village are supplied by neighbouring districts.
'he sellers carry their produce by boat and visit the
irrounding villages.

These pedlars start with only a general expectation
f a gross return and do not insist on a fixed price for
ich particular transaction. The seller offers a price,
ir instance, two coppers for three sweet potatoes. The
uyer will not negotiate on the money value, but after
ie money has been given to the seller she will take
veral extra pieces. The seller may resist or pretend
) resist, but I have never seen the transaction re-
idiated because the buyer takes too much. Such a
nd of bargaining is made possible by various factors :
ie seller has no rigid conception of price, and the
iyer no rigid idea of his demand. Moreover, there
. no immediate competition on the side of either the
ller or the buyer. The amount of extra goods taken
ill not exceed what seems reasonable to the buyer,
id also varies according to many factors. For in-
ance, men will not ask for extra pieces since, as they
it it, this would hurt their self-respect ; but their
ives are free to do so. Conversation and joking,
pecially between different sexes, will increase the
imber of extra pieces. In such çases, the seller will
iluntarily offer the extras without persuasion. Of
urse, the taking of extras cannot go too far, except

I*

the extras approximate to presents. In the long run it appears that the prices determined by this kind of bargaining are not higher than the market price in the town ; for if it is discovered that this is in fact the case the seller will not find it easy to sell his goods next time. Probably the price will also not be lower than the town price, for if the gross return obtained by the seller is less than he could obtain from selling to the stores in the town, eventually he will not come to the village. But this leaves a large margin for fluctuation in particular transactions.

There are two regular pedlars from the town : one sells tailoring and toilet articles and the other sells sweets for the children. The women in the village go to the town less frequently than the men, since they have duties in household work and care of the children. Tailoring and toilet articles are solely for women consumers. Moreover, these goods are connected with personal tastes. Women will not trust their agent or their husbands to buy for them, and it is this which gives the pedlar his market. Bargaining with such pedlar takes a different form from that described above. The buyer will not accept the price offered and then ask for extra pieces but will try to reduce the price for a fixed amount of goods. Thus the transaction may not take place if a price satisfactory to both parties cannot be arrived at. The lowest price which the pedlar will take is determined by the amount he pays for the goods, and the amount of profit necessary to maintain his living. Since the goods are not perishable, he can wait for better terms.

The pedlar selling sweets follows another method. The demand for such goods must be artificially created by the seller. A loud bugle is used to attract children. Usually not all the children possess petty cash. Many have to ask adults to buy for them. The pedlar thus often causes dramatic domestic scenes. Children's cries and mothers' curses are mixed with the transaction of buying and selling. Bargaining is not keen because the buyer is either the child who does not know how to hide his real interest or the mother whose main purpose is to get rid of the nuisance. Part of the sweets are made in the pedlar's own house. The raw material is cheap. The price is thus determined largely by the living expenses of the pedlar.

Each of these pedlars has a customary area of peddling which includes several villages, and the area of which is determined by the distance the pedlar can walk and the profit he can make. The frequency of his visits is also thus determined. The pedlar selling tailoring and toilet articles comes to the village every two or four days, while the pedlar selling sweets comes nearly every day.

4. RETAIL STORES

Pedlars do not live in the village. They visit the consumers periodically. Retail stores, on the other hand, are located at permanent places and attract buyers to the stores. This gives rise to a group of people who specialize in trading. They do not produce the objects which they sell, but buy them from the town and sell them to the villages. The following table shows the number of stores in their respective trades:

Grocers	3
Meat sellers	3
Bean cake sellers	2
Medicine seller.	1
Brick seller	1
TOTAL	10

The three groceries are located near the three bridges. They sell mainly cigarettes, matches, sweets, paper, candles, paper-money and other religious articles. I was not able to assess the total amount of their stock. Neither was I able to discover their average sales each day. The main difficulty is that they do not keep accounts. According to their information their daily sale varies from one dollar to twenty cents, and it is obvious that they are not able to supply the whole village with daily necessities of miscellaneous types. As we shall describe presently, the majority of purchases are made from the town by means of the agent boats. Chou described to me the function of these groceries, " We go to the groceries to buy cigarettes when we have guests." In other words, they are only supplements of the agent boats. The agent boats take a whole day to fulfil their customers' orders, and in urgent cases, people cannot wait until their return. They will then go to the stores. Religious articles are never needed at a very short notice, but are used at definite periods which can be foreseen. These appear in the retail stores because of the difficulty of transporting them in the agent boats. The paper-money is made of tin foils in the shape of old silver ingots. It is empty inside and so cannot be compressed. A larger space is therefore required for its transport than is available in the agent boats.

Meat is an important article of diet in the village. This is supplied by the butchers in the town through the meat dealers who go to the town at midnight and bring back to the village the amount needed in the morning. Consumers are thus able to get their meat when they cook their meal at noon. Since there is no means of preserving fresh meat, the dealer will not bring more than he is certain to sell. This is often exhausted before the last buyer comes to the store, and if one wishes to make sure of the supply one must order it the evening before.

Bean cake is used as fertilizer on the farm. This is heavy and takes up much space like bricks. The agent boat cannot be cumbered with this type of goods. Thus there are special stores for them in the village. The medicine store sells Chinese herbal medicines. These are usually sold at high retail prices and are often needed at a moment's notice, therefore the store finds a place in the village.

5. AGENT BOATS AS CONSUMERS' BUYING AGENT

The village stores cannot meet all the daily needs of the villagers. For instance, there is no place in the village from which such essential goods as salt and sugar can be bought. These must be fetched by agent boats. The agent boats offer a free daily service to purchase necessities from the town and derive their income from acting as selling agents of the villagers. They play an important function in the village economy. This institution is common in the region round the Lake Tai, and it has led to a special development of the neighbouring towns.

Every morning, about seven o'clock, the agent boats begin to be active. There are four boats in the village; two plying on Stream A and two on Streams B and C (II–4). As the boats move along the stream, the villagers give their orders to the agent, " Twenty coppers of oil for this bottle and thirty coppers of wine in that container, please." The agent collects the bottles and money. Without counting he throws the money on the floor of the hinder part of the boat. He will talk freely with his clients on other topics. When the boat reaches the west end of the village, from where it proceeds directly to the town, the agent has collected a few dozens of bottles and a large number of coppers. The people going to the town board the the boat as it passes their houses. They do not pay any fare.

Each boat has its own regular clients. The village can be divided into two areas each served by two boats. The two boats plying on the same stream draw their clients from the same area. Thus they are in competition with one another. But it is friendly competition. If there are few passengers in one boat, it will wait for the other and all the passengers will be transferred to the one boat. The boat is rowed by the young men passengers. The agent will classify the bottles and containers according to the orders and collect the coppers on the floor, he will join the passengers in talking or will help them to bind the silk in a proper form for selling.

From the village to the town takes two and a half hours. The boat arrives there at about ten o'clock. Each boat has connections with several stores in the town, and from these the agent will buy the articles ordered by the villagers. Salesmen in the stores come down to the boat to fetch the bottles and containers and to receive their orders from the agent. Before he returns to the boat in the afternoon, the agent will visit the stores and pay the bills. The boat begins to return at about two in the afternoon, and reaches the village between four and five. Villagers wait at their door to receive their goods as the boat passes.

One of the four boats had begun its service only about two months before I reached the village ; the

ther three have run for many years. One of the
gents, now an old man, himself inherited this pro-
ession from his father. Thus we can see that it is
. very old institution.

Theoretically anyone can start an agent boat. There
s no formal qualification for the agent. He has only
o announce to the public that he will be an agent and
vill receive orders. But once started, he must carry
on the business regularly every day regardless of how
nany orders he has received. One agent, Chou Fu-sen,
vas very sick when I was there, but he could not stop
iis service because all the clients depended on him for
heir daily supply. The new agent, Chou Chi-fa,
often went to the town without a single order. This
neans that the agent must devote his whole time to his
ob, and this is a requirement which most of the
villagers who have land to cultivate cannot fulfil.
Moreover, the agent must be connected with the stores
in the town, especially when he acts as the selling agent.
To acquire the knowledge and custom of the trade
takes time and practice.

The number of agents in an area depends on the
number of orders and personal ability of the agent.
An unusually able man like Fu-sen could, in the past,
monopolize the whole area around Stream A, more
than a hundred and fifty households. Personal ability
consists of clear-mindedness and a good memory which
enables an agent not to make mistakes in the numerous
oral orders. It is unbelievable at first sight that anyone
can manage so many orders without the help of written
notes. It is in fact possible only through a slow process
of becoming familiar with the particular bottle or
container of each client, and through training the
powers of memory. Mistakes are sometimes made.

Once a client claimed that he had given Fu-sen a dollar but Fu-sen could not remember the order. Although Fu-sen bore the responsibility for returning the money, the client complained. As Fu-sen's powers were thus gradually failing, Chi-fa was able to look forward to succeeding him in his area.

The agent does not ask for any commission from his clients for his service, nor make any profit therefrom except the periodical gifts and entertainments which the stores in the town offer him. Therefore the price of articles does not rise in passing through the hands of the agent. If the villagers go to purchase directly from the town, they may sometimes get worse and less goods than if they buy through the agents. The traders in the town may cheat the individual buyers, but he cannot so treat the agents. This is not due so much to the personal ability of the agent as to the competition among the town traders to secure constant customers. Most of the stores in the town depend on the agent boats for their wide market in the villages. Losing a single boat will mean a lot to the traders. They try to keep old customers and attract new. Thus the agents gain a favourable position in the transaction.

The existence of the agent boats has put the village stores into a supplementary position. Village stores cannot compete with the agent boats. They are too small to order goods directly from big wholesale stores in the cities, as the town stores do. They buy from the town stores like the agent boats. But the agent boats offer free services in buying while the village traders have to make a profit from retailing. As shown above, the village stores can only find a market in articles which are urgently needed and those which are too heavy to be transported by the agent boats.

The agents do not keep written accounts. I therefore found it rather difficult to assess the amount of their transactions. Fu-sen gave me his estimate as about ten to twenty dollars a day. The highest record was forty dollars a day near the end of the year. This seems to be a reasonable estimate, because it can roughly be checked with the general amount of goods that the village obtains from outside. According to the estimate given in the analysis of household expenditure (VII–8), this is about 80,000 dollars every year. If we exclude from this amount the expenses for clothing, vegetables, heavy tools, and mulberry leaves, which are not purchased through the agent boats, it amounts to 30,000 dollars, and this gives an approximate average similar to the above estimate.

I was not able to make a complete list of articles that the agent boats buy from the town. The list must be a very long one because all goods that can be bought in the town and can be transported by boat are ordered from the agent. Small quantities of those things such as bean cakes, bricks, and paper-money, during the time when the boat is not crowded, are also orderable. The most common goods found in the agent boats are food and ingredients for cooking.

To complete the description of the buying process, it is necessary to mention again the direct purchase by the consumers in the town market or from other villages. For instance, not enough mulberry leaves, the essential raw material for the silk industry, are grown in the village. The villagers must buy them from the other villages near the Lake Tai. The buyer goes personally and transports the goods himself. Every time people come to the town they will do some shopping. The amount of trade through this process is difficult to estimate. But as the villagers do not go to the town very often, it is thus limited.

6. AGENT BOATS AS PRODUCERS' SELLING AGENT

One important feature of the agent boat is that it does not make any profit as a buying agent of the consumers. Similarly passengers do not pay any fare (except that the young men are obliged to row the boat). The gift given by the town stores are far from enough to provide the agent with a living. The agents obtain their reward by acting as the selling agents of the producers.

The process of selling requires much skill and knowledge of the market which the villagers do not necessarily possess. When they sell their produce, they rely on the agents. The agents are constantly in touch with the collectors in the town and know every detail about the different collectors. Because the collectors are connected with different traders or weaving factories they have particular preferences in what they purchase. It is essential for the producers to get in touch with the right collector for his particular produce. Moreover, in collecting silk, there is an accepted practice by which the producer is allowed to add a certain amount of cotton and water to the silk in order to increase its weight. But if the conventional limit is exceeded the collector will deduct from his payment more than the weight of the cotton and the water added. Therefore the expert advice of the agent is needed.

The agent will help the producer to bind the silk in a proper way so that the same amount and quality of silk will yield the highest possible return. The producer goes with the agent to the collector. But the collector will recognize only the agent whose name

ppears on his account. If the producer does not
ccept the price, he is free to withdraw his produce.
ut generally he will follow the advice of the agent
hom he trusts. When the producer sells 100 Liang
1·3 lbs.) of silk, about 25 dollars at the present price,
e will pay the agent 1 dollar commission. In other
ords, the agent will get 4 per cent. commission from
ie amount of silk sold. The amount of the reward
oes not change according to the price. So when the
rice is high, the rate of commission is much lower.
n the case of rice, the commission is 5 cents for 3
ushels, which will yield about 7 dollars for the pro-
ucer. The percentage of commission is about 0·7.
'he total production of silk in this village is about
o,000 Liang which will give 900 dollars for the agents'
ommission. The total exported rice is about 7,000
ushels which will give a total commission for the
gents of about 650 dollars. If this amount is equally
ivided among the four agents, each will get about
oo dollars a year. That amount will provide them
ith a fairly good living.

Those who have paid commission to the agents on
ie sale of their produce are entitled to use the boats
or communication and to order goods through them.
'he payment for this service is thus distributed accord-
ig to the amount of production but not to the amount
f consumption of the clients.

The sheep raising recently introduced has added a
ew source of income to the agent ; but I do not know
ie exact system of commission for selling sheep.

The change in the silk industry had challenged the
ery existence of the institution. The new silk factory
oes not make use of the selling agents in the town
iarket. The produce is sold directly to Shanghai.

At the start, the agent appealed for compensation
The reformers regarded the agent boats as a usefu
institution in the village and decided to support it b
giving compensation according to the tradition:
amount of commission. Each member of the cc
operative society receives a card on which the amour
of his cocoon supply is recorded. The producer ca
give the card to the agent whom he uses as his buyin
agent. The agent in return receives compensatio
according to the total amount of cocoons recorded o
the member's card. In this way the institution of th
agent boat has been saved.

7. OTHER TYPES OF COLLECTING

The staple rural products are collected by the tow
through the agent boats or by the city through th
factory. But for minor objects—and waste goods-
such as old clothes, the ashes of paper money and ol
metal objects, there is yet another manner of collectio
Sometimes this takes the form of barter, that is, dire
exchange of objects. The collector carries with hir
porcelain articles or a special type of sweets to exchang
for old clothes and metal objects. Ashes of pape
money, which contain tin, are exchanged for shee
of tin foil from which the paper-money is made.

8. MARKETING AREAS AND THE TOWN

The size of a marketing area is determined by th
system of transport—the cost and time involved in th
movement of persons and goods. The primary marke
in which the consumers buy their goods directly,
limited to an area in which the buyer can get his goo
without spending so much time as to hamper his othe

ctivities. In this village we can distinguish two
rimary marketing areas. The people living near the
ridge on Stream B will not make purchases from the
ores near the bridge on Stream A. For instance,
arbers, meat sellers, groceries, and temples are all
egregated in these two areas, roughly corresponding
to the areas divided by the activities of the agent boats.
ut the silversmith, the shoemaker, and the medicine
ore are located near the west bridge on Stream A, the
entre of the intra-village route system (II–4). These
re the only stores of their kind in the village. To this
xtent, the village is also a primary market.

The secondary market is that from which the retail
ealers in the primary market draw their goods at
wholesale prices. In this region, the agent boat cannot
be considered as a retailer. It makes purchases on
ehalf of the consumers, but, as we have seen, without
making a charge for this service. The agent boat thus
estricts the function of the primary market in the
village and enables the distant town to be the centre of
rimary purchase of the consumers.

The agent, specializing in this function, can spend
all his time in this activity. Thus the distance
etween the buyer and the seller is lengthened to that
racticable for a daily return trip. The actual distance
epends on the rate of movement of the boat, which
estimated at about 1·6 miles per hour. The
urthest village that is able to send its agent boat to
he town cannot lie farther than 5 miles distant. The
iameter of such a marketing area is thus between 8 and
o miles.

At the centre of each marketing area is a town, the
ssential difference of which from the village lies in
he fact that the population in the town is mainly

occupied in non-agricultural work. The town is fo villagers the centre of exchange with the outsid world. The villagers buy most of their manufacture goods from the middlemen in the town and supply thei produce to the collector there. The development c the town depends on the number of customers that ca be attracted to it. As we have seen, the institutio of the agent boat enables the town in this region t concentrate the primary purchase from its tributar villages and thus reduce the function of the villag traders. The size of the marketing area of this typ is much larger than that found in North China, whei land transport is predominant and the agent system i not developed. A study by C. K. Yang [1] showed tha the marketing area, above that of the primary villag market, typical in North China, is about $1\frac{1}{2}$ miles t 3 miles in diameter. The marketing area of a highe order, consisting of six basic marketing areas, is abou 8 to 12 miles in diameter. The latter type is com parable in size to the town market in the region we ar investigating.

The town on which the village depends—that is, th town to which the agent boats go daily—is called Chê Tsê, about 4 miles south of the village. It is tru that the town does not monopolize all the marketin activities of the village. There is another town in th north, called Tai Miao Chiung, about $1\frac{1}{2}$ miles froi the village on the bank of Lake Tai (Map II). Th is a small town specializing in trade with the island in the lake. Near the town is a temple of the Go of Lake Tai from which the name of the town i derived. When the people visit the temple the

---

[1] *Marketing System in Chuping, Shantung*, Unpublished monograph of tl department of Sociology, Yenching University, China.

usually do some shopping in the town. To walk there takes about 1½ hours. But trade between the village and Tai Maio Chiung is insignificant as compared with that with Chên Tsê.

In the process of collecting rural produce, Chên Tsê monopolizes nearly all the rice trade of the village. But it has never completely monopolized the silk produce, and since the establishment of the silk factory in the village, manufactured silk has been directly transported to Shanghai. Even in former times, when the village supplied a large quantity of raw silk for the weaving industry in Sheng Tsê, a town about 12 miles east of the village, there was a boat which plied direct to that town. It was too far for a daily return trip, and the service was irregular, so the boat was only engaged in selling. It ceased to run more than ten years ago owing on the one hand to the decline of the weaving industry of the town, and on the other to the reform of the silk industry in the village.

An interesting study might be made of the competition of the towns to secure tributary territories. But a detailed analysis of this problem requires a wider investigation of the whole region than the present study could afford.

9. MARKETING AND PRODUCTION

Silk and sheep are produced entirely for selling. We have already seen how the price has affected the production in these industries. The low price of native silk stimulated the reform programme. As a result of the reform, the amount of the production of native silk was greatly reduced. But in recent years, the amount has not declined in proportion to the decline of price. On the contrary there are signs of an increase.

As explained, this is due to the lack of other work to
absorb the surplus female labour in the village.   Sheep
raising was started because of the new demand of the
market.   But the amount of production cannot be
increased while supply of grass is limited as at present.
Price is thus not the only factor determining the
volume of production.

Rice is produced partly for selling and partly for
consumption.   The amount of reserve does not necessarily fluctuate according to the price.   Each household will try to reserve enough rice for a year's consumption.   A high market price of rice will not induce
the producer to sell his reserves, because the future
price level is uncertain.   But a low price will force
people to sell more rice to the market ; this is because
the amount of money income needed by each household is more or less known at the time of harvest when
the tenants are required to pay their rent in terms of
money.   This fact is important for the rice collectors.
They usually try to force down the price in order to
increase the volume of trade.   The villagers' total
reserve is frequently so reduced as to be insufficient
for their own consumption.   In the following summer
the villagers will be dependent on outside supply
(XV–3).   This also is to the benefit of the trader.

The fluctuation of price does not affect the total production of rice.   The total amount is determined by
the size of the land, the technique of production, and
last, but not least, the supply of rainfall.   These are
matters over which the people have little control.
Change of occupation is difficult and even change of
crop seldom comes to the minds of the villagers.   Thus
the structure of production is a rigid one and does
not react elastically to the demand of the market.

When changes take place, they are gradual and far-reaching.

Let us take the silk industry as an example. The adjustment between the new demand of the market and the productive system has taken nearly ten years in spite of a well-planned programme and special efforts. From our analysis of the changing process (XII), we have seen that the effectiveness of supply and demand depends on a knowledge of the market which villagers do not always possess. Without some special agents to affect a change, the people would hardly understand the cause of the decline of price and still less define the type of goods that would meet the new demand of the market. To bring about a change in the industry, special knowledge and social organization are needed. All these factors delay an immediate and automatic adjustment of supply and demand in the rural economy.

Change of occupation in the village is more difficult than reform of an existing industry. No serious attempt has yet been made to find out the possibility of introducing new industries to the village besides sheep raising. Even the latter is only a supplement to the existing productive system and not a change of occupation. Villagers can change their occupation only by leaving the village. In other words, occupational mobility under the present situation means a mobility of population from the village to the town. In the village, those who go out to find new occupation are mostly young girls who have not yet entered into a fixed social place in the community. Even in this group, such mobility has already challenged the traditional kinship relation and the stability of the domestic group (XII-9). The reaction against the disruptive forces in social stability becomes a force to counteract the present mobility. It is difficult to say at the present stage how far the traditional forces will give way in the novel situation. But on the whole the slow mobility of population, especially of the male population, indicates the slow effect of the outside demand for labour and the rigidity of the traditional productive system in the village.

Nevertheless it is clear that the market affects production strongly. It has led to various changes which are not limited to economic life only. The reaction of the productive system to market conditions does not take a simple course but is a long and involved process which requires investigation in a wider perspective than that of a purely economic inquiry.

FINANCE

The problem of credit rises when, in the process of
:change, the return either in the form of goods and
:rvices or of money is delayed. Credit, in its simple
:nse, is the trust by one party in another for an
ventual return after a certain lapse of time.

In this sense non-immediate forms of exchange such
: mutual obligation, mutual accommodations, and
.ft-making, are forms of credit. The return of these
rpes of credit is secured by the principle of reciprocity
.herent in the social institutions and is bound up
ith the ties of kinship and friendship. For trans-
:tions outside the group thus related, the time for
:payment has to be explicitly agreed upon and credit
in only be received by the economic benefits of the
ansaction.

The loan may be used for any purpose or may be
mited to certain uses prescribed by the agreement.
ut the term credit cannot be limited to refer only to
lvances for future production. In the village, credit
in most cases for consumption or for payment of tax
id rent which is only indirectly related to the process
f production. Similarly it is difficult to regard (except
i a very metaphorical sense) the money borrowed to

263

finance a marriage ceremony as a help to the borrower's productive ability.

Professor Tawney, in his discussion on the problem of the credit system in rural China, says, " The characteristic feature of the system . . . is that neither borrower nor lender appears to make any clear distinction between loans needed to finance the business of farming, and loans sought to eke out the domestic budget. Everything goes down, so to speak, in a common account, with the result that there is no discrimination in the mind of either debtor or creditor between the borrowing and advancing of money for productive purposes, which should yield a return sufficient to meet the interest, and household expenses which ought, in the absence of exceptional misfortune to be met out of income." [1]

In this chapter, I shall use the term credit in its broad sense.

1. SAVING AND DEFICIENCY

Credit is possible only when there is saving on the one hand and deficiency on the other. Saving is the surplus of income over expenditure in an economic unit, in the village the Chia. Income is the total production of the Chia. It may or may not be converted into money. Expenditure includes all the goods, produced by the unit or purchased on the market, used by the members for consumption, for fulfilment of social obligation and for production.

The amount of production of each Chia in the village does not vary much because the groups are very similar in size, and in their technique of production. There is also uniformity in the amount of consumption

---

[1] *Land and Labour in China*, p. 62.

nong them (VII–1). The inequality in the dis-
ibution of wealth is, apart from special reasons in
dividual cases, mainly due to the system of land
nure. A tenant has to bear a heavy burden of rent.
wo-thirds of the land in the village is now in the hands
' absentee landlords. Each year the villagers pay
total 4,800 bushels of rice for rent. This burden
not shared equally by the villagers, but is spread
er about 70 per cent. of the people. Among these
ain the burden is not equal (XI–5). The system of
nd tenure has resulted in an annual outflow of a large
uantity of wealth from the village to the town and
unequal distribution of wealth in the village.

When the silk industry was prosperous the villagers,
spite of high rents, were able to enjoy a sufficient
andard of living and could in consequence save.
his saving was usually hoarded. The opportunity
r investment in the village is limited and there is
other means, except in rent, for the town to absorb
accumulated wealth. The goods or money hoarded
ere used firstly for a reserve against recurrent disaster
d secondly for financing expensive ceremonies. The
aborate ceremonies in connection with individual life
ises or periodical religious meetings of the local
oups were in fact an important outlet for the hoarded
ealth of the rural district. On ceremonial occasions
e idea of thrift gives place to competitive display.
ealth was lavishly expended in burials, on marriage
fts, on dowries and feasts, and especially in inter-
llage parades (VII–7).

The depression of the silk industry has caused a
ecline of one-third of the average income of the
llage (XII–2). On the side of expenditure, con-
umption and social obligations have remained largely

as they were. The only elastic item that can b
reduced or suspended is ceremonial expenditure ; an
according to my estimate, the minimum amount of suc
expense at present is only one-fifth of the total mon
expenditure (VII–8). With the rapid decline of t
income level, accompanied by a rigid level of expend
ture, deficiency is the result.

Deficiency may be urgent or may not be urgen
Urgent deficiency calls for immediate measures. It
found in such situations as food shortage, lack of capit
goods, and inability to pay rent and tax. Unle
financial aid in these cases is forthcoming there will l
disastrous consequences to the individuals concerne
Owing to the unequal distribution of rent obligation
deficiences of this urgent kind are confined to a pa
of the villagers. There is still a small group whic
even in present circumstances, is able to save ar
another group which is able to meet all the minimu
requirements of subsistence. But deficiency of a le
urgent nature, such as inability to pay for ceremoni
occasions, is more common even among the better-c
group. I have already described how the villagers ha
suspended their annual meeting, delayed their ma
riages, and reduced their ceremonial expenses.

The decline of the ability to save has caused
increasing need for outside financial help. The i
ternal credit system functions only as a means to co
with the unequal distribution of wealth within t
community. It cannot meet the situation of gener
insolvency. Thus external aid has become the urge
financial problem in the village.

In the following sections, I shall describe the worki
of various internal and external credit systems. B
the present material is not sufficient to define th

relative importance in quantitative terms. Such data, important as they are, require more extensive inquiries than I was able to make.

2. FINANCIAL AID SOCIETY

As with goods and services, small sums of money can be borrowed from relatives or friends for a short term without interest. This system of mutual allowance is found chiefly in cases of temporary deficiency, and the creditor is confident in the ability of the debtor to repay within a short time. But the term of such allowance may extend over a period of months. Such relatively long-term credit is frequently found among brothers after division of the Chia. Although they may have separate houses and properties, they are still bound by social ties to look after each other's welfare. To demand interest from a brother for any small loan is considered to be impossible.

But when a large sum is needed, it is difficult to borrow from one individual and to repay in a short time. Here the mutual help among brothers or other relatives becomes inadequate. Hence there is the financial aid society.

The financial aid society is a mechanism for collective saving and lending. It consists of a number of members and lasts for a number of years. The members meet several times a year. At each meeting, each subscribes a share. The total subscription of the members is collected by one of the members who can thus use the money to finance his activities. Each member in turn collects the sum. The first collector is the organizer. From the very beginning, he is a debtor to the society. He repays his loan bit by bit during the whole course with a certain amount of interest. The last collector is a depositor. He collects at the end the sum of his deposit and its interest. Other members change from depositor to debtor as they collect the sum. The order of collection is determined either by contract or by lot, or by auction. The system of calculating the amount of subscription of each member in each meeting is sometimes complicated by various factors which will be described later.

Such a society is organized on the initiative of the person who needs financial help. Members who join the society are considered as having rendered help to the organizer. According to the system described above, it would appear that all the members in turn would profit by the society. But we must remember that, with the limited opportunity of investment, to raise a loan and to pay interest on it may be uneconomical. Moreover, owing to the uncertainty of time of the collection, it may be difficult for the collector to find a profitable use for the money collected. Therefore, the organizer cannot appeal to members on economic grounds only. He must state his need of aid and ask for help. Membership is thus usually limited to certain groups of persons who are obliged to help the organizer and those who are willing to join for other purposes.

The usual purpose of organizing such a society is to finance marriage ceremonies. Repayment of a debt incurred for such proper reasons as the financing of a funeral ceremony may also be regarded as acceptable ground. But productive purposes, such as starting a business or buying a piece of land, are not so regarded.

Given a proper purpose, the organizer will approach his relatives ; father's brother, brother, sister's hus-

and, mother's brother, wife's father, etc. These
have an obligation to join the society. Even when
they are unable to subscribe, they will find some of
their relatives to take their place.

The number of members varies from eight to fourteen. In the village the kinship circle, in which intimate relations are maintained, is sometimes smaller.
Membership may then be extended to relatives' relative
or friends. These are recruited by appealing, not to
social obligations but to mutual benefits. If someone
needs financial help which does not justify organizing
a society by himself he will join a society formed by
others. Those who are known in the community to
be rich will respond to a justifiable appeal for help
in order to show generosity and to avoid public
criticism. For example, Chou has gained much prestige
by subscribing to more than ten societies.

But the nucleus of such a society is always the kinship
group. The person who has a larger sphere of relatives
has a better chance of gaining support in a financial
crisis. In this connection we can see that institutions
such as the *siaosiv* (III–8), which diminish the kinship
circle, will in the long run produce unfavourable
economic consequences. On the other hand, the
widening of kinship relation, even through such means
as pseudo-adoption, has an important economic significance (V–3).

In theory the organizer will be responsible for any
default by the members, and will pay the share of the
defaulters. But since he is usually in need of financial
help himself, his responsibility does not give a real
guarantee of security. Default is prevented not by
legal sanction but by the acknowledged social obligations between relatives. The possibility of default

K

is again diminished by the supplementary system o
mutual allowance. It is easy for a person to raise ai
allowance in such a situation, especially when he ha
the prospect of collecting a sum from the society
Reciprocity is also an essential consideration. Th
defaulter will find it difficult to organize his own societ
in case of need. Nevertheless defaults do occur, ani
have done so especially during the past few years. A
I have mentioned, the efficiency of the local credi
system depends on the general saving ability of th
villagers. The economic depression has caused default
to be increasingly frequent, and these have threatene(
the local credit system. This has had far-reachin;
consequences in disrupting the existing kinship ties
But as I did not make a detailed study of this problem
I can only leave it for further investigation.

There are three types of financial aid societies. Th(
most popular one is called Yao Hui. In this th
organizer gathers fourteen members, each of whon
subscribed 10 dollars. The organizer thus gets 14(
in all. The society will then meet twice a year : firs
in July or August when the silk industry is completed
and again in November or December, when rice i
reaped. At each meeting, the organizer will repay t(
the society 10 dollars of capital and 3 dollars of interest
He will thus clear his debt at the end of the fourtee:
meetings.

At each successive meeting, one of the members wil
collect a sum of 70 dollars. The one who has col
lected this sum is a debtor to the society and will repa}
at each succeeding meeting 5 dollars of capital an(
1·5 dollars of interest. The system of calculation i
complicated by the fact that the member's sum i.
reduced to half of the organizer's own. Thus half o(

the organizer's annual subscription will be equally divided among the members $(13/2 \div 14) = 0.464)$, this being called the organizer's surplus. The actual member's sum is $70 + 0.464$, and the actual debtor's annual subscription is 6.036 ($6.5 - 0.464$).

The organizer's and the debtors' annual subscriptions and the member's sum of collection are constant. Those who have not collected the member's sum are depositors of the society. Since at every meeting there is a member who collects the sum, the number of debtors increases and the number of depositors decreases accordingly. The depositors' subscription at each particular meeting is determined by the following formula : Member's sum $(70.464) - \{$Organizer's subscription $(13) + [$Number of debtors $\times$ debtor's subscription $(6.036)]\} \div$ Number of depositors.

The total amount of the depositor's subscriptions decreases at every meeting.[1] For each individual

[1] Order of Meeting	Number of Depositors	Amount of subscription of each Depositor
1st	13	4·420
2nd	12	4·286
3rd	11	4·126
4th	10	3·936
5th	9	3·702
6th	8	3·410
7th	7	3·035
8th	6	2·535
9th	5	1·838
10th	4	0·785

At the eleventh meeting, the sum of subscription of the organizer and the debtors has already exceeded member's sum of collection. The depositors need not pay anything but share the new surplus. The principle of distributing the surplus is that, excluding the organizer and the collectors of first four meetings, all the members will have a share in proportion to the order of their collection. For instance, in the eleventh meeting the collector of the fifth meeting will get a share of 0·11 dollars or 5/110 of the total surplus (2·432). But the three depositors in that meeting, whose orders of collection member, the total amount of subscription decreases according to the order of collection. Since the amount of collection is constant, the difference between the amount of subscription and the amount of collection is the interest either paid for the loan or received from the deposit. The rate of interest fixed for the debtor is 4·3 per cent. per annum. But owing to the combination of deposit and loan as well as the two kinds of surplus, the actual rate of interest is different among the members and from each year.[1] The collector at

are still not certain, will have an equal amount of 13/110 of the surplus The total amount of surplus of each meeting from the eleventh is :

11th	.	.	.	.	2·432
12th	.	.	.	.	8·004
13th	.	.	.	.	14·968
14th	.	.	.	.	21·004

[1] Order of Collection	Amount of Subscription	Amount of Collection	Average rate of Interest per Half Year (in Per Cent.)	
			For Loan	For Deposit
Organizer	182·00	140·00	2·2	—
1st	88·47	70·47	2·1	—
2nd	86·85	70·47	2·3	—
3rd	85·10	70·47	2·6	—
4th	78·96	70·47	2·0	—
5th	74·71	70·47	1·5	—
6th	71·99	70·47	1·0	—
7th	69·06	70·47	—	2·0
8th	65·62	70·47	—	3·4
9th	62·70	70·47	—	2·8
10th	57·08	70·47	—	3·1
11th	51·41	70·47	—	3·4
12th	44·91	70·47	—	3·6
13th	38·43	70·47	—	3·8
14th	31·06	70·47	—	4·0

Average rate of interest is calculated by dividing the total difference between subscription and collection by the amount of collection and the difference between the numbers of times of deposit and repayment.

each meeting is determined by lot. Each member throws two dice, and the one who scores the highest points is the collector. A feast is prepared at each meeting by the organizer and paid by the collector of that particular meeting. Lot drawing comes after the feast, when all the subscriptions, having been collected, are in the hand of the organizer.

This system is rather complicated. But it has its merits—

(1) The members who join the society have no definite prospective use for the sum collected. By reducing the member's sum, the burden of the members is reduced. Thus it diminishes the risk of default. (2) To determine who is to be the collector by lot gives every depositor an equal hope of collecting. This induces subscription by those who are in need of financial help. (3) The rapid decrease of subscriptions of the depositors compensates their delayed collection. (4) The rich feasts attract the members. Some people had modified the system by offering the feast once a year in the winter, and the collector for the next period was determined beforehand. It has been found that collection of the shares in the spring was very difficult. Therefore the practice was given up.

The complexity of this system is too difficult for every ordinary villager to understand. In fact, very few persons in the village know the system of calculation. They have therefore to invite the village heads to instruct them. To meet this difficulty, another and simplified system was introduced a relatively short time ago. This is called Hui Hui, because it is supposed to have originated in Anhwei Province. According to this system, the order of collection and the amount to be subscribed by each member is fixed in advance.[1]

The total collected at each meeting is constant. This is 80 dollars, including the collector's own share. This system is convenient for calculation, and each member can foresee his turn of collecting and adjust it to his need.

A third type is called Kwangtung Piao Hui, an auction system supposed to be originated in Kwangtung. All depositors will offer a sum expected to collect from the meeting. The one who offers the lowest bid will be the collector. The surplus of subscription, after the sum for the collector is deduced, will be equally divided among the members, both the debtors and the depositors. This type is not popular in the village because, as my informant put it, there is too much gambling.

3. AGENT BOATS AS CREDIT AGENT

Kinship ties between the village and the town are very limited. The number of villagers living in the town is small. Those who have been resident in the town for some generations, have allowed kinship ties with their clansmen in the village to become very loose. As I have mentioned, the clan is usually divided when the members disperse (V–1). Marriage between village and town is rare, except in the case of

---

[1] Order of Collection

	Amount of Subscription for Each Meeting
Organizer	13·5
2nd	12·5
3rd	11·5
4th	10·5
5th	9·5
6th	8·5
7th	7·5
8th	6·5

maid servants in the town who may return to the village upon marriage. It appears to me that the relation between the town people and the villagers is mainly of an economic nature. It may, for example, be the relation between landlord and tenant, which under the present system of land tenure, is impersonal. More intimate relations are found between the master and the servant who temporarily works in the town ; but on the whole, the social relation between townsmen and villagers is not strong enough to maintain a system of mutual allowance or the financial aid society. When the villagers need external financial help, they usually resort to the system of rice-lending and usury.

Deficiency of food supply is extraordinary in a village where rice is the staple produce. It is a result of the decline of price of rural produce. To receive the same money income as formerly, the amount of output must be increased. As a result, the rice reserve of the villagers is sometimes exhausted before the new rice is ready. In this connection the agent boat plays an important function in the village economy.

The villagers sell their rice to the town collectors through the agent boat. The collector deals with the agent, not with the real producers. To secure a constant supply, especially against the competition of the town market, the collector must maintain good relations with the agent. On the other hand, the agent is indispensable to the producers. They rely upon him for selling and buying. These relations enable the agent to bring the collector and the villagers into financial relationship in case of need.

The agent will ask the collector on behalf of his clients to lend rice and he will guarantee the return when the new rice comes to market. His guarantee

is effective because the rice produced by the debtor
will pass through his hand. Moreover, by extending
credit, the collector can not only make a profit, but
ensures his future supply.

The rice borrowed from the collector is valued at
12 dollars per 3 bushels, which is higher than the
market price. The debtor repays an amount of rice
equivalent to 12 dollars at the market price (which
during the winter is about 7 dollars per 3 bushels).
The rate of interest works out at about 15 per cent.
per month if the term is two months. This rate is
comparatively low. It is made possible because the
creditor does not run much risk owing to the institution
of the agent boat and the economic value for the collector of insuring his future supply. The existence
of a number of collectors on the market makes the
supply of credit more elastic and gives the debtor a
better position in negotiation.

This credit system is comparatively a recent one
It has not been developed beyond the sphere of rice-
lending. But by the same principle it might be
gradually extended to money-lending through rice
and silk collectors as a payment in advance for produce
which is relatively stable and can be counted on
beforehand.

4. USURY

Money-lending from the town to the village is indispensable when the village finance is in distress.
Villagers borrow money from wealthy people in the
town with whom they have relations. The interest
on such a loan varies according to the closeness of the
personal relation between the debtor and the creditor
But, as I have mentioned, the personal relation between

villagers and townsmen is limited, and the townsmen with whom the villagers have personal relations may be unable to lend money. As a result there emerge professional money-lenders in the town. Professional money-lenders advance money to the villagers on very high rates of interest. This traditional institution we may term usury.

A person who finds himself unable to pay land tax, for instance, and is not prepared to spend the whole winter in prison, has to borrow money. The usurer's door is open to him. The money from the usurer is expressed in terms of an amount of mulberry leaves. At the time of the transactions, there are no mulberry leaves at all and a market price does not exist. The price is arbitrarily set at 70 cents per picul (114 lbs.). For instance, a loan of 7 dollars will be regarded as a loan of 10 piculs of mulberry leaves. The term of the loan expires at Ch'ing Ming (April 5th), and it must be repaid not later than Ku Yü (April 20th). The debtor has to pay an amount of money according to the market price of mulberry leaves, which at that time is about 3 dollars per picul. Thus a loan of 7 dollars or 10 piculs of mulberry leaves, concluded in October, yields a return of 30 dollars to the creditor in April. During these five months, the debtor is paying an interest of 65 per cent. per month. This system of money-lending is called " living money of mulberry leaves."

At the time of Ch'ing Ming the people are just starting their silk industry. This is a financially vulnerable period in the village. Persons who were unable to pay their rent in the winter are not likely to be able to pay the amount back to the creditor. In the previous five months, they have been engaged on no major pro-

K*

ductive enterprise, except trade ventures. In these circumstances, the debtor may ask the creditor to renew the loan in terms of rice. This process is called " changing to rice." The price of rice is counted, irrespective of the market, at 5 dollars per 3 bushels The term is extended to next October. Repayment will be made according to the highest market price of the rice, which is about 7 dollars per 3 bushels The person who borrowed 7 dollars in one October will thus repay 48 dollars in the next October. The rate of interest is thus about 53 per cent. per month on the average.

If the debtor is still unable to clear up his debt, no prolongation of the term will be allowed. The debtor must settle by handing the legal title of his land to the creditor. In other words, he will transfer the right of ownership of the subsoil of the land to the creditor The price of land is counted as 30 dollars per *mow* From then on, he is no longer a debtor but a permanent tenant. Instead of paying interest, he will pay an annual rent (XI–4).

The rent is 8 pints (2·4 bushels) of rice or about 4·2 dollars per *mow*. If we take Professor Buck's estimate of the average rate of interest from the investment in rural land as 8·5 per cent,[1] we find that a *mow* of land has a money value of 56 dollars. Thus a loan of 7 dollars will ultimately in one year yield as return to the creditor a piece of land worth 89 dollars.

Through the usurer, the ownership of the subsoil is transferred from the hand of the cultivators to the absentee landlords who buy the land titles from the usurer. Upon this financial institution, the system of absentee landlordship is based (XI–4).

[1] *Chinese Farm Economy*, p. 158.

Usury is an extra-legal system. According to law, if the rate of interest agreed upon exceeds 20 per cent. per annum, the creditor is not entitled to claim any interest over and above 20 per cent.[1] Therefore, the contract must be enforced by other means than legal force. The usurer employs his own collector to force the debtor to pay when the term has expired. If payment is refused, the collector will use violence and take off or destroy anything at his disposal. In one case, I know, on the death of the debtor, the creditor took off a girl of the deceased to town as his slave. The debtor is usually too ignorant to seek the protection of the law and the community gives him no support. He is actually at the mercy of the usurer. If the debtor really has nothing to pay the debt with, and possesses no subsoil of land, the creditor will find it to be wiser to let him continue farming and reserve his claim on the future produce. In the worst situation, the debtor may commit suicide at the house of the usurer. The usurer will then face the revenge of the spirit and also the pressure of public resentment which will force him to forfeit his claim. This drastic means, though rarely used, is, to a certain extent, effective in preventing the usurer from going too far.

Usurers live in the town. Each has a nickname. The one connected with the village of our study is Sze, the Skin-tearer. This nickname indicates the public hatred. But he is an important source available to the villagers in case of urgent need. The supply of credit is very limited while the demand is urgent. The consequence of being imprisoned or losing the entire silk crop is more immediate and irreversible

[2] The Civil Code, Article 205.

To borrow money from the usurer at least leaves open the possibility of repaying when the time comes.

I was not able to calculate the total amount of loans from usurers outstanding in the village. Since there are few, if any, other ways for the ownership of the subsoil to pass out of the village, the extent of tenancy might be an indication of the extent of the usury system (XI–5).

The existence of the system is due to the lack of a better financial organization between the town and village. Under the present system of land tenure, the villagers supply an increasing amount of produce to the town in terms of rent while there is no means for the villagers to draw back an equivalent amount from the town. Formerly when the chief textile industries in China, such as silk and cotton, were developed in rural districts, the villagers were able to offset the outflow of rural wealth by the profit made from the industrial export. The rapid deindustrialization of the rural district has dislocated the financial balance between town and village. The rural problem, broadly speaking, originated in deindustrialization, finds its concrete expression in financial insolvency and is crystallized in the issue of land tenure. In the village, effort for an immediate solution has been directed to the rehabilitation of the silk industry. The partial success of this industrial reform is significant also as a factor relieving the acute land problem.

5. CO-OPERATIVE CREDIT SOCIETY

In this connection I should also mention the well-intentioned measure by the government for stabilizing rural finance through the co-operative credit system. The co-operative credit system, introduced into the village, in fact, is not an organization of the villagers themselves but a means for them to borrow money from the national bank at low interest rates. A sum was allotted by the Provincial Peasant Bank for credit to the villagers. This system promised a fundamental solution of the problem of rural finance. But the success of this system depends on its administration, and the capacity of the government to afford the credit. In our village, I found that a few thousand dollars had been borrowed by the people from the " co-operative society." But owing to the financial insolvency of the debtors, they were not able to repay their debt when the term expired. The creditor does not possess the same extraordinary means as the usurer to compel the debtor to pay, and the small interest on the loan is not enough to finance an elaborate administration. When the small sum allotted was exhausted, the society ceased to function and had a full list of black debts.

The present failure of the experiment, at least in the village, teaches the importance of a full knowledge of the local financial organization. It might be better if the government could use the existing system, such as the agent boat and the financial aid society, to finance the people. To introduce a new credit system requires a new system of sanctions. In the local credit system, sanctions are ready. There seems better chance of success if the traditional channel can be utilized and improved by governmental effort.

CHAPTER XVI

AGRARIAN PROBLEMS IN CHINA

The above account of the economic life of a Chinese village is the result of a microscopic examination of a specimen. The phenomena observed in this confined area undoubtedly are of a local character. But they also have wider significance because this village shares a common process with most other Chinese villages. Hence we can learn some of the salient features of the agrarian problems in China.

The essential problem in Chinese villages, putting it in the simplest terms, is that the income of the villagers has been reduced to such an extent that it is not sufficient even to meet the expenditure in securing the minimum requirements of livelihood. It is the hunger of the people that is the real issue in China.

In this village, the immediate cause of the present economic depression is the decline of domestic industry. The present depression is not due to a deterioration of quality nor to a decrease of the quantity of production. Had the villagers produced the same type and the same amount of silk, they could not get the same amount of money from the market as before. The cause of depression lies in the relation between the village industry and the world market. It is the lack of adjustment between production and demand that accounts for the fall in the price of silk.

In view of the decline of domestic industry, the only

alternatives open to the peasants are to improve their produce or to give up the industry. To improve the produce, as I have shown, is not only a matter of technical improvement but also a matter of social reorganization. Even this is not enough. A successful reorganization of rural industry depends ultimately on the prospects of industrial development in China. The present analysis is a warning to reformers who tend to underrate the force of international capitalist economy.

If there is no immediate recovery of rural industry, the peasants will be forced to adopt the second alternative. They will in despair give up their traditional source of income, as has already happened in the weaving industry. If the labour released from the doomed domestic industry could be used in other productive activities, the situation would not be so desperate. It must be recognized that in industrial development there are certain industries which it may not be advisable to retain in the village. But in so far as there is no new occupation to take the place of the old, the waste of labour will mean a further reduction in family income.

As their income is diminishing and as there is no hope of immediate recovery, the peasants can naturally only resort to a corresponding reduction of expenditure. In expenditure, as the Chinese peasants are concerned, there are four categories : necessary daily account, periodical ceremonial expenses, capital for production, and interest, rent, and tax. As we have seen, the villagers have already suspended ceremonies as far as possible, and even sold their rice reserve when necessary. It appears that the most rigid category is the last one. If the people are not able to pay their ever-increasing interest, rent, and tax, they will be threatened by brutal treatment from the usurers, and rent and tax collectors, and by legal enforcement through imprisonment. But when hunger is stronger than the fear of being shot, peasant revolts take place. Perhaps, this is the situation that has resulted in the disturbance of the Red Spear Club in North China and the Communist movement in Central China. If the author of *Red Star Over China* is right, the main force that drove millions of peasants in the heroic long march was nothing but hunger and its derived hatred of landowners and tax collectors.

In the present study, I have tried to show that it is incorrect to condemn landowners and even usurers as wicked persons. When the village needs money from outside to finance their production, unless there is a better system to extend credit to the peasants, absentee-landlordism and usury are the natural products. Without them, the situation might be still worse. At present, owing to the insecurity of rent, there is already a tendency for urban capital to move into the treaty-ports instead of into rural districts, as seen in the recurrence of crises in Shanghai speculative enterprises. The scarcity of capital available in rural districts encourages the development of usury in the town. The more depressed is the country, the less capital is available, and the more active is the usury—a vicious circle which saps the life of the peasants.

There was another dilemma in the Chinese land problem. The national government with all its promises and policies on paper was not able to carry out any practical measures owing to the fact that most of the revenue was spent in its anti-communist campaign, while, as I have pointed out, the real nature of the communist movement was a peasant revolt due to their dissatisfaction with the land system. Despite all kinds of justification on either side, one thing is clear : that the conditions of the peasants are getting worse and worse. So far no permanent land reform has been accomplished in any part of China since the recovery of the Red Area by the government.

It must be realized that a mere land reform in the form of reduction of rent and equalization of ownership does not promise a final solution of agrarian problems in China. Such a reform, however, is necessary and urgent because it is an indispensable step in relieving the peasants. It will give a breathing space for the peasants and, by removing the cause leading to " revolt," will unite all forces in finding the way to industrial recovery.

A final solution of agrarian problems in China lies not so much in reduction of expenditure of the peasants but in increasing their income. Therefore, industrial recovery, let me repeat once more, is essential. The traditional industry of China was mainly rural, for example, the entire textile industry was formerly a peasant occupation. At present, China is, in fact, facing a rapid decay of this traditional industry directly due to the industrial expansion of the West. By arresting this process, China comes into conflict with the Western Powers. How this conflict can be solved peacefully is a question I would like to leave to other competent scientists and politicians.

But one point connected with the future industrial development in China must be stressed here. Being a late comer in the modern industrial world, China is in a position to avoid those errors which have been committed by her predecessors. In the village, we have seen how an experiment has been made in developing a small-scale factory on the principle of co-operation. It is designed to prevent the concentration of ownership of means of production in contrast with the capitalist industrial development in the West. In spite of all difficulties and even failures, such an experiment is of great significance in the problem of the future development of rural industry in China.

Finally, I would like to emphasize that the above-mentioned problems have not disappeared since the present Japanese invasion. The tragedy is unavoidable in building our new China. It is a part of our international adjustment that sooner or later we must face. Only by going through it, can we hope for a real reconstruction of our country. During the struggle, the agrarian problems in fact have become more vital. Our victory against foreign aggression can be insured only by removing internal conflicts through relieving the peasants by a reasonable and effective land reform. Now Japan has offered us an opportunity to break our old vicious circle in the land problem. It is true that thousands of villages have already, like Kaihsienkung, been destroyed by the invaders, but in their ruin our internal conflicts and follies should find their last resting-place. From the ruin, a new China will emerge. The coming generation will, I sincerely hope, credit us with facing the problems of our age in a spirit of understanding and sympathy ; our sacrifices and the hardship we are undergoing shall stand vindicated only if we look forward to the future with oneness of purpose and clarity of vision.

APPENDIX

A NOTE ON CHINESE RELATIONSHIP TERMS

In view of the special interest in anthropology on the problem
f relationship terms, I would like to add an appendix to the
resent book as a supplement to the chapter on kinship
xtension.

It is essential to make clear that a structural analysis of
elationship terms, at best, covers only a part of the whole
roblem of kinship system and that a mere presentation of a
hart of terms is of little use by itself because it fails to show
heir sociological implications. Such a treatment, which most
f the previous studies have followed, from the old work of
Torgan and Hart up to the recent publication of H. Y. Feng,[1]
s resulted from the unsound conception of language which
iews words as representations of reality. Therefore it is
elieved that an analysis of the relationship terms will be
nough to understand the organization of kinship.

Relationship terms, like all other linguistic data, should be
tudied in their contexts. They are used for progmatic
urposes in establishing claims, in expressing affectional
ttitudes and, in short, as a part of the behaviour of the speaker
owards his relatives. An adequate analysis must be carried
ut by direct observation of how the terms are actually used.[2]
ut in the present note it is not possible to treat the problem
1 detail; I only intend to suggest an outline for further
vestigation.

Chinese relationship terms can be classified into four cate-
ories based on the general contexts of speech : (1) the context

[1] My criticism on the historical-literary method in studying Chinese
nship system, cf. " The Problem of Chinese Relationship System,"
onumenta Serica, Vol. II, 1936–37, Fac. 1 ; and my review of H.Y.
eng's The Chinese Kinship System, Man, August, 1938, p. 135.
[2] Theory of language, cf. Malinowski, Coral Gardens and Their Magic,
ol. II.

in which a person addresses his relatives directly, (2) the context in which a person refers his relative indirectly, (3) the
context in which a person describes the relationship as such
in colloquial language, and (4) that in literary language.

I. TERMS OF ADDRESS

Terms of address are the first set of relationship terms used
in individual life. A child is taught to name different persons
in contact by relationship terms. The first group of persons
whom the child will come into contact and whom he will
address are his fellow members in the Chia—his parents,
father's parents, sometimes father's brothers and their wives
and children, and father's unmarried sisters. Most of the
time the child is in the arms of its mother, but when the mother
is busy in her household work, she will put it in the arms
of other persons. The child's grandmother, father's sister,
own elder sister, and wives of father's brothers are candidates
to take up the mother's function.

Male members of the Chia have less direct a duty in caring
for the child. But when it grows up, the father as a source
of discipline becomes more and more important. (The
relation of the child with its relatives, cf. III-4 and V-1, 2)
Terms used for this group of fatherside relatives are given in
the following table.

The terms recorded in the table are sometimes only radicals
of the terms actually used. For an addresser, each term stands
for a definite person. If there are two or more persons bound
with him in a similar relationship, such as two elder brothers
of his father, modifiers will be added to the radicals for par-
ticularization. He will call the eldest as *DA PAPA* (*Da*
meaning large or elder) and the second as *N'I PAPA* (*N'i*
meaning the second). Modifiers are of two types : numbers
and personal names. As a rule, in reference to intimate and
senior relatives, such as father's brother and sister, elder brother
and sister, numbers are used, while for remote relatives and
younger brother and sister personal names are used.

Several principles in classifying paternal relatives can be
seen in the above list :

(*a*) Distinction of sex : No exception of this principle is
found. The correlation between linguistic distinction and
sociological distinction is high in this case. Sex differentia-

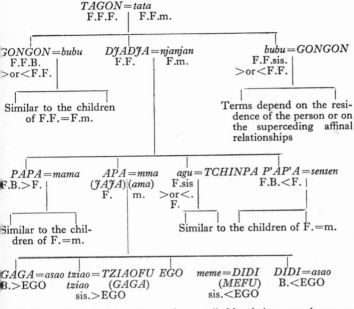

All the relatives of descending grade are called by their personal name or by simple numbers.

Terms for males in capitals ; for females in small type : = for marriage bond, F. for father, m. for mother, B. for brother and sis. for sister, > for elder and < for younger, ( ) for the terms recently introduced.

tion in the household work and in other social functions, privileges and duties has been shown in above description.

(*b*) Distinction of kinship grade : [1] The differentiation of social obligations and privileges according to kinship grade is well expressed in kinship sociology. The grandfather, for instance, does not exercise authority very often as the father over the child but very frequently indulges him and acts as mediator between the father and son. The grandson has no specific economic obligation towards his grandfather so long as his father is living. But the terms for male relatives of the second and third ascending grade, except father's father, have the same root, *GON ; TA* being a modifier meaning great. In fact, the term *TAGON* is very seldom used in direct

[1] Kinship grade, following Raymond Firth, differs from generation in the sense that " the former implies a biological classification, based upon birth ; the latter is of the sociological order, based upon genealogical ranking. *We the Tikopia*, p. 248.

address because it is rarely seen that four kinship grades exist in the same group.

(c) Distinction between consanquinity and affinity : Relatives resulted from marriage are always distinguished from relatives resulted from procreation. For instance, father's sister is differentiated from father's brother's wife. This distinction is maintained in daily life. Father's brother's wife, does not live very far if not in the same house, while father's sister after marriage usually lives in another village. The former is available to take up the mother's function in case of need while the latter is met mostly in occasional visitings.

(d) Distinction between the elder and younger relatives in reference to ego or ego's direct ascending male relatives : This distinction holds good only in ego's own grade and the first ascending grade. But in the latter, it is not so pronounced because father's elder and younger brothers are distinguished only by a slight change in articulation of the sounding PA, shorter for the younger and longer for the elder although such difference is always distinguishable. Father's sisters are called by the same term without distinction of elder and younger and similarly their husbands.

The distinction between elder and younger brothers may be correlated with the special privilege and obligations of the eldest son (IV-3). The less differentiation in social relation with the relatives of higher grade also reflects in the fusion of terminology.

(e) Distinction of family groups. This principle does not effect ego's own grade. In the first ascending grade, the term for father has the same root, PA, as found in the terms for father's brothers. Only recently, a new term JAJA has come into use. JA is the term for father used in the context of describing the relationship as such. Terms for mother and father's elder brother's wife have also the same root ma. Nevertheless, the maintainence of the distinction shows the same fact as indicated above that the family nucleus is not entirely submerged in the larger kinship unit Chia.

From this examination, we can see there is a rough correlation between kinship language and kinship sociology. This correlation is found only in the general principle of classification but not in specific terms.

The second group of relatives come from the child's mother's kindred who usually live in some neighbouring village. Although his mother's mother assists his mother in child delivery, she does not stay long in the house; this is one of the few occasions when the mother of a daughter-in-law will spend a night in her daughter's husband's house. The child will however very often go to his mother's parents' house with his mother and will stay there several times a year for periods of ten days or more. In his mother's parent's house, he is a guest and enjoys indulgences (V–2). He learns the relationship terms for his mother-side relatives in a context which is different from that in which he learns the terms for his own kindred. The sentiments attached to these terms are thus different.

The list of maternal relatives is given in the following table :

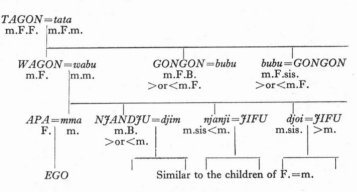

Special terms used for maternal relatives as distinguished from paternal relatives are found mostly in the first ascending grade, except mother's own parents. As I have shown above, those maternal relatives who have intimate association with ego are limited to mother's parents, mother's brothers and sisters and their children. Special terms are limited to them too, except the relatives of ego's own grade. The distinction of elder and younger is found only in the terms for mother's sisters and this distinction is made by different modifiers. No difference in social relation with ego is found between them.

Usually a person will learn the whole set of relationship terms during childhood except sometimes those terms for younger brothers and sisters. Few new terms are added after one gets married.

A married woman is introduced to her husband's relatives soon after the wedding ceremony. In the introduction, she addresses them in the same manner as does her husband, except her father-in-law, who she calls *TCHINPA*, and the wife of her husband's brother, whom she calls by the same term as her own sister. At the beginning of her married life she is a newcomer and refrains from making intimate and frequent contacts with her husband's relatives. She does not even address her husband. There is in consequence no special term used by them for one another. For instance when she has prepared the dinner, she simply calls the whole house as *tagale*, meaning all come here. This is the accepted manner of annonymous address. When she wishes to refer to her husband, a simple pronoun is enough. But when she must address the relatives, she uses her husband's system of terms. When a child is born to her, her contacts with her husband's relatives increase on behalf of her child. She also has the obligation to teach her child, who is constantly attached to her. Kinship terminology is a part of this education. On these occasions, when making inquiries for or about her child and teaching her child to recognize relationships, she uses the terms that should be used by her child. For instance, she will call her father-in-law *DJADJA* the term for grandfather, in this context. But this does not mean the abandonment of the special term *TCHINPA*, which is used on other occasions. In fact, she has a choice of her own special term, her husband's term and her child's term, according to the context.

A man will call his wife's father as *TCHINPA* and mother as *tchinm*. The term *TCHINPA* is also used for father's sister's husband. Since it is also used by a daughter-in-law to call her father-in-law, it indicates both types of cross-cousin marriage—the up-hill type and the reverting type (III–8). In practice the reverting type is not preferable. Therefore, the identification of terms cannot be interpreted only by the married system.

The other relatives of his wife will be addressed by the term used by his wife or his children, according to the appropriate contexts.

The number of terms actually used depends on the size of the kinship groups. In the village, the size of the Chia is small, therefore, the number cannot be large. Moreover, for the child of a mother who had been married through the institution of *siaosiv*, the entire group of mother-side relatives may be eliminated.

2. TERMS OF REFERENCE

If a person talks about a certain relative to another person, what term will he use for that relative? There are three persons involved: A the speaker, B the person A speaks to, and C the person A and B talk about.

A may refer C to B

   (I) by the term he uses to address C, or
  (II) by the term which B uses to address C, or
 (III) by the term used to describe the relationship between A and C or B and C in colloquial or in literary language (see next section), or
 (IV) by the terms referring to the non-relatives (see V-4).

Application of these principles depends on the relation existing among A, B, and C—whether they belong to the same kinship group and who is senior in kinship grade and in social status.

The general rules can be formulated as follows but space does not allow me to give examples of each case and to qualify them with exceptions.

(1) A, B, and C are of the same Chia:
    (a) $C<A$ and B—personal name of C
    (b) $C=A$ and B—I
    (c) $C>A$ and B, $A<B$—I
              $A=B$—I
              $A>B$—II

(2) A, B, and C are of the same extended kinship group:
    (A) C is in A's Chia:
        (a) —III or personal name,
        (b) —III or personal name,
        (c) $A<B$—I or III
           $A=B$—III
           $A>B$—II

    B) C is in B's Chia:
        (a) —personal name of C
        (b) —II, III, or IV
        (c) $A<B$—I
           $A=B$—I or III
           $A>B$—II, III, or IV

(3) A and B have no kinship relation, (Seniority is counted according to age and social status) :

(A) C is a relative of A,
  (*a*) —III or personal name,
  (*b*) —III or personal name,
  (*c*) A<B—I or III
  A=B—III
  A>B—III or IV

(B) C is a relative of B,
  (*a*) —III or personal name,
  (*b*) —III or personal name,
  (*c*) A<B—IV
  A=B—III or IV
  A>B—II, III or I·V

In the contexts listed above, A and B are in direct conversation while C is indirectly referred to. There is another type of context in which A addresses C taking B as the centre of reference. I have already pointed this out in the case of a child for whom somebody else is acting as spokesman. His mother addresses her father-in-law as *DJADJA*, grandfather, for the child. In these contexts, A is speaking not as himself or herself but for somebody else. But this must not be confused with the terms used in direct address.

3. TERMS TO DESCRIBE RELATIONSHIPS

Terms of this type differ from those of the above types in that the latter refer to particular persons and the former refer to relationships as such. A child calls his mother *mma* but the relationship between them is described as *NITZE* (son) and *njian* (mother).

These terms are also used, as shown in the above section, in indirect reference. For instance, a child may be asked by a senior, " How is your *njian* ? " or " Is his *njian* well ? " In such a case, a pronoun is usually added, unless in a context no confusion can be made.

The general term for describing relationship may be " classificatory," because there may be a group of persons related to ego in similar relationships. For example, if there are two father's younger brothers, the relationship existing

etween them and ego are the same, that is, *SOSO* (father's
ounger brother) and *ADZE* (brother's son).

The classification of relatives expressed in using the same
adical in the terms of address may be different from the
lassification given in the terms to describe relationships.
'or instance, mother's brother's son is called by the same term
sed for brother. But the former is described as *PIAOGA*
nd the latter as *AGA*. All the relatives of descending grades
re called by personal names or by numbers, but they are
lassified by the terms to describe relationship, one's own son
s *NITZE*, brother's son *ADZE*, sister's son *WASEN*, etc.

In this type of terms, decrepencies may be found between
olloquial and literary languages. A general distinction
etween colloquial and literary language is that the former is
poken by local people and the latter is written by all the
terate Chinese. Indeed, both of them can be spoken and
rritten, but in actual usage the distinction is on the whole
aaintained. Although recently there is an attempt to develop
olloquial literature, in other words, to write in spoke form,
othing has been done besides the Pai-hua actually the " Peking
ialect." On the other hand the literary language, which has
een used through thousands of years and by all the literate
'hinese, are expressed in system of written characters which
an be read differently according to local phonetic peculiarities.
t remains on paper and ready to be read. Since the grammar
f the literary language is different from that of the colloquial
anguage, the former cannot be understood by ordinary people
a its reading form. The literary terms enter in the spoken
anguage only in special context. The literary term for a thing
r a relation may be different from the colloquial term for the
ame thing or relation. This difference may be illustrated
y the relationship terms. Take the term describing the
elationship of father as an example : the literary term is
'U, but the colloquial term in the village is *JA*. Moreover,
ie classes of relatives made in literary language may be
ndifferentiated in colloquial language ; for instance, the
elationships of father's brother's son and father's father's
rother's sons' son are all described in colloquial terms as
'-*ZOSHONDI* (brothers of my clan) but are distinguished in
terary terms as *TONSHON* and *ZETONSHON* respectively.

I cannot in my present note discuss in full on the problem
f the relation between the literary and colloquial relationship

terms. I have given elsewhere a summary of my view. " I
the written system the theorists had systematically an
throughly carried out those principles of classification, whic
had been noticed by them empirically in the process of chang
in the relationship system. Each generation is designated b
the same stem, vertically split into two groups of older an
younger, and then the family group is distinguished, by usin
modifications of the terms, from the other groups which ar
again differentiated according to their closeness to the famil
group. Such logical construction has not only over-shadowe
the existence of the senior-junior classification, especially th
fact of the absence of special terms of address for the junic
class, but also mis-represented the relative working influenc
of these principles. As a result of such a construction, th
literary system went too far from the actually practised system:
Of course, the process of change in the above mentione
direction has been greatly helped by the literary systen
However, new changes in the Chinese social organization, suc
as the partial disintegration of the clan organization, the growin
importance of the mother clan, and the change of the soci
status of the females, as shown in the analysis of the Wukian
system, has resulted in a direction of change which was nc
foreseen by the old theorists and is not to be found in th
codified written system. Thus, the new social change wi
carry the actual practice still further from the written one."[1]

[1] " The Problem of Chinese Relationship System," p. 148. In the abo
quotation, the actual practised system refers to the colloquial terms whi
the written system the literary terms. A full list of literary terms can l
found either in Chen and Shryock, " Chinese Relationship Terms
American Anthropologists, N.S., Vol. 34, No. 4, 1932 ; or H. Y. Feng, *op. ci
Harvard Journal of Asiatic Studies*, Vol. 2, No. 2, 1937.

INDEX

Agent boat :
  as buying agent, 249 f.
  as selling agent, 254 f.
  as credit agent, 274 f.
  and marketing area, 257
Ancestor :
  worship, 30
  sacrifice, 76
  mourning for, 77 f.

Birth ceremony, *menyu*, 35, 86
  and neighbourhood, 98–9
  expenses of, 132
Boat, its importance in communi-
    cation, 19, 123
BODDE, DERK : on calendar, 146
BUCK, J. L. :
  on grave land, 75
  on ceremonial expenses, 133
  on rate of interest, 278

Calendar :
  lunar system, 145
  section or Chieh system, 146 f.
  Western solar system, 148
  time table of economic and other
    social activities, 152–3
CHANG TA TI (God of flood) :
  his birth day, 150
  mythology of, 167
CHEN HAN SENG :
  on land leasing, 180
  on transference of land right, 183
  on permanent tenancy, 184
  on collective ownership of land,
    187
  on land policy, 190
Chia, expanded family :
  definition, 27–8
  constitution, 28, 29 note 1
  average size, 29
  division of, 28, 65 f.
  authority in, 37, 48, 63, 234
  property of, 59–63
  economic power of the head, 62–3

Clothing :
  social distinction, 124
  expenses of, 125
Communication : in relation to
    village plan, 19
Credit :
  defined, 263–4
  financial aid society, 267 f.
  agent boat, 274 f.
  usuary, 276 f.
  co-operative society, 280 f.
Cross-cousin marriage
  parental selection, 42
  up-hill type, *saonseodiu*, and re-
    verting type *wesienodiu*, 50–1, 89
Cultural change :
  nature of Chinese, 1–2
  function of social science in, 2
  difficulties in, 3
  seen in village plan, 21

Daughter-in-law :
  her relation with husband and
    other relatives, 45–6, 233 f.
  stabilizing her new position, 46–7
  difficulties in adjustment, 47–9
  desertion and committing suicide,
    49
  new legislation, 81
Definition of a situation, 3–4
Descent :
  principle of, 31
  and sex equality, 3–4, 32, 81
  obliterations of, 70 f.
  new legislation on, 81
Division of labour :
  occupational differentiation, 138 f.
  among men, women, and chil-
    dren, 170

Exchange :
  defined, 240
  types of, 240 f.

Family :
  defined, 27
  nucleus of a Chia, 29
  property of, 61

297

The International Library of

Sociology

and Social Reconstruction

Edited by W. J. H. SPROTT
Founded by KARL MANNHEIM

ROUTLEDGE & KEGAN PAUL
BROADWAY HOUSE, CARTER LANE, LONDON, E.C.4

CONTENTS

PRINTED IN GREAT BRITAIN BY HEADLEY BROTHERS LTD
109 KINGSWAY LONDON WC2 AND ASHFORD KENT

GENERAL SOCIOLOGY

Brown, Robert. Explanation in Social Science. *208 pp. 1963. (2nd Impression 1964.) 25s.*

Gibson, Quentin. The Logic of Social Enquiry. *240 pp. 1960. (2nd Impression 1963.) 24s.*

Goldschmidt, Professor Walter. Understanding Human Society. *272 pp. 1959. 21s.*

Homans, George C. Sentiments and Activities: Essays in Social Science. *336 pp. 1962. 32s.*

Jarvie, I. C. The Revolution in Anthropology. *Foreword by Ernest Gellner. 272 pp. 1964. 40s.*

Johnson, Harry M. Sociology: a Systematic Introduction. *Foreword by Robert K. Merton. 710 pp. 1961. (4th Impression 1964.) 42s.*

Mannheim, Karl. Essays on Sociology and Social Psychology. *Edited by Paul Keckskemeti. With Editorial Note by Adolph Lowe. 344 pp. 1953. 30s.*
Systematic Sociology: An Introduction to the Study of Society. *Edited by J. S. Erös and Professor W. A. C. Stewart. 220 pp. 1957. (2nd Impression 1959.) 24s.*

Martindale, Don. The Nature and Types of Sociological Theory. *292 pp. 1961. 35s.*

Maus, Heinz. A Short History of Sociology. *234 pp. 1962. 28s.*

Myrdal, Gunnar. Value in Social Theory: A Collection of Essays on Methodology. *Edited by Paul Streeten. 332 pp. 1958. (2nd Impression 1962.) 32s.*

Ogburn, William F., and **Nimkoff, Meyer F.** A Handbook of Sociology. *Preface by Karl Mannheim. 656 pp. 46 figures. 38 tables. 5th edition (revised) 1964. 40s.*

Parsons, Talcott and **Smelser, Neil J.** Economy and Society: A Study in the Integration of Economic and Social Theory. *362 pp. 1956. (3rd Impression 1964.) 35s.*

Rex, John. Key Problems of Sociological Theory. *220 pp. 1961. (2nd Impression 1963.) 25s.*

Stark, Werner. The Fundamental Forms of Social Thought. *280 pp. 1962. 32s.*

FOREIGN CLASSICS OF SOCIOLOGY

Durkheim, Emile. Suicide. A Study in Sociology. *Edited and with an Introduction by George Simpson. 404 pp. 1952. (2nd Impression 1963.) 30s.*
Socialism and Saint-Simon. *Edited with an Introduction by Alvin W. Gouldner. Translated by Charlotte Sattler from the edition originally edited with an Introduction by Marcel Mauss. 286 pp. 1959. 28s.*
Professional Ethics and Civic Morals. *Translated by Cornelia Brookfield. 288 pp. 1957. 30s.*

Gerth, H. H., and **Wright Mills, C.** From Max Weber: Essays in Sociology. *502 pp. 1948. (5th Impression 1964.) 35s.*

Tönnies, Ferdinand. Community and Association. *(Gemeinschaft und Gesellschaft.) Translated and Supplemented by Charles P. Loomis. Foreword by Pitirim A. Sorokin. 334 pp. 1955. 28s.*

SOCIAL STRUCTURE

Andrzejewski, Stanislaw. Military Organization and Society. *With a Foreword by Professor A. R. Radcliffe-Brown. 226 pp. 1 folder. 1954. 21s.*

Cole, G. D. H. Studies in Class Structure. *220 pp. 1955. (3rd Impression 1964.) 21s.*

Coontz, Sydney H. Population Theories and the Economic Interpretation. *202 pp. 1957. (2nd Impression 1961.) 25s.*

Coser, Lewis. The Functions of Social Conflict. *204 pp. 1956. 18s.*

Glass, D. V. (Ed.). Social Mobility in Britain. *Contributions by J. Berent, T. Bottomore, R. C. Chambers, J. Floud, D. V. Glass, J. R. Hall, H. T. Himmelweit, R. K. Kelsall, F. M. Martin, C. A. Moser, R. Mukherjee, and W. Ziegel. 420 pp. 1954. (2nd Impressions 1963.) 40s.*

Kelsall, R. K. Higher Civil Servants in Britain: From 1870 to the Present Day. *268 pp. 31 tables. 1955. 25s.*

Ossowski, Stanislaw. Class Structure in the Social Consciousness. *212 pp. 1963. 25s.*

SOCIOLOGY AND POLITICS

Barbu, Zevedei. Democracy and Dictatorship: Their Psychology and Patterns of Life. *300 pp. 1956. 28s.*

Benney, Mark, Gray, A. P., and Pear, R. H. How People Vote: a Study of Electoral Behaviour in Greenwich. *Foreword by Professor W. A. Robson. 256 pp. 70 tables. 1956. 25s.*

Bramstedt, Dr. E. K. Dictatorship and Political Police: The Technique of Control by Fear. *286 pp. 1945. 20s.*

Crick, Bernard. The American Science of Politics: Its Origins and Conditions. *284 pp. 1959. 28s.*

Hertz, Frederick. Nationality in History and Politics: A Psychology and Sociology of National Sentiment and Nationalism. *440 pp. 1944. (4th Impression 1957.) 32s.*

Kornhauser, William. The Politics of Mass Society. *272 pp. 20 tables. 1960. 25s.*

Laidler, Harry W. Social-Economic Movements: An Historical and Comparative Survey of Socialism, Communism, Co-operation, Utopianism; and other Systems of Reform and Reconstruction. *864 pp. 16 plates. 1 figure. 1949. (3rd Impression 1960.) 50s.*

Mannheim, Karl. Freedom, Power and Democratic Planning. *Edited by Hans Gerth and Ernest K. Bramstedt. 424 pp. 1951. 35s.*

Mansur, Fatma. Process of Independence. *Foreword by A. H. Hanson. 208 pp. 1962. 25s.*

Myrdal, Gunnar. The Political Element in the Development of Economic Theory. *Translated from the German by Paul Streeten. 282 pp. 1953. (3rd Impression 1961.) 25s.*

Polanyi, Michael, F.R.S. The Logic of Liberty: Reflections and Rejoinders. *228 pp. 1951. 18s.*

Verney, Douglas V. The Analysis of Political Systems. *264 pp. 1959. (2nd Impression 1961.) 28s.*

Wootton, Graham. The Politics of Influence: British Ex-Servicemen, Cabinet Decisions and Cultural Changes, 1917 to 1957. *320 pp. 1963. 30s.*

FOREIGN AFFAIRS: THEIR SOCIAL, POLITICAL AND ECONOMIC FOUNDATIONS

Baer, Gabriel. Population and Society in the Arab East. *Translated by Hanna Szöke. 288 pp. 10 maps. 1964. 40s.*

Bonné, Alfred. The Economic Development of the Middle East: An Outline of Planned Reconstruction after the War. *192 pp. 58 tables. 1945. (3rd Impression 1953.) 16s.*

State and Economics in the Middle East: A Society in Transition. *482 pp. 2nd (revised) edition 1955. (2nd Impression 1960.) 40s.*

Studies in Economic Development: with special reference to Conditions in the Under-developed Areas of Western Asia and India. *322 pp. 84 tables. (2nd edition 1960.) 32s.*

Mayer, J. P. Political Thought in France from the Revolution to the Fifth Republic. *164 pp. 3rd edition (revised) 1961. 16s.*

Schlesinger, Rudolf. Central European Democracy and its Background: Economic and Political Group Organization. *432 pp. 1953. 40s.*

Thomson, David, Meyer, E., and Briggs, A. Patterns of Peacemaking. *408 pp. 1945. 25s.*

Trouton, Ruth. Peasant Renaissance in Yugoslavia, 1900-1950: A Study of the Development of Yugoslav Peasant Society as affected by Education. *370 pp. 1 map. 1952. 28s.*

SOCIOLOGY OF LAW

Gurvitch, Dr. Georges. Sociology of Law. *With a Preface by Professor Roscoe Pound. 280 pp. 1947. (2nd Impression 1953.) 24s.*

Renner, Karl. The Institutions of Private Law and Their Social Functions. *Edited, with an Introduction and Notes by O. Kahn-Freund. Translated by Agnes Schwarzschild. 336 pp. 1949. 28s.*

CRIMINOLOGY

Cloward, Richard A., and Ohlin, Lloyd E. Delinquency and Opportunity: A Theory of Delinquent Gangs. *248 pp. 1961. 25s.*

Friedländer, Dr. Kate. The Psycho-Analytical Approach to Juvenile Delinquency: Theory, Case Studies, Treatment. *320 pp. 1947. (5th Impression 1961.) 28s.*

Glueck, Sheldon and Eleanor. Family Environment and Delinquency. *With the statistical assistance of Rose W. Kneznek. 340 pp. 1962. 35s.*

Mannheim, Hermann. Group Problems in Crime and Punishment, and other Studies in Criminology and Criminal Law. *336 pp. 1955. 28s.*

Morris, Terence. The Criminal Area: A Study in Social Ecology. *Foreword by Hermann Mannheim. 232 pp. 25 tables. 4 maps. 1957. 25s.*

Morris, Terence and **Pauline,** assisted by **Barbara Barer.** Pentonville: a Sociological Study of an English Prison. *416 pp. 16 plates. 1963. 50s.*

Spencer, John C. Crime and the Services. *Foreword by Hermann Mannheim. 336 pp. 1954. 28s.*

Trasler, Gordon. The Explanation of Criminality. *144 pp. 1962. 20s.*

SOCIAL PSYCHOLOGY

Barbu, Zevedei. Problems of Historical Psychology. *248 pp. 1960. 25s.*

Blackburn, Julian. Psychology and the Social Pattern. *184 pp. 1945. (6th Impression 1961.) 16s.*

Fleming, C. M. Adolescence: Its Social Psychology: With an Introduction to recent findings from the fields of Anthropology, Physiology, Medicine, Psychometrics and Sociometry. *271 pp. 2nd edition (revised) 1963. (2nd impression 1964) 25s.*
  The Social Psychology of Education: An Introduction and Guide to Its Study. *136 pp. 2nd edition (revised) 1959. 11s.*

Fleming, C. M. (Ed.). Studies in the Social Psychology of Adolescence. *Contributions by J. E. Richardson, J. F. Forrester, J. K. Shukla and P. J. Higginbotham. Foreword by the editor. 292 pp. 29 figures. 13 tables. 5 folder tables. 1951. 23s.*

Halmos, Paul. Solitude and Privacy: a Study of Social Isolation, its Causes and Therapy. *With a Foreword by Professor T. H. Marshall. 216 pp. 1952. 21s.*
  Towards a Measure of Man: The Frontiers of Normal Adjustment. *276 pp. 1957. 28s.*

Homans, George C. The Human Group. *Foreword by Bernard DeVoto. Introduction by Robert K. Merton. 526 pp. 1951. (4th Impression 1963.) 35s.*
  Social Behaviour: its Elementary Forms. *416 pp. 1961. 30s.*

Klein, Josephine. The Study of Groups. *226 pp. 31 figures. 5 tables. 1956. (3rd Impression 1962.) 21s.*

Linton, Ralph. The Cultural Background of Personality. *132 pp. 1947. (5th Impression 1964.) 16s.*
  See also Yang, M.

Mayo, Elton. The Social Problems of an Industrial Civilization. With an appendix on the Political Problem. *180 pp. 1949. (4th Impression 1961.) 18s.*

Ridder, J. C. de. The Personality of the Urban African in South Africa. A Thematic Apperception Test Study. *196 pp. 12 plates. 1961. 25s.*

Rose, Arnold M. (Ed.). Mental Health and Mental Disorder: A Sociological Approach. *Chapters by 46 contributors. 654 pp. 1956. 45s.*
Human Behavior and Social Processes: an Interactionist Approach. *Contributions by Arnold M. Ross, Ralph H. Turner, Anselm Strauss, Everett C. Hughes, E. Franklin Frazier, Howard S. Becker, et al. 696 pp. 1962. 60s.*

Smelser, Neil J. Theory of Collective Behavior. *448 pp. 1962. 45s.*

Spinley, Dr. B. M. The Deprived and the Privileged: Personality Development in English Society. *232 pp. 1953. 20s.*

Wolfenstein, Martha. Disaster: A Psychological Essay. *264 pp. 1957. 23s.*

Young, Professor Kimball. Personality and Problems of Adjustment. *742 pp. 12 figures. 9 tables. 2nd edition (revised) 1952. (2nd Impression 1959.) 40s.*
Handbook of Social Psychology. *658 pp. 16 figures. 10 tables. 2nd edition (revised) 1957. (3rd Impression 1963.) 40s.*

SOCIOLOGY OF THE FAMILY

Banks, J. A. Prosperity and Parenthood: A Study of Family Planning among the Victorian Middle Classes. *262 pp. 1954. 24s.*

Chapman, Dennis. The Home and Social Status. *336 pp. 8 plates. 3 figures. 117 tables. 1955. 35s.*

Klein, Viola. The Feminine Character: History of an Ideology. *With a Foreword by Karl Mannheim. 256 pp. 1946. 16s.*

Myrdal, Alva and Klein, Viola. Women's Two Roles: Home and Work. *238 pp. 27 tables. 1956. (2nd Impression 1962.) 25s.*

Parsons, Talcott and Bales, Robert F. Family: Socialization and Interaction Process. *In collaboration with James Olds, Morris Zelditch and Philip E. Slater. 456 pp. 50 figures and tables. 1956. 35s.*

THE SOCIAL SERVICES

Ashdown, Margaret and Brown, S. Clement. Social Service and Mental Health: An Essay on Psychiatric Social Workers. *280 pp. 1953. 21s.*

Hall, M. Penelope. The Social Services of Modern England. *416 pp. 6th edition (revised) 1963. 28s.*

Heywood, Jean S. Children in Care: the Development of the Service for the Deprived Child. *256 pp. 1959. (2nd Impression 1964.) 25s.*
An Introduction to teaching Casework Skills. *192 pp. 1964. 28s.*

Jones, Kathleen. Lunacy, Law and Conscience, 1744-1845: the Social History of the Care of the Insane. *268 pp. 1955. 25s.*
Mental Health and Social Policy, 1845-1959. *264 pp. 1960. 28s.*

Jones, Kathleen and Sidebotham, Roy. Mental Hospitals at Work. *220 pp. 1962. 30s.*

Kastell, Jean. Casework in Child Care. *Foreword by M. Brooke Willis. 320 pp. 1962. 35s.*

Rooff, Madeline. Voluntary Societies and Social Policy. *350 pp. 15 tables. 1957. 35s.*

Shenfield, B. E. Social Policies for Old Age: A Review of Social Provision for Old Age in Great Britain. *260 pp. 39 tables. 1957. 25s.*

Timms, Noel. Psychiatric Social Work in Great Britain (1939-1962). *280 pp. 1964. 32s.*
Social Casework: Principles and Practice. *256 pp. 1964, 25s.*

Trasler, Gordon. In Place of Parents: A Study in Foster Care. *272 pp. 1960. 25s.*

Young, A. F., and **Ashton, E. T.** British Social Work in the Nineteenth Century. *288 pp. 1956. (2nd Impression 1963.) 28s.*

SOCIOLOGY OF EDUCATION

Banks, Olive. Parity and Prestige in English Secondary Education: a Study in Educational Sociology. *272 pp. 1955. (2nd Impression. 1963.) 28s.*

Collier, K. G. The Social Purposes of Education: Personal and Social Values in Education. *268 pp. 1959. (2nd Impression 1962.) 21s.*

Edmonds, E. L. The School Inspector. *Foreword by Sir William Alexander. 214 pp. 1962. 28s.*

Evans, K. M. Sociometry and Education. *158 pp. 1962. 18s.*

Fraser, W. R. Education and Society in Modern France. *150 pp. 1963. 20s.*

Hans, Nicholas. New Trends in Education in the Eighteenth Century. *278 pp. 19 tables. 1951. 25s.*
Comparative Education: A Study of Educational Factors and Traditions. *360 pp. 3rd (revised) edition 1958. (4th Impression 1964.) 25s.*

Mannheim, Karl and **Stewart, W. A. C.** An Introduction to the Sociology of Education. *208 pp. 1962. 21s.*

Musgrove, F. Youth and the Social Order. *176 pp. 1964. 21s.*

Ortega y Gasset, Jose. Mission of the University. *Translated with an Introduction by Howard Lee Nostrand. 88 pp. 1946. (3rd Impression 1963.) 15s.*

Ottaway, A. K. C. Education and Society: An Introduction to the Sociology of Education. *With an Introduction by W. O. Lester Smith. 212 pp. Second edition (revised). 1962. (2nd Impression 1964.) 18s.*

Peers, Robert. Adult Education: A Comparative Study. *398 pp. 2nd edition 1959. 35s.*

Pritchard, D. G. Education and the Handicapped: 1760 to 1960. *258 pp. 1963. 28s.*

Samuel, R. H., and **Thomas, R. Hinton.** Education and Society in Modern Germany. *212 pp. 1949. 16s.*

Simon, **Brian** and **Joan** (Eds.). Educational Psychology in the U.S.S.R. *Introduction by Brian and Joan Simon. Translation by Joan Simon. Papers by D. N. Bogoiavlenski and N. A. Menchinskaia, D. B. Elkonin, E. A. Fleshner, Z. I. Kalmykova, G. S. Kostiuk, V. A. Krutetski, A. N. Leontiev, A. R. Luria, E. A. Milerian, R. G. Natadze, B. M. Teplov, L. S. Vygotski, L. V. Zankov. 296 pp. 1963. 40s.*

SOCIOLOGY OF CULTURE

Fromm, Erich. The Fear of Freedom. *286 pp. 1942. (8th Impression 1960.) 21s.* The Sane Society. *400 pp. 1956. (3rd Impression 1963.) 28s.*

Mannheim, Karl. Diagnosis of Our Time: Wartime Essays of a Sociologist. *208 pp. 1943. (7th Impression 1962.) 21s.*
Essays on the Sociology of Culture. *Edited by Ernst Mannheim in co-operation with Paul Kecskemeti. Editorial Note by Adolph Lowe. 280 pp. 1956. (2nd Impression 1962.) 28s.*

Weber, Alfred. Farewell to European History: or The Conquest of Nihilism. *Translated from the German by R. F. C. Hull. 224 pp. 1947. 18s.*

SOCIOLOGY OF RELIGION

Argyle, Michael. Religious Behaviour. *224 pp. 8 figures. 41 tables. 1958. 25s.*

Knight, Frank H., and **Merriam, Thornton W.** The Economic Order and Religion. *242 pp. 1947. 18s.*

Watt, W. Montgomery. Islam and the Integration of Society. *320 pp. 1961. (2nd Impression.) 32s.*

SOCIOLOGY OF ART AND LITERATURE

Beljame, Alexandre. Men of Letters and the English Public in the Eighteenth Century: 1660-1744, Dryden, Addison, Pope. *Edited with an Introduction and Notes by Bonamy Dobree. Translated by E. O. Lorimer. 532 pp. 1948. 32s.*

Misch, Georg. A History of Autobiography in Antiquity. *Translated by E. W. Dickes. 2 Volumes. Vol. 1, 364 pp., Vol. 2, 372 pp. 1950. 45s. the set.*

Silbermann, Alphons. The Sociology of Music. *224 pp. 1963. 28s.*

SOCIOLOGY OF KNOWLEDGE

Hodges, H. A. The Philosophy of Wilhelm Dilthey. *410 pp. 1952. 30s.*

Mannheim, Karl. Essays on the Sociology of Knowledge. *Edited by Paul Kecskemeti. Editorial note by Adolph Lowe. 352 pp. 1952. (3rd Impression 1964.) 35s.*

Schlesinger, Rudolf. Marx: His Time and Ours. *464 pp. 1950. (2nd Impression 1951.) 32s.*

Stark, W. The History of Economics in its Relation to Social Development. *104 pp. 1944. (4th Impression 1957.) 12s.*

America: Ideal and Reality. The United States of 1776 in Contemporary Philosophy. *136 pp. 1947. 12s.*

The Sociology of Knowledge: An Essay in Aid of a Deeper Understanding of the History of Ideas. *384 pp. 1958. (2nd Impression 1960.) 36s.*

Montesquieu: Pioneer of the Sociology of Knowledge. *244 pp. 1960. 25s.*

URBAN SOCIOLOGY

Anderson, Nels. The Urban Community: A World Perspective. *532 pp. 1960. 35s.*

Ashworth, William. The Genesis of Modern British Town Planning: A Study in Economic and Social History of the Nineteenth and Twentieth Centuries. *288 pp. 1954. 25s.*

Bracey, Howard. Neighbours: Neighbouring and Neighbourliness on New Estates and Subdivisions in England and the U.S.A. *220 pp. 1964. 28s.*

Cullingworth, J. B. Housing Needs and Planning Policy: A Restatement of the Problems of Housing Need and "Overspill" in England and Wales. *232 pp. 44 tables. 8 maps. 1960. 28s.*

Dickinson, Robert E. City and Region: A Geographical Interpretation. *608 pp. 125 figures. 1964. 60s.*

The West European City: A Geographical Interpretation. *600 pp. 129 maps. 29 plates. 2nd edition 1962. (2nd Impression 1963.) 55s.*

Dore, R. P. City Life in Japan: A Study of a Tokyo Ward. *498 pp. 8 plates. 4 figures. 24 tables. 1958. (2nd Impression 1963.) s.*

Jennings, Hilda. Societies in the Making: a Study f Development and Re-development within a County Borough. *F eword by D. A. Clark. 286 pp. 1962. 32s.*

Kerr, Madeline. The People of Ship Street. *240 pp. 1958. 23s.*

RURAL SOCIOLOGY

Bracey, H. E. English Rural Life: Village Activities, Organizations and Institutions. *302 pp. 1959. 30s.*

Infield, Henrik F. Co-operative Living in Palestine. *With a Foreword by General Sir Arthur Wauchope, G.C.B. 170 pp. 8 plates. 7 tables. 1946. 12s. 6d.*

Littlejohn, James. Westrigg: the Sociology of a Cheviot Parish. *172 pp. 5 figures. 1963. 25s.*

Saville, John. Rural Depopulation in England and Wales, 1851-1951. *Foreword by Leonard Elmhirst. 286 pp. 6 figures. 39 tables. 1 map. 1957. 28s. (Dartington Hall Studies in Rural Sociology.)*

Williams, W. M. The Country Craftsman: A Study of Some Rural Crafts and the Rural Industries Organization in England. *248 pp. 9 figures. 1958. 25s. (Dartington Hall Studies in Rural Sociology.)*
The Sociology of an English Village: Gosforth. *272 pp. 12 figures. 13 tables. 1956. (3rd Impression 1964.) 25s.*

SOCIOLOGY OF MIGRATION

Eisenstadt, S. N. The Absorption of Immigrants: a Comparative Study based mainly on the Jewish Community in Palestine and the State of Israel. *288 pp. 1954. 28s.*

SOCIOLOGY OF INDUSTRY AND DISTRIBUTION

Anderson, Nels. Work and Leisure. *280 pp. 1961. 28s.*

Blau, Peter M., and **Scott, W. Richard.** Formal Organizations: a Comparative approach. *Introduction and Additional Bibliography by J. H. Smith. 328 pp. 1963. (2nd impression 1964.) 28s.*

Gouldner, Alvin W. Patterns of Industrial Bureaucracy. *298 pp. 1955. 25s.*
Wildcat Strike: A Study of an Unofficial Strike. *202 pp. 10 figures. 1955. 16s.*

Jefferys, Margot, with the assistance of Winifred Moss. Mobility in the Labour Market: Employment Changes in Battersea and Dagenham. *Preface by Barbara Wootton. 186 pp. 51 tables. 1954. 15s.*

Levy, A. B. Private Corporations and Their Control. *Two Volumes. Vol. 1, 464 pp., Vol. 2, 432 pp. 1950. 80s. the set.*

Levy, Hermann. The Shops of Britain: A Study of Retail Distribution. *268 pp. 1948. (2nd Impression 1949.) 21s.*

Liepmann, Kate. The Journey to Work: Its Significance for Industrial and Community Life. *With a Foreword by A. M. Carr-Saunders. 230 pp. 40 tables. 3 folders. 1944. (2nd Impression 1945.) 18s.*
Apprenticeship: An Enquiry into its Adequacy under Modern Conditions. *Foreword by H. D. Dickinson. 232 pp. 6 tables. 1960. (2nd Impression.) 23s.*

Millerson, Geoffrey. The Qualifying Associations: a Study in Professionalization. *320 pp. 1964. 42s.*

Smelser, Neil J. Social Change in the Industrial Revolution: An Application of Theory to the Lancashire Cotton Industry, 1770-1840. *468 pp. 12 figures. 14 tables. 1959. (2nd Impression 1960.) 40s.*

Williams, Gertrude. Recruitment to Skilled Trades. *240 pp. 1957. 23s.*

Young, A. F. Industrial Injuries Insurance: an Examination of British Policy. *192 pp. 1964. 30s.*

ANTHROPOLOGY
(Demy 8vo.)

Crook, David and **Isabel.** Revolution in a Chinese Village: Ten Mile Inn. *230 pp. 8 plates. 1 map. 1959. 21s.*

Dube, S. C. Indian Village, *Foreword by Morris Edward Opler. 276 pp. 4 plates. 1955. (4th Impression 1961.) 25s.*
India's Changing Villages: Human Factors in Community Development. *260 pp. 8 plates. 1 map. 1958. (2nd Impression 1960.) 25s.*

Fei, Hsiao-Tung. Peasant Life in China: a Field Study of Country Life in the Yangtze Valley. *Foreword by Bronislaw Malinowski. 320 pp. 14 plates. 1939. (5th Impression 1962.) 30s.*

Gulliver, P. H. The Family Herds. A Study of Two Pastoral Tribes in East Africa, The Jie and Turkana. *304 pp. 4 plates. 19 figures. 1955. 25s.*
Social Control in an African Society: a Study of the Arusha, Agricultural Masai of Northern Tanganyika. *320 pp. 8 plates. 10 figures. 1963. 35s.*

Hogbin, Ian. Transformation Scene. The Changing Culture of a New Guinea Village. *340 pp. 22 plates. 2 maps. 1951. 30s.*

Hsu, Francis L. K. Under the Ancestors' Shadow: Chinese Culture and Personality. *346 pp. 26 figures. 1949. 21s.*

Lowie, Professor Robert H. Social Organization. *494 pp. 1950. (3rd Impression 1962.) 35s.*

Maunier, René. The Sociology of Colonies: An Introduction to the Study of Race Contact. *Edited and translated by E. O. Lorimer. 2 Volumes. Vol. 1, 430 pp., Vol. 2, 356 pp. 1949. 70s. the set.*

Mayer, Adrian C. Caste and Kinship in Central India: A Village and its Region. *328 pp. 16 plates. 15 figures. 16 tables. 1960. 35s.*
Peasants in the Pacific: A Study of Fiji Indian Rural Society. *232 pp. 16 plates. 10 figures. 14 tables. 1961. 35s.*

Osborne, Harold. Indians of the Andes: Aymaras and Quechuas. *292 pp. 8 plates. 2 maps. 1952. 25s.*

12

Smith, Raymond T. The Negro Family in British Guiana: Family Structure and Social Status in the Villages. *With a Foreword by Meyer Fortes. 314 pp. 8 plates. 1 figure. 4 maps. 1956. 28s.*

Yang, Martin C. A Chinese Village: Taitou, Shantung Province. *Foreword by Ralph Linton. Introduction by M. L. Wilson. 308 pp. 1947. 23s.*

DOCUMENTARY
(Demy 8vo.)

Belov, Fedor. The History of a Soviet Collective Farm. *250 pp. 1956. 21s.*

Meek, Dorothea L. (Ed.). Soviet Youth: Some Achievements and Problems. *Excerpts from the Soviet Press, translated by the editor. 280 pp. 1957. 28s.*

Schlesinger, Rudolf (Ed.). Changing Attitudes in Soviet Russia.
1. The Family in the U.S.S.R. *Documents and Readings, with an Introduction by the editor. 434 pp. 1949. 30s.*
2. The Nationalities Problem and Soviet Administration. Selected Readings on the Development of Soviet Nationalities Policies. *Introduced by the editor. Translated by W. W. Gottlieb. 324 pp. 1956. 30s.*

Reports
of the Institute
# of Community Studies

(*Demy 8vo.*)

Cartwright, Ann. Human Relations and Hospital Care. *272 pp. 1964. 30s.*

Jackson, Brian and Marsden, Dennis. Education and the Working Class: Some General Themes raised by a Study of 88 Working-class Children in a Northern Industrial City. *268 pp. 2 folders. 1962. (2nd Impression.) 28s.*

Marris, Peter. Widows and their Families. *Foreword by Dr. John Bowlby. 184 pp. 18 tables. Statistical Summary. 1958. 18s.*
Family and Social Change in an African City. A Study of Rehousing in Lagos. *196 pp. 1 map. 4 plates. 53 tables. 1961. 25s.*

Mills, Enid. Living with Mental Illness: a Study in East London. *Foreword by Morris Carstairs. 196 pp. 1962. 28s.*

Townsend, Peter. The Family Life of Old People: An Inquiry in East London. *Foreword by J. H. Sheldon. 300 pp. 3 figures. 63 tables. 1957. (2nd Impression 1961.) 30s.*

Willmott, Peter. The Evolution of a Community: a study of Dagenham after forty years. *168 pp. 2 maps. 1963. 21s.*

Willmott, Peter and Young, Michael. Family and Class in a London Suburb. *202 pp. 47 tables. 1960. (2nd Impression 1961.) 21s.*

The British Journal of Sociology. *Edited by D. G. MacRae. Vol. 1, No. 1, March 1950 and Quarterly. Roy. 8vo., £2 p.a.; 12s. 6d. a number, post free. (Vols. 1-12, £3 each.)*

All prices are net and subject to alteration without notice